PRAISE FOR
WHEN GRIT IS NOT ENOUGH

"*When Grit Is Not Enough* does a truly remarkable job of providing a framework for both aspiring entrepreneurs and seasoned executives to drive increased performance and progress across their respective organizations. The suggestions and blueprints are not only easily digestible but are provided with empathy and understanding of the challenges one faces during the company-building process. I would highly recommend this book to any entrepreneur or business operator looking for guidance on how to level up their performance and drive significant tangible results."

—THOMAS SWALLA, CEO of Dotmatics

"*When Grit Is Not Enough* is a master class in building a thriving software business from the ground up. Dean Guida shares battle-tested insights and systems, revealing the art of bootstrapping with tenacity, creativity, and strategic acumen. This book is a treasure trove of wisdom, offering pivotal moments—from crucial decisions on culture to setting big hairy audacious goals—that shaped his company's trajectory. For founders and investors alike, this is the ultimate guide to building an enduring business. A must-read for those who dare to dream big and build bigger."

—JOANNE YUAN, partner at Turn/River Capital

"Dean Guida's journey is a testament to the power of combining grit with strategic thinking. *When Grit Is Not Enough* is a practical guide filled with actionable advice. It's a must-have resource for any business leader looking to break through barriers."

—SEAN ELLIS, author of *Hacking Growth*

"One of the lasting lessons CEOs have learned over the past few years is that there will always be unknowns when it comes to business. Whether it is artificial intelligence, inflation, or global conflict, being prepared for unexpected issues can make or break a company. Dean Guida's book is a guide with actionable information for every business leader/entrepreneur to deal with the complexities of the business world."

—**SAM REESE,** CEO of Vistage Worldwide

WHEN
GRIT
IS
NOT
ENOUGH

AN ENTREPRENEUR'S PLAYBOOK

FOR TAKING YOUR BUSINESS

TO THE NEXT LEVEL

DEAN GUIDA

WHEN
GRIT
IS
NOT
ENOUGH

AN ENTREPRENEUR'S PLAYBOOK

FOR TAKING YOUR BUSINESS

TO THE NEXT LEVEL

DEAN GUIDA

ENOUGH

AN INC.
ORIGINAL

An Inc. Original
New York, New York
www.anincoriginal.com

This work is being published under the An Inc. Original imprint by an exclusive arrangement with Inc. Magazine. Inc. Magazine and the Inc. logo are registered trademarks of Mansueto Ventures, LLC. The An Inc. Original logo is a wholly owned trademark of Mansueto Ventures, LLC.

Distributed by River Grove Books

Design and composition by Greenleaf Book Group
Cover design by Greenleaf Book Group
Cover images: ©iStockphoto/Savushkin

Publisher's Cataloging-in-Publication data is available.

Paperback ISBN: 978-1-63909-023-5

Hardback ISBN: 978-1-63909-025-9

eBook ISBN: 978-1-63909-024-2

First Edition

CONTENTS

ACKNOWLEDGMENTS

This book would not have been possible without the people who have helped me and supported me on my journey of building a successful tech company. I wish I could include all of them, but I have space for only some. Let me start with my mom. She taught me how important it is to keep learning and seeking out knowledge. Mom's support allowed me to believe that anything is possible in life if you want it badly enough. She also taught me that hard work and focus are key ingredients to success.

I am so appreciative of the love and support of my wife, Karen. She has always been there for me, no matter what happens—since before I started my company all the way to the present day.

I have also been inspired by my kids, Michael, Jenny, and Rachel. I am in awe of their energy, playfulness, and spirit to love life. Thinking of them always keeps me motivated to push through the ups and downs of being an entrepreneur.

I thank the people of Infragistics. Over the last thirty-five years, they have continued to innovate, take care of our customers, and work as a team against all odds. They exemplify all the learning, experimenting, and operational experience expressed in this book.

I also thank my executive team, Jason Beres, Holly Fee, Chris Rogers, and Phil Dinsmore, and my assistant, Diane Shea. They are the best and brightest in the industry and are instrumental in running Infragistics. In addition, I thank my board of directors for all the tough conversations.

My thanks go to the Infragistics design team and everyone who helped proofread the book and gave feedback along the way.

Finally, I thank my book team: Larry Rothstein, Matt George, and Christine Dunn. We spent many hours together discussing the contents of each chapter. They made the process fun and enjoyable. We started off as business collaborators and ended up as friends.

INTRODUCTION

All successful entrepreneurs have had this feeling at least once: You're in triage mode. Every new problem that arises takes more and more of your attention. You try to stave off the deluge by plugging as many leaks as possible through an individual Herculean effort, but the dam is about to burst and soon the problems will drown the enterprise.

My "Dutch boy" moment came during what should have been a time of triumph for my company, Infragistics. We had recently merged with one of our competitors—a company that was nearly bankrupt but had a large customer base. It also had a number of talented employees in design development, sales, and marketing to add to our team.

It seemed like the right move to get us to the next level as a company. What could go wrong?

Plenty, as it turned out.

Within months, we were draining cash. One day, we hit rock bottom. We had $618.00 in the bank and $580,000 in monthly expenses. Suddenly, we were the ones who were about to go out of business.

So I did what I had always done—hurled myself throughout the company. I was coding, writing software, traveling the country and the world pitching our products, conducting public relations, cutting my pay, and on and on. Every day was a whirl of activities, but it still wasn't enough to turn us around. I was burning out rapidly. My life had become an agony. But with my physical and mental exhaustion came a realization: We were now a much bigger company, but we lacked the processes and procedures to execute at this level. I had to discover a new way to help Infragistics win.

Learning new ways has never been easy for me. Like most entrepreneurs, I am hardwired to overcome challenges personally, no matter how difficult they are. I am also usually single-mindedly focused on success. I worked tirelessly for years, always displaying what is commonly described as "grit," a mixture of passion and perseverance.

Grit comes naturally to me—ever since I began working at the age of eight. My parents had divorced two years earlier, and wanting to help my mother, I convinced our condo's maintenance man to let me sweep floors and clean the pool. By the second grade, I was using an eight-track player to create mixtapes of Pink Floyd, Bachman–Turner Overdrive, and Styx, which I would sell to other kids. Over the next few years, I continued to hustle—making burritos at Fiesta Taco and working as a busboy and barback at TGI Friday's—eventually earning enough money to pay half of our monthly rent.

By sixteen, I bought my first fully loaded computer system and used it to launch a business with a friend's older brother, who was a CPA. We created an accounting software program. Despite never releasing it to the public, it was a great learning experience for me. Hustling was now firmly ingrained in my blood.

After high school, I attended the University of Miami. Always in need of money, I worked nights operating the school's IBM mainframe and interned in the human resources department, whose $8 million payroll system was deeply flawed and ineffective. I convinced the HR vice president to let me improve it. To his amazement, I quickly solved all of the system's problems. The delight in his eyes when the system hummed along was something I have tried to replicate with every Infragistics customer.

Following graduation, I headed to Wall Street. For several years I freelanced for such major companies as IBM and AIG. Financially I was doing well, but I wanted my own company—one that would create simple and beautiful products.

I saved $25,000 and with my friend Don Preuninger launched a business that eventually became Infragistics. Don worked from his mom's house on Staten Island coding night and day. My days were spent writing code for IBM, and my nights, like Don's, were focused on coding so our dream could come true.

Eventually, Infragistics's UX and UI tools, which we sold to application developers and designers, were used by major international companies, including Intuit, Morgan Stanley, Credit Suisse, Bank of America, Fidelity, Ikea, Exxon, and Charles Schwab, as well as by all 911 systems in the United States. Success after success.

But now this crisis over the merger. Would Infragistics be buried under the flood of new problems? Would all the efforts of my lifetime be swept away?

I knew I had to learn new ways to run a company and be more strategic about it. I knew Infragistics had to change dramatically if it was to compete in an ever-changing market.

The practices and procedures I have discovered since that moment of crisis are described in this book. They are the foundation of what I have come to call a vNext Business.

What do I mean by vNext? vNext is a software idea I have adapted to describe my belief that a company is like an organic being, endlessly needing to adapt and change. It must continually create the next version of itself, adapting at a relentless pace to survive and prosper.

At each stage of your business growth, you will have to adapt, learn, and improve your operations to grow and be profitable. I wrote this book to give you actionable information to improve and create resilience in your business.

And a vNext Business is what you need to build if you want to thrive and win in the next era of business.

So, what kind of company is Infragistics now?

It is a company that produces beautiful products and services that delight customers and enable us to sustain our profitability over many years.

Our culture is based on ethics and values, where teams collaborate productively and efficiently at meetings while maintaining deep human connections. Here employees feel passionate about their work and help one another through honest and nonjudgmental feedback. This enables us to find and retain the best talent available.

Moreover, Infragistics supports this culture by being data driven, operationally efficient, and financially rigorous.

Infragistics is now agile enough to respond to the relentlessly changing marketplace. We are a company whose leadership is self-reflective, transparent, and constantly creating an organization where learning is a primary purpose and goal.

That is the kind of company Infragistics has become—a vNext Business!

When I began my business more than thirty years ago, I never realized how much I had to learn to enable Infragistics to continue to win. If only I had known then what I know now.

If my life and the success of Infragistics is any proof of concept, your journey can be as enjoyable and successful as ours. When a fresh crisis hits your company, or the market turns dramatically, there will be no need to plug the holes to prevent the flood of problems. Your teams will share the burden and solve the problems one by one as you create a stronger and more resilient company—positioned to ride the upside when the crisis passes. It is then you will know you have become a vNext Business.

1

CULTURE, DESIGN, AND OPERATIONS

When I was looking for a new Infragistics headquarters some time ago, I was shown a number of buildings that once housed thriving enterprises but that were now closed and boarded up. Amid mounds of dust and stacked chairs, each darkened firm left behind statements still taped on walls stating the firm's values and objectives in an attempt to create a corporate culture. The founders of these businesses, undoubtedly, had tried to develop a culture that would enable them to achieve profitability and to sustain long-term success.

What had happened? Did they not understand all the dimensions of what constitutes an outstanding company culture? Did they not design a culture that was tied to operational goals so as to achieve the superior outcomes necessary for a vNext Business?

Many CEOs think culture is important and attempt to develop a positive one. However, because they usually view culture as "fluffy," their efforts are often half-hearted; they fall behind other priorities and end up entailing little more than putting up posters, ordering T-shirts with the corporate logo, and sending out an occasional e-mail blast.

This level of effort is a recipe for financial disaster. An outstanding culture *dramatically* affects the bottom line. Carolyn Dewar and Reed Doucette, consultants at McKinsey and Company, researched more than one thousand organizations that collectively employed more than three million workers. Companies in the top quartile of outstanding cultures posted a 60 percent higher return to shareholders than companies in the medium quartile and 200 percent higher than those in the bottom quartile.[1]

Dewar and Doucette argued that what separates the highest-performing organizations from the rest is culture, because it enables a company's competitive advantage to sustain itself and grow over time.[2]

Culture is inherently difficult to copy because it adapts automatically to changing marketplace conditions as companies seek to find new ways to succeed. High-performing organizations thrive on change. On the other hand, low-performing cultures do not respond well to change. Dewar and Doucette's research shows that 70 percent of transformations fail, and 70 percent of those failures are due to culture-related issues.[3]

Moreover, companies with weak cultures suffer from a disengaged worker force. A 2023 Gallup report surveying more than 160 countries, titled "State of the Global Workplace," indicated that only 23 percent of workers feel engaged, which means that 77 percent feel disengaged.[4] Try creating great products and services with employees who are just going through the motions so they can pick up a paycheck.

When I started Infragistics, I intuitively realized how important an outstanding culture would be for our success. My belief wasn't, however, based on research or global surveys but was the result of hard-earned lessons learned at some of the most successful enterprises in America.

Prior to launching my own company, I worked on Wall Street as a freelance consultant, where I encountered numerous colleagues who lacked passion about what they were doing and rarely strove to achieve anything important. At one firm, I was teamed with thirty people and charged with developing a new software product. Two associates and I did *all* the work. Our teammates mindlessly chatted away during meetings and wasted time writing reports nobody read.

At other companies, I worked with many individuals whose sole focus was career advancement. To achieve their aims, they withheld vital information so they could acquire power within the company. If that didn't help them land in the C-suite, they used intimidation to get their ideas and decisions implemented. Their behavior created an environment where I rarely looked forward to going to work.

Such negative experiences fueled insights into the kind of culture I wanted at Infragistics. I believed it should be a company where everyone could have fun, all employees were passionate about their work, and they were devoted to delighting the customer. Further, it should be a company where people build great, simple, and beautiful software. In addition, I wanted employees who desired to learn new things, who talked through problems to solve them, and who were consistently helpful to their teammates and other employees. Finally, I wanted us to attract talented employees and retain them for a long time.

But how would I do this?

As an avid reader, I devoured as many books as I could about all the elements needed to create a great culture. I also attended lectures and conferences to hear some of the best business minds in the world speak. I culled the thoughts of my executive team. And I spent time reflecting on what worked and didn't work at Infragistics.

From all these diverse sources, I concluded that an outstanding culture involves:

- Defining in clear terms what a company culture should be

- Creating a learning organization

- Hiring smart, open-minded, lifelong learners who get things done

- Designing a warm, helpful, safe, welcoming, and relaxed environment—physically and emotionally in the way people interact with each other

- Hiring, firing, nurturing, and rewarding people and teams, an important job for your executive team, managers, and indirect leaders

- Achieving alignment and ownership by clearly defining the outcomes you want, and giving your leaders and teams the autonomy to achieve your company's goals

- Articulating company values along with a mission statement, a vision statement, and a purpose statement

- Using the principles of intelligent design to achieve a culture that supports operational excellence and execution

- Accomplishing outstanding business outcomes

OUR VALUES

Let's start our discussion with the definition we use in Infragistics: *Culture* is how we get projects done and how we work and behave with each other. Specifically, we created spaces—interpersonal and physical—and processes that allowed us to leverage everyone's excellence to achieve our goals.

Next, we developed our company's values and created our mission, vision, and purpose statements.

Then we devoted time to figuring out how best to implement them in a way that can be embodied by employees and management.

At Infragistics, our overarching values are innovation, commitment, and respect.

These values inform twenty-two behaviors and actions through what we call the Infragistics Way. (For a full list, see the appendix.) Some of these behaviors and actions include the following.

Do the Right Thing

At Infragistics, we have an unwavering commitment to doing the right thing in every action we take and in every decision we make, especially when no one's looking. We tell the truth, no matter what the consequences. If we make a mistake, we own up to it, apologize, and correct it.

Deliver Results

While we appreciate effort, we reward and celebrate results. We follow up, and we take responsibility to ensure tasks are completed. We set high goals, measure our progress, and hold ourselves accountable for achieving those results.

Delight the Customer

We believe in doing all the big and little things that delight our customers. We want to exceed expectations and deliver the "wow" factor to them in every interaction. We achieve this by focusing on beauty and simplicity in all our products and services.

Be Fanatical about Response Time

We respond to our customers' questions and concerns quickly, whether in person, on the phone, or by email. We acknowledge their questions and concerns and inform them that we're "on it." We keep them continuously updated on the answers to their questions and how we will resolve their concerns.

Be Curious and Innovate

We are a learning organization, always searching for the best solutions. We are driven by our curiosity. We ask why and listen intently to the answers. We take risks and are constantly innovating and improving our products and services.

We are not afraid to make mistakes—and we learn from them.

Check Your Ego at the Door

We don't let our egos get in the way of doing what's best for the team. We believe worrying about who gets credit or taking things personally is counterproductive. Every decision is based solely on advancing a team's goals and doing what's best for the customer.

COMMUNICATING OUR VALUES

Our commitment to the Infragistics Way—a detailed statement of our values—is sustained and deepened by a series of actions.

- The statement is published on our website.

- We give every employee a physical card with the statement printed on it.

- Our flip charts have the Infragistics Way written on them.

- Whenever I speak to our teams, whether it's the whole company or in smaller meetings, I always mention the Infragistics Way.

- The executive team and I rotate writing a weekly email to the whole company, talking about the values in the Infragistics Way and telling stories that validate what we're doing and why we're doing it.

Orientations

In addition to the above measures, every quarter I conduct an orientation with all the new hires, usually in groups of five to ten, but sometimes up to fifteen. In that forty-five-minute meeting, I talk about the history of Infragistics, about myself, about the company's values and culture, about our strategies, and about our successes and our challenges. I emphasize we are all unique people, and we should show up as our authentic selves every day and help each other. I add it is important for them to have fun and enjoy their workday as we compete and try to win. If we do not, then none of us will get paid.

At the beginning of my talk, I inform them that when I finish, I want them to tell the group what they found meaningful and interesting about what I said. This provides me with useful feedback and is a way for them to hear what their colleagues think. In addition, this helps align everyone and bonds us around how we want to behave and work together to win, to have fun, and to compete as a team. They need to realize it is up to them to nurture our culture. Their behavior will determine whether or not we can actually keep our great culture going.

These talks are rewarding to me personally, and they reinforce what we are trying to achieve culturally. We are an international, multicultural firm with offices in the United States, Japan, India, South America, and Europe. We build software for the world. We want diversity in thinking. We don't want "yes people."

My efforts bore fruit at a recent meeting when one participant objected to the way I was acting because I'd violated one of the tenants of the Infragistics Way. She was right. I thanked her for holding me accountable. To make a culture great, everyone must buy in—including the CEO!

Mission, Vision, and Purpose Statements

We have consciously injected our values into both our mission statement and our vision statement.

Many entrepreneurs and company leaders believe the two are interchangeable. They are not. A *mission statement* summarizes your company's goals and values while a *vision statement* inspires your employees to dream about where the company should go rather than how to get there.

Over time, we found that trying to continuously communicate and remember three different statements was difficult for us. We decided to collapse the three statements into one and focus on our purpose—*to create simplicity, beauty, and happiness in the world, one app at a time* (see Chapter 14).

Research has indicated that when a company has a clear purpose, it results in a higher level of employee engagement and a more positive work culture. It also keeps talent at your company. Purpose-driven workers are 54 percent more likely to stay for five years at a company and 30 percent more likely to grow into high performers compared to those who arrive at work with only a paycheck as their motivator.[5]

Our purpose statement helps us in a variety of ways:

- Decision-making: Our employees and managers in all areas use the purpose statement as a guide in all critical business choices we make.

- Attracting talent: We have so many talented employees because of the strength of our purpose.

- Maintaining focus: Our purpose statement helps us face challenges in the marketplace by keeping us on track.

- Maintaining employee morale: By adhering to our mission statement, we continue to excite and motivate our employees.

EXPERIENCE DESIGN AND OPERATIONAL EXCELLENCE

Two other concepts—experience design and operational excellence—also help us infuse our culture into all our company processes.

I know the importance of experience design from years of working in the software industry. To create great software, *every single interaction* must be considered, and then these interactions have to be coordinated and strategically implemented.

A highly effective culture interweaves the seventeen seemingly disparate elements I discuss in this book—from creating a data-driven organization, to running effective meetings, to constructing strategic plans, to effective personal care—while helping us determine how to operationalize these elements.

When that happens, the "fluffy" notion of culture gives way to making hard business sense.

How you operationalize your culture depends on what kind of business you are in. For a business that focuses on products, operations involve how you purchase, store, make, and ship merchandise. For a business that is service oriented, operations can mean communicating, collaborating, and managing projects in the most efficient manner.

For a software enterprise like Infragistics, where we have both products and services, value lies in our personnel. For us, operations involve finding optimal ways of hiring, training, and mentoring our employees and creating effective teams. Our efforts to retain talented employees and keep them highly motivated is also how we see operations.

Physical Environment

Let's see how this concept of operations helped us design a better Infragistics culture. Some time ago, we lost one of our most talented employees. I asked a number of people at the company what had happened and discovered it wasn't about how much we were paying him. Rather, he said he left because another company was "cooler" than we were.

Cooler than Infragistics?! That could not stand! I became determined to rethink how to build an even stronger Infragistics culture.

That is why we spent heavily on our new building. When potential employees enter, they immediately find a warm, welcoming, innovative, and high-end physical environment.

We also have a fun-filled social environment designed to increase the bond between us in a variety of ways. For example, when I see a product manager, a software developer, and a marketing specialist playing pool or ping pong and really enjoying themselves, I know we have created an activity that stimulates cross-collaboration. I play a lot of pool myself, having learned the game when I was eight years old from my grandfather. I am still pretty good, and I have a lot of fun winning!

During lunchtime, I develop relationships and our culture by sitting down with employees to chat, as well as to learn how they are progressing on various projects.

Great Food

Food plays a major role in creating our culture. At Infragistics, we have many great cooks from different ethnic backgrounds, so the food is always delicious, flavorful, and interesting. We have frequent potluck meals.

I really enjoy cooking, and I bring in my own specialties. One is stuffed peppers. The recipe: Fill bell peppers with a mix of yellow rice, mozzarella cheese, ground beef, and whatever spices you desire, and bake them for 45 minutes at 375 degrees Fahrenheit. It's that easy.

My other specialty is the so-called DG burger—half a pound of beef, ranch dressing, thick bacon chopped up, cheddar cheese, and jalapeno peppers, all put in a burger bowl and then grilled with the hood shut.

The folks at Infragistics love it.

The DG burger even has international appeal. When one of our biggest clients from Japan along with several of his colleagues came to our New Jersey headquarters, I made DG burgers for them. They gulped them down and wanted another round. They even snapped pictures of them, which they posted on Facebook.

Sometime later when I went to Tokyo to meet with our customers, they all started to call me the "DG burger guy." That is one way to spread a company's culture!

Hosting Events

Community activities are another element of building our culture. We host lots of after-hours events involving local schools and continuing education. Once a month, we provide food and drinks and teach about software development and design at no charge.

We also host events for schools and their clubs in our building. I believe it inspires the kids and maybe even the parents to study engineering, design, and computer science. The parents, kids, and Infragistics employees really enjoy it.

Our Rhythm

Our company's culture, like all firms, has a rhythm. As vigilant as we try to be at Infragistics, there are times when we fail to pay attention to it. Sometimes the pressure of work and deadlines gets in the way. Sometimes we get distracted by personal issues. As we grew bigger, it became more difficult to sustain our culture, particularly when we became international.

But as the research shows and the success of Infragistics demonstrates, there is tremendous value in a strong company culture. It motivates our employees, it drives our innovation, it attracts the talented and caring people who work here, it underpins our profitability, and it delights our customers.

Culture is much more than words taped to a wall. It is the essence of who you are. And it is the key to your business becoming a vNext Business. The steps to achieving success lie in each of the following chapters.

 KEY POINTS FOR CREATING A VNEXT BUSINESS

1. Define your company culture in clear terms.

2. Create a learning organization.

3. Hire open-minded, lifelong learners—smart people who like to get things done.

4. Create a warm, helpful, safe, welcoming, and relaxed environment both physically and with regard to how people interact with each other.

5. Nurture your culture through hiring, firing, recognizing, and rewarding people and teams. This is an important job for your executive team, managers, and indirect leaders.

6. Create alignment and ownership by clearly defining the desired outcomes and giving company leaders and teams the autonomy to achieve the firm's goals.

7. Articulate company values along with a mission statement, a vision statement, and a purpose statement.

2

BUILDING TRUST
IN A TEAM

After thirty-five years of running Infragistics, I believe the most important ingredient for achieving a cohesive and high-performing team can be summed up in just one word: trust.

When I first began in business, I had an intuitive idea about trust, but I had no idea how critical it is in building high-performing teams.

Trust is the magic glue that keeps you together when things get tough.

Trust enables two-way communication and knits together individuals with different approaches to work and problem-solving to form a cohesive, strong company fabric.

In addition, trust opens up a team's talents and creativity, and, ultimately, it enables a team and a company to win in the marketplace.

Trust takes time to create but can easily slip away. If this happens, you must work diligently to re-create it.

RESEARCH ON TRUST

I have done extensive reading about trust. Interestingly, two of the best books on the subject were written in the 1930s during the Great Depression, when many Americans had lost trust in themselves and in the country. Both books rely on insights gained from observing human behavior. And a remarkable current book provides further examples about the importance of trust during war and in civilian life. And recently, a massive Google study about teams, which utilizes detailed data analysis, added another layer to my understanding of trust.

The first book that impressed me was Dale Carnegie's *How to Win Friends and Influence People*, a 1936 bestseller that remains popular today.[1] Raised on a farm in Missouri, Carnegie went to New York City to become an actor after completing college. While living from hand to mouth at the YMCA on 125th Street, he conceived the idea to teach public speaking. Out of this grew what became the Dale Carnegie Course—which is still being taught today—and his famous book, wherein he details ten lessons useful in establishing trust. These concepts are so universal and so enduring that they have helped me establish trust not just in my business relationships but also in my personal ones.

I particularly like these concepts and principles:

1. *Do not criticize, condemn, or complain.* This is not always easy in business or in personal life. But I look for the positives in people at work and at home, which almost always results in improving a relationship.[2]

2. *Be generous with praise.* Whenever I encounter people at Infragistics doing an excellent job by working hard or delivering a great experience to our customers, I always tell them how much I appreciate their efforts. Too many managers and executives are indifferent to the achievements of others.[3]

3. *Remember their name.* As Carnegie wrote, "A person's name is to that person the sweetest and most important sound in any language."[4] A simple rule but a powerful one. Use people's names in conversations as often as you can—it is a sign of respect and that you value them. Infragistics is a multinational company, so sometimes I find it difficult to pronounce people's names correctly,

but I always try. Even if I don't get it quite right, they appreciate my attempt.

4. *Be genuinely interested in other people.* The best way to connect with people is to learn about them.[5] At Infragistics, we think of ourselves as a family and are open to sharing both our personal and our professional sides.

5. *Be quick to acknowledge your own mistakes.* Summing up another of Carnegie's lessons, Frances Bridges points out, "Having strong and stable personal and professional relationships relies on you taking responsibility for your actions, especially your mistakes. Nothing helps end tension or a disagreement more than a swift acknowledgment and apology on your part."[6] I own up to my mistakes. We all make them. Acknowledging them creates a strong bond with your colleagues.

A year after Carnegie's book appeared, another optimistic treatise was published titled *Think and Grow Rich.*[7] It has become one of the ten best-selling self-help books of all time. Written by Napoleon Hill, it lays out thirteen principles for success. Each one resonated with me when I read them.

Among Hill's most important ideas was what he called principle 9: the power of the master mind. Hill thought no two minds ever come together without creating a third, invisible, intangible force that he labeled as a third mind—when discussing something with another person or persons, good ideas suddenly appear.[8]

The power of the master mind occurs daily at Infragistics as teams develop new software or generate new customer solutions. No matter how smart someone is or thinks they are, a team whose members trust each other always makes better decisions than an individual acting alone.

Flashing forward, a recent book that influenced me was *Extreme Ownership: How U.S. Navy SEALs Lead and Win* by former officers Leif

Babin and Jocko Willink.[9] The authors discuss the importance of creating trust in teams that engage in life-or-death combat missions. They propose the key to achieving trust is that each team member must be completely responsible for their own actions. There are no excuses. Whether a mission succeeds or fails (particularly if it fails), leaders must hold themselves accountable. By accepting full responsibility, that individual gains a team's complete trust. Navy SEALs put a higher value on trust than even the skills of warfare.[10]

At Infragistics, all executives and managers take full responsibility for their actions and decisions. Experience has taught us, like Willink and Babin, that this is the best way to build and maintain trust in the company.

Willink and Babin's concepts have been confirmed by a major Google study dubbed Project Aristotle, after the great Greek philosopher who famously said, "The whole is greater than the sum of the parts."[11] Google analysts examined dozens of teams and interviewed hundreds of executives, team leaders, and team members. The researchers then evaluated team effectiveness in four different ways: (1) executive evaluation of the team, (2) team leader evaluation of the team, (3) team member evaluation of the team, and (4) sales performance against quarterly quota.[12]

What did they find? By measuring participant and leader perceptions against actual sales performance data, they concluded that what really mattered was not so much who was on the team, but how the team worked together. And the most important factor contributing to a team working well together? You guessed it—trust.[13]

In a team with high psychological safety, teammates feel safe to take risks around their team members.

For the Google researchers, trust was the outgrowth of what they termed "psychological safety."[14] I prefer the term "safe environment" because it encompasses more than just interpersonal dynamics by incorporating all elements in a work situation, including physical spaces.

The Google researchers defined psychological safety as an individual's perception of potentially taking a risk, and the response their teammates may have to them taking that risk. They described it this way:

> *In a team with high psychological safety, teammates feel safe to take risks around their team members. They feel confident that no one on the team will embarrass or punish anyone else for admitting to a mistake, asking a question, or offering a new idea.*[15]

ELEMENTS OF TRUST

In addition to this report and the books I mention, over the course of my career I have learned about other elements essential in building trust.

First, a leader and all team members must bring their authentic selves to work every day—all day. This may seem obvious, but in business employees often believe they should hide their feelings and be "professional." But let's be honest: This is not who most of us really are.

Thinking of yourself as a "professional" can cause you to suppress your emotions and natural instincts. When you are authentic, you spontaneously and effectively establish rapport, trust, and relationships with others. When you share something personal and behave naturally, you will be a catalyst for others to do the same. Authentic behavior can be modeled and encouraged.

Being a leader means disclosing your honest feelings when things are going well and (equally important) when they are not going well. If you need help, ask for it. Modeling this behavior allows other team members to do the same. For such honesty to occur, as Google's Project Aristotle shows, you must intentionally create a safe place for employees.

Recently one of our software developers, a brilliant engineer, was stuck on an architecture design problem. He spun his wheels for weeks, afraid to admit to the team that he couldn't find a solution. Finally, when questioned at a meeting as to why he was so far behind the deadline for the project, he confessed his bewilderment about what to do. Members of the team came to his assistance and within an hour the issue was solved.

This positive result occurred because we'd created a safe space and established an environment where failure isn't punished—it's simply the start of a new conversation. Creating a safe space requires effort. It requires consistency. And it requires a commitment to supporting your teams— not just when they succeed but especially when they're struggling.

At Infragistics, we have gone beyond just proclaiming that meetings are safe spaces to discuss feelings; we have consciously designed our building in ways that actively promote feelings of warmth, community, and openness. This extends to the colors of walls and the use of wooden floors and bookcases and comfortable chairs and sofas. We have created a number of small rooms where groups of four to six employees can meet and collaborate. Behind the building, we have "the bamboo room"—a backyard with teak furniture, music, and lots of food. What better place to relax and connect with your team? Good for business and makes getting work done fun!

While the responsibility of creating trust starts with the team or company leader, everyone must be involved. Each person's behavior influences, positively or negatively, others on the team. Everyone must create an environment that feels as if "we are in this together" to get things done and leverage the strength of the team.

After all, trust takes a long time to build but only an instant to lose.

KEY BEHAVIORS THAT BUILD TRUST

Over the years, I have found there are key behaviors that create trust among people and teams. My observations, just like the ones Dale Carnegie made long ago, underscore what is essential for people to learn so that others will like you and want to work with you. They are discussed in the following sections and summarized in Figure 2.1.

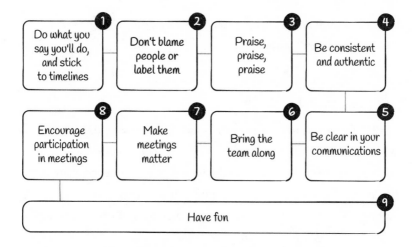

Figure 2.1. Nine key behaviors that create trust among people and teams

Do What You Say You'll Do, and Stick to Timelines

If you cannot complete something by when you said it would be done, inform the team of the issues you're facing, ask for help, and set a new target date. Be vividly transparent in this.

Don't Blame People or Label Them

No one *wants* to fail. Everyone wants to do a good job. Develop a culture that doesn't blame individuals for failure. Help them get things done through coaching, education, support, and by adding skills from other members that they may lack.

Praise, Praise, Praise

When a team succeeds, praise them publicly. For every time you talk about areas for improvement, multiply those four times when providing positive feedback to an individual or to a team. Thank them for work and behaviors that align with your company's core values and for achieving their stated objectives. Celebrate their wins! I constantly remind folks of all the great companies that use our software and how we continuously solve our customers' problems.

Be Consistent and Authentic

Trust is built on consistent behavior. You can't come in to work one day a whirling tornado and the next day completely laid-back. If I did that, my colleagues and employees would wonder which Dean they are dealing with. Every day I try to be a thoughtful, listening, caring leader, always thinking about how I am expressing my attitudes in my body language, my tone of voice, and the words I choose.

This must be done authentically. What people see should be what they get. If you model authenticity, others will follow suit, ultimately creating a nurturing and trusting environment.

Be Clear in Your Communications

Both leaders and members of teams must communicate clearly, or trust will evaporate. When communications work well, individuals have peace of mind because they understand what is being asked of them and what they are supposed to do. Moreover, decision-makers feel confident things will get done and projects will move forward.

Bring the Team Along

The coronavirus crisis was a great test of how to consistently communicate decisions in a highly politicized environment and with constantly changing advice from medical and governmental authorities. At Infragistics, we closed our office and worked remotely when the virus first struck in March 2020. As vaccines became widely available in early 2021, we looked forward to returning to our building by fall and once again seeing each other in person. But when the Delta variant struck, I decided to keep our people home as death rates once again rose. When we reopened our offices in April 2022, we were a hybrid workplace.

I communicated these decisions through email and in our monthly company-wide meetings. I consistently followed up with more emails, making sure I kept conveying my awareness of the isolation that many employees were feeling and the need for us to be together again. And I constantly thanked everyone for their continued efforts to make Infragistics operate and even improve during this most difficult period.

Make Meetings Matter

On a practical level, I recommend meeting at least once a week as a team. But instead of launching into the agenda, start the meeting off by having everyone check in and share something personal for two or three minutes or longer. There is no right amount of time for this—whatever works for you and your team.

Our executive team has a two-hour agenda meeting scheduled every week. We are a team of five and we spend the first forty-five minutes, about nine minutes each, checking in professionally and personally. This has really helped our team bond and become much closer. The rest of the time should be centered on an agenda set by the CEO or executive team members. (For more, see Chapter 12.)

Encourage Participation in Meetings

For me, silence in meetings is a waste of time. As a leader you are always striving to get your team to understand ideas, align on these ideas, solve problems, and share their opinions. To get full participation, ask people who are not talking what they think.

Communicating that you expect participation from everyone helps even the most reserved team member offer his or her best thoughts and opinions. Everyone's point of view is important, particularly those who are silent. Many times they are not aligned with the direction the others in the meeting favor. Adding their viewpoints makes for more lively and fun meetings and, occasionally, contentious ones.

Every team member should have the opportunity to shine, regardless of their job title or time with the company. This leverages the group's diversity of thinking, which, in turn, helps solve problems.

Side conversations, which delay execution and divide a team, should be discouraged. Ultimately, the team must align as a group around decisions.

Have Fun

For me, this is vitally important in building trust with a team. We spend so much time at work that to have a fulfilling life you must have fun during these hours. At Infragistics we enjoy going to dinner and then to a movie, particularly those by Marvel Studios. We also have parties and events. Such activities make the day more enjoyable and bring team members closer.

These bonding experiences result in increased efficiency and better group problem-solving. Create a budget for these activities so managers and executives have money to plan them with their teams as they see fit.

HOW TRUST CAN BE LOST AND FOUND AGAIN

No matter how hard you try to build trust, it can easily and quickly slip away.

A software company founder I know made every effort to build trust throughout her company and with her executive team. She felt close to her team and believed that they felt the same toward her.

As she viewed the future of the company, however, she became convinced it needed to head in a totally new (and admittedly risky) direction. When she told her team her thoughts, she faced strong opposition from the company's head of sales. He said, "Your new approach could lose us significant market share." Other team members sided with him almost instantly. No consensus was reached that day about the company's future.

The conflict soon turned personal and extremely contentious.

Throughout the next few months, the head of sales consciously worked to marshal other employees' opposition to upend the founder's vision for the company. Despite the founder's and the company's deep commitment to creating safe spaces so that employees could express their opinions freely, the head of sales acted so negatively and eroded trust so substantially that the founder felt he had to be dealt with in a strong manner.

The founder removed all his direct reports, dramatically reducing his power and indicating that the next step—firing—was around the corner.

That worked. Shaken, the head of sales agreed to see what would happen if the company headed in this new direction and to work in good faith to achieve this goal. Over time, the founder was proven correct. She and the head of sales eventually repaired their relationship, and executive meetings went back to being productive and creative. Trust flourished again.

From my point of view, trust never entirely left the relationship. When the breakdown happened, a kernel of trust remained that enabled the leader to find a positive solution.

In this case, as with SEAL teams and so too with Infragistics teams, trust is the essential component that enables a company or a military unit to withstand the most difficult of circumstances and continue to win.

 ## KEY POINTS FOR CREATING A VNEXT BUSINESS

1. Keep trust uppermost in all interactions. Trust is the fabric and critical foundation for innovation, teamwork, taking risks, and team performance.

2. Observe the trust level on the team, nurture it, and work to repair it when it erodes. Trust is ever a work in progress and is hard to establish but easy to undo.

3. Build trust by doing what you say you'll do.

4. Showing up as your authentic self and sharing personal things about yourself and your life will create a bond with your team.

5. Your physical environment, body language, tone, and words all contribute to trust or detract from it.

6. Conflict and points of view should not be avoided but should be discussed fully. This ultimately helps align a team in one direction. Everyone in the team may not be 100 percent aligned, but because a decision was made fairly, team members will work toward the best outcome for the company.

7. Having fun and doing social things together is good for business. It creates a bond that helps teams collaborate, trust, align, and get work done. Set aside a budget for these activities.

8. Talking about problems shouldn't dominate your conversations with team members. Be sure to point out and praise the great work being done about four times more often than you address areas for improvement.

9. Be genuinely interested in people and learn about them. Using someone's name in a conversation communicates respect, and it makes them feel heard and seen. And we all love hearing our names!

10. Don't label folks. Everyone wants to do a good job, so help them succeed. When things go badly or when people make mistakes, have them own up to it. Then everyone should move on.

3

GOALS AND OKRS

Quick: Can you name your company's major objectives? Now, what about your team? Can they name them?

If your answer is yes, congratulations!

If your answer is no, don't worry. You are not alone. In a 2015 survey of eleven thousand senior executives and managers, the majority *couldn't* state their company's top priorities.[1]

Describing your company's objectives is vital for long-term business success. A 2015 Deloitte study showed that no single factor had more impact on business success because "clearly defined . . . goals create alignment, clarity and job satisfaction."[2]

CASCADING GOALS

To handle the problem of employees being unable to describe a company's objectives, many organizations implement a process called *cascading goals*.[3] After determining their company's strategic goals, top executives identify "second-tier" goals and then drive them throughout the organization.

This focus moves goals more effectively to lower levels, but it still has major flaws. These include the following:

1. Because there is no communication flow upward, executives cannot easily see how the company's goals are progressing or who is working on which goals.[4]

2. Under this process, strategies are usually adjusted only once per year. In our unpredictable economy, a yearly focus dramatically increases the probability a company will fail to achieve its goals, or it will go out of business because it doesn't pivot quickly enough when dealing with marketplace changes.[5]

3. Even if an individual and their team are aligned with the company's goals, under the cascading goals model, it is difficult to determine what other teams are doing. They might be paralleling a particular team, at odds with them, or duplicating efforts. No one knows.

There is a better way!

OKRS

Infragistics has always been goal-oriented—even in our early days.

As we grew, we adopted the cascading approach to goal setting but found difficulty, as others had, in implementing them down to our frontline workers. Our goals didn't give enough guidance, they didn't capture sufficient amounts of data, and they were not flexible enough to help those who had to implement them on a daily basis.

What has worked best for us is a process called *objectives and key results* (OKRs). OKRs have focused our efforts, increased coordination between departments, promoted feedback, and expanded our vision of what we can accomplish. They have helped us set priorities (all goals are not equal), aided us in becoming a learning organization, and increased our ability to be agile and nimble. Over the last five years, by using OKRs, our objectives have become more precise, our progress more measurable, and our ability to achieve our goals much greater. (See Figure 3.1.)

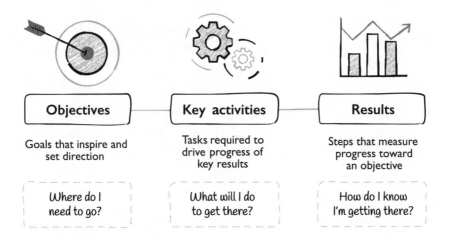

Figure 3.1. The OKR framework

Our experience is not unique. In recent years, leading technology companies such as Google, Dropbox, LinkedIn, Oracle, Slack, Spotify, and Twitter have adopted OKRs, as well as such major companies as Anheuser-Busch, BMW, Disney, Exxon, and Samsung.[6]

Many startups are also using OKRs because, as consultant Andrew Constable wrote in *Forbes* magazine, "early-stage companies are often cash poor and struggle with too much to do with limited resources; therefore, it's vital to maximize the return of investment of their time and focus on the right actions at the right time."[7]

The defining book on OKRs is *Measure What Matters*, written by John Doerr, chair of the venture capital firm Kleiner, Perkins.[8] Since 1980, he has invested in some of the world's most successful companies, including Amazon, Google, Intuit, and Netscape.

Doerr first became aware of OKRs in 1975 when he joined Intel after graduating from Harvard Business School. He attended an Intel course on OKRs taught by Andy Grove and quickly became his protégé. Grove was a Hungarian refugee who rose to become Intel's CEO and chair of the board. As CEO, Grove encouraged his managers and employees to be actively engaged in experimentation and to always be prepared for continual changes in the marketplace. Grove preferred open channels of communication between managers and employees and urged employees to express their true feelings and thoughts. OKRs exemplify Grove's philosophy of open and transparent communication.[9]

Doerr described how, after investing $12 million in Google when it was a startup, he introduced OKRs to founders Larry Page, Sergey Brin, and thirty other employees (which, at the time, was almost the entire company).[10] Doerr summarized Grove's thinking to them through a formula:

I will [objective], as measured by [set of key results].

Doerr explained to Page, Brin, and the others that objectives (or goals) are memorable *qualitative* descriptions of what you want your company to achieve. They must be written, short (one sentence), engaging, easy to understand, and if possible, inspirational, so they will motivate and challenge a team.[11]

Key results are a set of metrics that measure a company's or a team's progress toward achieving these objectives. Doerr argued there should be just three to five key results per objective. Any more, and no one will remember or accomplish them.[12]

Finally, he described two other OKR characteristics—they should be *transparent* and *bidirectional*.[13]

"Transparent" means that OKRs should be made accessible to everyone in a company at all levels. This aligns team objectives with a company's goals and improves cross-team communication.[14]

"Bidirectional" implies that goals should emerge from the *bottom up*, as well as from the *top down*. Anyone should feel empowered to suggest a new OKR, or to alter established ones, provided he or she presents analysis and evidence for needing such changes.[15]

For me, OKRs really came to life when I started to look at examples. The following is one of Infragistics's OKRs.

Marketing Goals

Owner: Executive team

Objective: Deliver 50,130 new seats (customers) a year.

Key activities: Execute an action plan across different channels to ensure we are bringing in high-quality leads that will convert and will have an exceptional customer experience. These channels include:

- Google Ads campaign

- Account-based marketing (ABM)

- Email marketing

- Search engine optimization (SEO) and content strategies

- Getting links from other websites to our website (backlinking)

- Virtual events

- Sponsored events

- Social media

- Affiliated programs

Key results:

- 4,028 new seats per month

- Deliver 28,000 quality leads per month; 336,000 leads a year

- Deliver qualified leads that yield a minimum close ratio of 21 percent

This OKR clearly establishes a goal (50,130 new customers per year), who is responsible for attaining this goal (the executive team), how it is to be accomplished (through different channels), and the steps necessary and expected to reach the goal (4,028 new seats per month; 28,000 quality leads per month, etc.).

Although this OKR is simple and clear, it is the result of considerable hard work and analytical thinking. Designing OKRs is a journey, requiring considerable thought and leadership. (We explore other OKRs in detail later in this chapter.)

Key results don't need to be complicated, but there should be clear and attainable ways to track progress toward the objective. Our key results for this objective describe how we accomplish our growth goals by segmenting progress and by defining how many leads we'll need—based on our internal growth-hacking data (more on growth hacking in Chapter 4)—to accomplish the conversion rate we desire.

Even the most useful objective is meaningless unless it is visible throughout the company—or at least to those responsible for achieving its key results.

At Google, CEO Sundar Pichai leads the entire company every quarter in evaluating its progress in achieving top-level objectives and key results. In November and December, each team and product area develops its own plans for the coming years and distills them into OKRs. The following January, Pichai articulates the company's strategic plan and its OKRs for the coming year. They are written down, displayed, and made available throughout the organization.[16]

Over the following weeks and months, thousands of Google employees formulate, discuss, revise, and grade their team and individual OKRs. They can browse the company intranet and see how other teams are measuring success. Once team members have consulted with their managers and committed to their OKRs for the quarter, any add-on must fit into the established agenda: How does the new goal stack up against the existing ones? Should something be dropped to make room for the new commitment?[17]

So where do objectives come from? At Infragistics, we discover them during the creation of our strategic and annual plans.

STRATEGIC AND ANNUAL PLANS

At Infragistics, we make an extensive company-wide effort to craft thoughtful and effective OKRs. Like most mature companies, we have a rhythm to what we do. Our OKRs originate from our strategic and annual plans, whose purpose is to align everyone around our goals, from the board of directors to the executive team to individual teams—marketing, sales, design, development, and so on.

We begin creating our strategic plan in the first quarter, which must be approved by the board in the third quarter; our annual plan starts in the second quarter and must be approved by the board in the fourth quarter.

Each element in our strategic and annual plans flows from our mission statement, which is: To create simplicity, beauty, and happiness in the world, one app at a time.

Everyone at Infragistics must be committed to achieving this mission in all aspects of their work.

I begin work on our strategic plan with a small group from our board. Our strategic plan is developed with three-year financial objectives and describes our business revenue/gross sales, states our profits and losses, and indicates what our cash on hand is and how it will be employed over those years. Our planning is based on sales targets, which are broken down by regions, product line, new business, and renewals. Once we finish our analysis, our expense structure is revealed as we answer these questions: How are we going to spend our money to achieve those sales targets? Do we need to be profitable? Do we need to be cash flow positive? (For a detailed description of how to create strategic plans and their importance, see Chapter 14.)

To create simplicity, beauty, and happiness in the world, one app at a time.

Once the board agrees on the strategic plan, we have our financial direction. I then work with my executive team to create our annual plan for the coming year. The annual plan's purpose is to align all our executives and all our teams so they can execute the strategic plan. (For a detailed discussion of how to create annual plans, see Chapter 15.)

OKRs are born during this process. They are how we turn our strategy into reality and execute our annual plan.

The executive team is responsible for communicating and executing the annual plan and the OKRs at all levels of the company. Our employees' duty is to implement the annual plan and the OKRs, which can be adjusted based on new economic conditions and customer feedback.

We have been designing strategic and annual plans for a long time. We have been constructing OKRs for only about five years. At first, OKRs were not easy to do. We have become much more efficient by drawing on previous ones—we build on, reuse, or throw out past OKRs. We are better now at defining what matters, changing things that weren't realistic, and finding objectives that were creating the wrong behaviors.

One objective for us was to reduce our digital marketing cost per click. Through experience, we realized we didn't want to reduce costs to such a degree that we were not gaining new customers or lowering our close rate. When we became aware of this problem, we adjusted the OKR.

Creating OKRs, along with strategic and annual plans, takes time, but it must be done. How can you adjust course without a North Star? How can you pivot and align people who work in a company without OKRs? How can you stay agile without knowing your direction?

At the same time, don't spend too much time organizing work instead of *doing* work. If devising OKRs significantly affects your work output, question your process. If it takes six months to plan and get everyone's agreement, and you have only six months to execute the goals, your process must be adjusted to the realities of work.

IMPACT OF OKRS

In my experience, OKRs are a powerful tool with multidimensional impact.

They help everyone from the executive team through frontline workers understand if they are doing a good job or not, determine what success looks like for individuals and teams, and detail a rational plan of attack to achieve success.

OKRs also help break down silos—business divisions that operate independently and avoid sharing information. As management author Patrick Lencioni wrote in his book *Silos, Politics and Turf Wars*, "Silos— and the turf wars they enable—devastate organizations, they waste resources, kill productivity and jeopardize the achievement of goals."[18] In a *Forbes* magazine article, author Brent Gleeson argues that silos are a growing issue for most organizations of all sizes and must be addressed.[19]

I agree. I have found that because OKRs require participation across teams, they significantly solve the silo problem. In addition, at Infragistics, OKRs have helped us develop a sense of common purpose. They can have a similar impact on your company, particularly when used in a learning organization such as Infragistics. We collaborate on problems and solve them blamelessly by creating a hypothesis, testing the hypothesis by gathering data, analyzing the data, and then constantly adjusting.

Without breaking down silos, it is extremely difficult to achieve company goals—the subject of our next section.

MOONSHOTS, BHAGS, COMMITTED, AND ASPIRATIONAL GOALS

There are four major types of objectives: moonshots, big hairy audacious goals (BHAGs), committed goals, and aspirational goals. The best businesses employ a mix of all four.

Moonshots

A *Harvard Business Review* article titled "What a Good Moonshot Is Really For" traces the origins of the term and its use in business.[20] It was written by Scott D. Anthony, a managing partner, and Mark Johnson, a senior partner, both at Innosight, an innovation consulting firm. The authors attribute the term to President John F. Kennedy, who captured the world's imagination when, in 1961, he declared a national goal of "landing a man on the moon and returning him safely to the Earth." The term *moonshot* was born as a shorthanded way of describing "a difficult or expensive task, the outcome of which is expected to have great significance."[21]

The term has been used to label such highly ambitious projects as Google's driverless cars, Jeff Bezos's Blue Origins, Elon Musk's Space X attempts at commercial space travel, and even the extraordinarily rapid development by Pfizer and Moderna of vaccines to mitigate the effects of COVID-19.

Anthony and Johnson argue organizations need moonshots to propel a "future-back" approach to strategy, unlike the "present-forward" nature of most strategic-planning processes.[22]

In their article, they propose that a good moonshot contains three ingredients. First, it inspires. President Kennedy's goal roused the spirit of the country and motivated people to do extraordinary things. Second, it's credible. Before his speech, Kennedy had a detailed assessment made to ensure the goal had a reasonable chance of success. Finally, it's imaginative. Kennedy's dream was a significant break from the past possibilities of flight.[23]

The same three ingredients can be found in a business moonshot. Netflix's moonshot idea was to create a service that allowed people to watch the movies they wanted when they wanted. It inspired a new and imaginative form of distribution—sending rented DVDs by mail. Its founders, Reed Hastings and Marc Randolph, tested the idea and found that it was feasible. Eventually, Netflix turned into a streaming service and a producer of numerous movies and television shows. It now has 151 million paid subscribers in 190 countries. By 2010, its main rival, Blockbuster, filed for bankruptcy, signaling the end of the video rental store.[24]

For me, a moonshot spurs everyone in a company to try to achieve an impossible, amazing goal. It generates innovation and motivation if everyone knows that *not* achieving the moonshot is not a failure. In fact, Doerr described success as reaching just 70 percent of a moonshot goal and argues that compensation should not be tied to moonshots. I agree. Otherwise, employees will be demotivated if they miss the moonshot.[25]

BHAGs

Big hairy audacious goals (BHAGs) are compelling, long-term goals that energize and motivate employees in a similar way to a moonshot but are slightly less ambitious. For me, the BHAG is an inspiring, crazy goal, but one that gives individuals and a company direction while motivating everyone. Like a moonshot, if you don't succeed completely, it is not a failure, and it should not be tied to compensation.

Management consultant Jim Collins and Stanford Graduate School of Business professor Jerry Porras coined the term in their book *Built to Last: Successful Habits of Visionary Companies.* They argue a BHAG time frame should be at least ten years, since it is designed to propel people out of short-term thinking. In addition, a BHAG should have at least a 50 percent chance of succeeding, and it should be action-oriented, exciting, and motivate employees in a sustained way.[26]

Collins and Porras break BHAGs into four main categories:

1. *Role model:* Companies seek to emulate the success of a business in their industry.

2. *Common enemy:* Companies seek to overtake a competitor in their industry.

3. *Targeting:* Companies seek a specific status marker, such as becoming a billion-dollar company or ranking number one in their industry.

4. *Internal transformation:* Companies seek to revitalize their people, their mission, or their business model.[27]

Several of the most prominent and successful companies have articulated BHAGs. Starbucks's BHAG was "Become the most recognized and respected consumer brand in the world." Amazon's initial BHAG was "Every book ever printed in any language, all available in less than 60 seconds." Microsoft's BHAG was "A computer on every desk in every home." Meta, formerly Facebook, has articulated several BHAGs over time, including "To make the world more open and connected" and "To give everyone the power to share anything with anyone."[28]

Committed and Aspirational Goals

Aspirational goals are stretch goals. They are hard, but they can be achieved, and they drive growth and commitment.

Companies and teams can arrive at an aspirational goal by thinking: "What could we do if we had more staff, or more funding or reallocated funding, or achieved higher market reputation?" One way teams can arrive at aspirational goals is by looking at opportunities from a customer's point of view: "What would my customer's world look like in the future if we are not limited by existing constraints in creating our product or services?"[29]

Committed goals can be achieved when a team fully utilizes its resources and applies the right approach toward achieving these goals. These are logistical, daily-work-driving goals. By the end of an estimated time, a team should be able to accomplish a significant amount of them, at least 70 percent, if not 100 percent.[30]

Committed goals form most of the goals we use in the Infragistics annual plan. When first introducing OKRs, committed goals should be the focus, since they're attainable. There's a clear connection between setting the goal and seeing a way to complete it. Usually having one or two aspirational goals is sufficient.

Let's look at these four kinds of goals through the launch of Infragistics's Slingshot in 2022, which is collaboration software designed to increase the efficiency of business teams.

The market we were entering was dominated by well-established players like Microsoft Teams, which had 250 million users and 50 percent of a $100 billion market in 2022.[31]

Our Slingshot BHAG is to have

Figure 3.2. Slingshot BHAG

Given the enormous lead Microsoft had in the collaboration software space, Infragistics's moonshot was to "beat" Microsoft. By that, I mean reviewers of Slingshot, along with customers, should rate it as the better product to enable seamless collaboration between teams that deliver extraordinary business results. Is this moonshot possible? Sure. Is it likely? Not really. Does it communicate to my team exactly where we should be aiming our efforts? You bet.

Our Slingshot BHAG is to have one million active users within twenty-four months of launch (see Figure 3.2). Possible? Sure. Likely? Difficult but attainable. Much more possible than the moonshot of overcoming the behemoth Microsoft Teams in the marketplace. If everything goes our way, if our teams perform perfectly, if our software delivers on its promise, and if we get a fair bit of luck, we might be able to accomplish our BHAG.

On the other hand, an aspirational goal for Infragistics would be that by the end of 2025, Slingshot has five hundred thousand users. Possible? Definitely. Likely? Very.

And our committed goal should be to generate enough leads to acquire five hundred thousand active customers in the first twenty-four months.

These aren't just examples. In fact, these are our goals directly from our annual plan. Hard yet achievable.

TRACKING OKRS

I have always been a very visual learner, and I find color coding helps to identify quickly and clearly different stages of completion. That's why Infragistics uses a three-color system to track our OKR progress. These colors also make it very clear to everyone which OKRs are proceeding as planned and which ones need a bit more care and attention.

Red: This color means we're not making any or adequate progress. Red is not necessarily bad, especially if it's attached to a moonshot goal. But it does indicate that our teams need to rethink their approach toward achieving their key results by identifying what challenges are impeding their progress.

Yellow: When a team has made considerable progress, but that progress is not complete, we code the OKR as yellow. A lot of aspirational goals and BHAGs wind up yellow at Infragistics. For committed goals, yellow signals the team must reallocate their resources, reassess their challenges, and reimagine their initiatives to find out what kept them from reaching the goal.

Green: Goal completed. We try to ensure every committed goal winds up green.

At Infragistics, team members are encouraged to use their OKR assessments as guides, not as grades. The colors are less important than the process of self-analysis, garnering effective feedback, and facilitating a nonjudgmental discussion by the team.

Questions I find useful after OKR assessments are these:

- Was the goal harder to achieve than you thought it would be when you set it? Was it the right goal in the first place?

- If you accomplished all of your objectives, what contributed to your success?

- If you did not accomplish all of your objectives, what obstacles did you encounter?

- What did you learn in the process of achieving the OKR that you might be able to apply to future objectives?

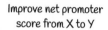

Improve net promoter
score from X to Y

Increase repurchase
rate from X to Y

Maintain customer
acquisition cost under Y

*Figure 3.3. Ways the key results directly support the
objective of creating an awesome customer experience*

Team leaders can use these questions as a guide for team discussions. Team members should be provided with avenues for effective feedback and should share their specific observations and experiences.

Let's look at two general examples of OKRs.

Example One

An objective might be "Create an awesome customer experience." A worthy goal, but how do you measure if a customer experience is awesome? Two ways: net promoter score (NPS) and repurchase rate.

NPS ascertains customer satisfaction based on one question: How likely is it that you would recommend (organization/product/service) to a friend or colleague? It is scored in the range of –100 to +100. The repurchase rate is the percentage rate of a cohort having placed another order within a certain period. The higher the repurchase rate, the more satisfied customers are.

But measuring NPS and repeat purchases alone can send the wrong message. It might encourage team members to make customers happy at any cost. A countermeasure such as customer acquisition cost should be added as a key result.

The OKR would be:

Objective: Create an awesome customer experience.

Key results (see Figure 3.3):

- Improve net promoter score from X to Y.

- Increase repurchase rate from X to Y.

- Maintain customer acquisition cost under Y.

Example Two

Objective: Launch a new digital product successfully in Q1.
Key results:

- Obtain at least twenty new product customers with an average order size of >$25,000.

- Obtain Leader Status in the Gartner Magic Quadrant.

- Win the "Best Product of the Year" award at an industry conference.

Unlike the first OKR, these key results may all be difficult to achieve, particularly Gartner Leader Status and Product of the Year. It still might be a successful launch, but unless two more reasonable metrics are added, the team might lose motivation to hit the sales target.

OKRS AT INFRAGISTICS

Let's look at several OKRs we just completed for our 2022 Annual Plan, which is specific to our industry.

Objectives

Under our strategic and annual plans, we had two major objectives.

1. Our first objective was a company-wide aspirational goal: We wanted to create the most innovative digital experiences and have the world's best designers and developers use Ignite UI and AppBuilder to build simple and beautiful apps. Our committed goal was for Infragistics to be number one in the web UI framework market by the end of the year.

2. Our second objective was to launch Slingshot, which we believe unleashes the power of the team and drives extraordinary business growth for all who use it. Our committed goal for Slingshot is to have more than five hundred thousand active users by the end of 2024. Our aspirational goal is to have one million active users by 2024.

Goals Driving Core Strategies

These goals drove our core strategies:

- Deliver the fastest grids and charts in the web stack.

- Deliver products from design to code that integrate with popular tools to produce incredible app experiences on modern UIs for web, cloud, and mobile.

- Through one app, connect everyone in a digital workplace to data analytics, and organize projects, content, and communications to boost team and company results.

- Focus on beauty and simplicity to help the software development team embed dashboards and analytics to drive business insights on modern web and cloud technology.

- Nurture a learning organization to drive growth through growth hacking.

- Execute a three-pronged approach to grow sales via transactional engagements, and create opportunities in key accounts through account-based marketing (ABM) and account-based sales (ABS) methodology to create a new sales 2.0 structure with Slingshot and Reveal market.

Resulting Goal and Additional OKRs

Under these core strategies, we established the following goal and OKRs. *Goal:* Leverage new sales 2.0 structure of always-on coaching, AI sales and marketing tools, and sales analytics to drive transactional and enterprise account growth.

Objective: Hire fifteen new Slingshot salespeople and sales operations manager; install intent data system and always-on sales coaching software by the end of Q1.

Owners: Debbie, Phil, Holly from the exec team

Key results:

- Hire and train fifteen salespeople by end of Q1.

- Hire sales operations manager by Q1.

- Begin to use intent data to focus our marketing account-based campaigns by Q1.

- Sales managers spend a minimum of one hour a day coaching each sales rep in each region where we have a presence.

Transactional and enterprise account growth needs to be supported by increasing brand awareness and trials of Infragistics. That was expressed in the following OKR.

Objective: Effective paid efforts to increase brand awareness and trials of our products

Owners: J.J., Holly, Poojitha

Key results:

- Deliver 20,000 leads a year; 1,680 per month.

- Cost per lead does not exceed $93.

- Cost per new seat is 35 percent or less of the LTV (lifetime value).

Note that in software, you have to think about the lifetime value of a customer—the reoccurring revenue, lifetime subscription software. When you acquire a new account for $1,000, you need to evaluate that cost in terms of knowing that customer will normally stay with Infragistics for ten years, so that customer has a $100,000 lifetime value.

A third OKR that was formulated to help Infragistics achieve its sales goals seeks to improve conversion rates.

Objective: Improve conversion rates of customer experience through growth hacking.

Owners: Holly, Jason Z., J.J.

Key activities:

- Deliver an exceptional end-to-end customer experience through UX, beauty, and digital properties (as measured through product and site surveys).

- Improve customer journey by knowing the "why" and where the leaks are, and increase product stickiness and satisfaction scores.

- Maintain a customer journey map that covers all the paths and avenues a user can take to discover our products—coming into our domain, trying them, and converting.

Key results:

- Improve conversion rates to 20 percent.

- Improve commerce experience from 15 percent to 20 percent conversion rate.

- Achieve a customer satisfaction score greater than 85 percent.

INDIVIDUAL OKRS

In the workplace, individual OKRs can help keep you on task and focused on delivering results for your team and clients.

Betterworks, a site devoted to helping implement OKRs, has extensive material on how to create individual OKRs. According to them, such OKRs should detail the tangible benefits to both the company *and* the person. Employees should identify specific learning outcomes from each of their OKRs and also set performance objectives that align their learning and development with business priorities.[32]

How do you create OKRs for individuals? Betterworks believes one approach is to determine the skills and traits that employees and their managers want to develop to drive business results. Employees can then set OKRs for personal development over several years that align with a company's strategic imperatives. They should also collaborate with their managers to identify one objective per quarter that produces specific learning outcomes aligned to talent strategy.[33]

Ideally, the key results required to achieve the objective should produce a specific, targeted learning outcome. Completing an OKR might involve taking on a new responsibility within the team or leading team members in a new area of learning.

To maximize personal learning and development, employees should set OKRs that give them exposure to roles or tasks they're interested in. The chance for experimentation with different tasks across the organization enables them to discover their ideal fit, where they can feel most fulfilled while benefiting the business.

OKRs aren't just for business goals. You can use them in your personal life as well. They're a great framework to learn a new skill or take on new tasks. I never thought about this possibility until recently, when I met a graduate of West Point who utilized OKRs to become a better father and husband.

They can even help in achieving goals such as losing weight. Take the usual goal of dropping five to ten pounds. Set that as the objective and create a time frame, say three months. Then put down key results—reduce carbohydrates by 50 percent, drink eight glasses of water a day, go on a one-hour walk daily.

As you read on, you will see heavy use of OKR in strategic planning, annual planning, and go-to-market (GTM) planning, which are all important elements to achieving successful outcomes and a vNext Business.

KEY POINTS FOR CREATING A VNEXT BUSINESS

1. OKRs give teams autonomy to execute strategic and annual plans by providing them with guidance on priorities to achieve those objectives.

2. Not all key results are equal, but they can help prioritize a team's work. Key results and objectives can be measured (but not all the time, and that is okay).

3. OKRs are flexible. They can flow from the top down in a hierarchical, cascading way where one objective is a key result of the OKR above it, or they can be used on a personal and team level, or flow top-down from a strategic level.

4. OKRs are a great framework to get work done; use them to minimize the time spent planning work and maximize the time you spend doing work.

5. A moonshot is a very aspirational, even unrealistic goal but serves the purpose of aligning your team around something extraordinary. Great things will happen in the pursuit, even if you don't achieve it.

6. A BHAG is similar to a moonshot, but it is a little more specific while remaining inspirational. Good things will happen even if it isn't achieved.

7. Your objectives should be focused primarily on committed or aspirational goals. If all your objectives are moonshots or BHAGs, they might demotivate your team because they're unattainable. Use all four types of objectives to motivate and align.

8. Always give your teams autonomy to execute an objective. This drives innovation, intrinsic motivation, and ownership of how to achieve an objective.

9. Communicate your OKRs clearly to the teams who will be working on them. OKRs are a great organizing principle but work only if everyone knows about them.

4

FINDING THE WHY: THE SCIENTIFIC (GROWTH-HACKING) METHOD OF RUNNING A BUSINESS

When most of us think of a scientist, certain images pop into our minds. Perhaps Albert Einstein, with his otherworldly look and swirl of white hair. Or Bill Nye, decked out in safety goggles and bow tie, standing over a Bunsen burner. Or more recently the women of the movie *Hidden Figures*—Dorothy Vaughan, Mary Jackson, and Katherine Johnson—whose abilities helped propel the early days of the American space program.

We may even remember the scientific method from our high school classes: Make an observation, ponder why something caused an occurrence, form a hypothesis to answer the question, test the hypothesis with a series of experiments, and then confirm the hypothesis or formulate a new one.

Most people don't normally associate scientists or the scientific method with business. But they should! Whether you are a startup, a growing company, or a large company, the scientific method is essential to your success as a vNext Business (see Figure 4.1).

I consider myself a business scientist, and I am surrounded by business

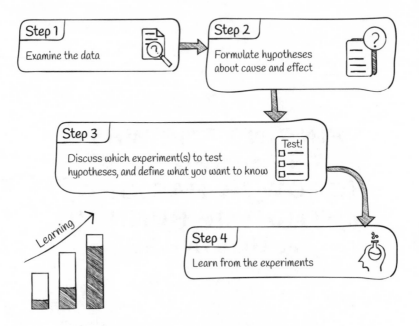

Figure 4.1. The scientific method for business

scientists at Infragistics! We don't wear white lab coats or have chemicals boiling in beakers, but every day we examine the data and signals we are receiving from the market and customers. Then we ask *why* these circumstances occur. I am particularly relentless with this aspect of the method because the same level of curiosity that drives scientists to make great discoveries propels me and my team to find answers to pressing problems.

The next step involves formulating hypotheses about the cause and effect of the signals and data we are observing. The executive team and I keep talking until we reach alignment on these hypotheses. Sometimes this happens quickly; sometimes it is more difficult to reach shared conclusions.

We then discuss which experiment or experiments we should conduct to test our hypotheses based on cost and anticipated outcomes. And we define what we want to know and decide on the metrics to assess those goals.

We learn from these experiments. If an experiment worked, we devote more resources to it. If it only partially worked, we modify the experiment and try again. If it did not work at all, we pivot and implement a new one.

Slingshot is designed to conduct the scientific method of driving better business outcomes and is vital to our ability to discover customer needs and why things are happening or not happening in the market.

Finding the *why* of any business situation is very difficult. You have to have the right data and the right amount of data to do any effective analysis. But even with those conditions satisfied, understanding cause and effect is hard because we exist in a world of constant market change and uncertain economic conditions.

Given our past successes, however, we believe in each other and in the efficacy of the scientific method, despite the obstacles and frustrations we always encounter.

Moreover, we have learned, like all scientists, to enjoy the adventure of solving a difficult problem, knowing that when we do, we will unlock growth and profitability for Infragistics.

GROWTH HACKING

A variant of the scientific method we use is called *growth hacking*, which is particularly relevant to early-stage startups that need to grow rapidly and quickly on tight budgets. Sean Ellis coined the term in a blog post in 2010 and featured it in his book *Hacking Growth*, cowritten with Morgan Brown.[1] Sean is an entrepreneur, an angel investor, a startup adviser, and my trusted friend.

Growth hacking uses various types of marketing and product iterations to rapidly test persuasive copy, email marketing, search engine optimization (SEO), and similar viral strategies, among other tools and techniques. Based on the results, companies replicate and scale the ideas that work while modifying or abandoning the ones that don't.[2]

In recent years, a number of startups became major companies using growth hacking. For example, Dropbox grew from one hundred thousand users to nearly four million, thanks to a referral program strategy—they offered users 250 MB of extra storage if they would invite other users in through social media or through automatic email invitations.

Other companies that employed growth hacking include Airbnb, Yelp, PayPal, Twitter, HubSpot, Pinterest, YouTube, and Groupon. These companies still utilize this process to build their brands, solve product challenges, serve their customers, and improve their profits.[3]

Infragistics's scientific method parallels much of what Sean teaches, with variations learned from long experience. Our process begins by assembling a group of business scientists that includes myself, the executive team, and others drawn from a wide range of Infragistics departments, such as marketers and salespeople, developers, designers, engineers, and product managers.

Whether we are launching a new product or supporting the continued growth of an existing one, such as Reveal, the scientific method undergirds the work we do and involves a number of phases. The early phases are determining market fit for our product, creating a hypothesis and a goal, and building awareness of the product. The later phases consist of acquisition, activation, retention, and referrals (see Figure 4.2).

Figure 4.2. The Infragistics seven growth-hacking phases

To gain a deeper understanding of how the scientific method is utilized at Infragistics, let's look closely into how we applied it when we developed Slingshot.

First Phase: Determining Market Fit

In this initial phase, we tried to understand the market we wanted to enter and how Slingshot would most closely align with the needs and wants of a potential or current customer—that is, the market fit. This is akin to the observation phase of the scientific method.

Despite the availability of other team-oriented software, we believed we could create a superior digital workplace experience that would help teams achieve extraordinary results to support companies' rapid growth.

Our idea was based on our own experiences at Infragistics, the readings and seminars the executive team and I have engaged in over the years, our talks with authorities on the subject (including venture capitalists who sat on boards of similar products), the successes our competitors had, and the analysis conducted by the Infragistics UX research team.

All of this research indicated that the market for collaboration software was growing exponentially with more than 400 million users per month and was generating more than $30 billion in revenues every year.[4]

Furthermore, our research found that companies that achieved extraordinary results had five elements:

1. They use data to make decisions.

2. They achieve high levels of trust.

3. They align on objectives and goals and have the autonomy to execute them.

4. They hold individuals and teams accountable.

5. They keep everyone in the know—information is flowing freely.

With this information in hand, we created Slingshot, which incorporated all of these elements.

But despite our significant competitive advantage, we also realized we should not "boil the ocean"—that is, increase the scope of the project until it is practically impossible to accomplish as envisioned.

We also had to factor in the size of Infragistics and our resources because we would be competing against much bigger companies capable of spending significantly more money than we could.

For Infragistics to succeed, we had to find "green fields," where the bigger players hadn't moved in yet. We needed to get momentum, awareness, and usage for Slingshot before we could be targeted. We thus concluded that we would focus 80 percent of our efforts on marketing teams and the rest of our efforts on the general market.

We selected these targets for a variety of reasons. Marketing teams usually have money to spend, they manage many projects, they work with outside firms, and they use lots of analytics. Moreover, marketing is a creative, collaborative effort—exactly what Slingshot was designed to facilitate.

The rest of our efforts were designed to help us learn about the needs of other segments of the marketplace.

Hypothesis and Goal Phase

With Slingshot in hand and a market focus on a particular segment, we created our hypothesis: There is a significant market for a new comprehensive, digital team software product aimed at marketing departments. Then we set a goal for the product: By 2024, the end of the second year after being launched, Slingshot should have one million users.

Awareness Phase

Our next task involved creating *awareness* about Infragistics and Slingshot. Although we had been in business for thirty-five years, we had sold tools to software developers and designers. We are now selling a business application to businesspeople. This was a brand-new market, and we had a lot to learn.

Whenever you need to learn anything, the scientific method should come into play. We designed a series of experiments. For example, we created a content calendar that included:

- *Blogs:* We wrote blogs on such topics as data-driven businesses and highly effective teams. When potential customers looked for these topics via the internet, they would connect with us through relevant search terms. Numerous potential customers clicked on our link and checked out our blogs. Of those, many read our white papers on these topics, which increased our brand awareness.

- *Direct digital marketing:* We tried to drive potential customers to our website through ads so we could inform them about Slingshot.

- *Public relations:* We looked to attract potential customers by getting stories about Infragistics and Slingshot in traditional media, such as newspapers (the *Wall Street Journal, Financial Times*), television and radio business networks (Bloomberg, NPR's *Marketplace*), and business magazines (*Harvard Business Review, Forbes, Bloomberg Business Week*).

During the awareness phase, we tracked impressions, website visits, and Google searches. Throughout the entire process, we kept asking questions about the efficacy of our campaign:

- Are we reaching the customers we targeted? If not, why not?

- Are they receiving our messages clearly? If not, do we need to create new messages?

- Do they understand our value proposition? If not, what needs to be changed so they understand it?

Acquisition Phase

The acquisition phase was the first real involvement by customers with Slingshot. This allowed us to collect information from the leads we were accumulating through our website, direct digital advertisement, and traditional public relations, as well as from our promotion efforts. That information included personal details, such as names or emails, and demographic data such as geographical locations.

In the acquisition phase, we continued to ask our potential customers questions so we could achieve market fit. These questions included:

1. Did you come to Infragistics because you were curious?

2. Are you trying to solve a specific problem?

3. If yes, what problem are you trying to solve?

4. Do you think Slingshot will solve your problem?

We also asked ourselves these questions:

- Are the market segments we have been targeting trying Slingshot?

- If not, why not? What do we need to do to reach the right segments?

- What aspects of Slingshot do they like? What elements don't they like?

Activation Phase

The goal of this phase is to turn potential customers into *real* customers. When people have to pay money for a product or service, you learn their real level of interest very quickly. That's why we focused on attaining an "aha" moment for our potential customers. After they entered our app, we only had a few minutes to make them say, "Wow, I didn't know I could do that."

To achieve a "wow" effect, we looked closely at our acquired data, which detailed potential customers who tried our app. This included:

- What is their role, department, and title?

- What problem are they trying to solve?

- Have they invited colleagues or collaborators to join Slingshot?

- What did they do? Create tasks, use dashboards, chat, and/or use discussions?

Within minutes of entering our app, we asked potential customers if a member of our success team could talk with them. If they gave us permission, we would discuss their interest in Slingshot, find out how we could help them with their business problems, and create proofs-of-concept based on their success criteria.

Retention Phase

The next phase involves *retaining* the customers who sign on to use our product. Given that we have a "freemium" business model, our retention goals are to keep them using Slingshot and convert them from using Slingshot for free to being a paid subscriber.

Following a product lead growth strategy, we want customers to have an "aha" moment as soon as possible within the app. We do this by educating them on how best to use the app to solve the problems that brought them into the app.

Our next goal is to expand to other teams and organizations they work with. Our customer acquisition cost (CAC) is based on the lifetime value (LTV) we get from a customer. If a customer is retained for ten years and the subscription is $240 a year, the LTV is $2,400. Many companies in the SaaS world spend two to three times sales to acquire customers, and the model works because of LTV.

In my experience, retention is a value calculation on the part of customers. Customers are constantly asking whether they are getting enough value *from* an engagement to continue paying *for* that engagement. This is why vNext companies must always be innovating—always be searching to improve experiences and products. At the same time, vNext firms need to understand customer needs, not as one homogeneous group but by segmented groups to better address their needs in product and service design. All of these business processes are aided by using the scientific method of driving better business outcomes.

We constantly ask our customers if Slingshot is helping them achieve extraordinary results and the level of teamwork they need to grow and increase profitability. If they are having any issues or need any additional help, we ask them to be open and tell us. In our case, because we are a digital product company, we can determine this through our data usage and cohort analysis.

Referral Phase

We want our existing customers to act as brand ambassadors for us by *referring* Slingshot to other potential customers. Customers are more likely to purchase from a business that their friends and family recommend.

Companies can create brand ambassadors through referral programs or social media campaigns. Contests are also popular. But in my opinion, the best is when customers have a great experience with a product that solves a real need in their lives. They are the ones most likely to advocate on behalf of one of our products.

Referrals create a *network effect*. This means a customer who is using Slingshot invites the entire company or particular departments to use it. This is a major way we do marketing.

In the referral phase, we continue to ask questions. We want to learn about the customer's journey and their company's needs. We ask questions such as:

1. How many people are using our product in your organization or department?

2. Are these people from the same or different teams?

3. How big is your organization?

4. Who is the person in your company who regularly connects with most people in the organization?

5. What business problems is your organization facing, and can our product solve it?

TRY AGAIN AND AGAIN

As we launched Slingshot and went through all these phases, several members of the executive and sales teams and I spent a considerable amount of time trying to determine our product market fit, which normally takes time. For Uber, it took two years. For Airbnb, it took only a year.[5] The search for your company's "why" is dynamic. You have to have faith in the process even when an initial hypothesis doesn't prove itself.

In our internal discussions, some argued the only way to increase sales was to ramp up our expenditure to twice or even three times what it was. I responded that because we were not gaining the retention levels we had envisioned, we needed to segment the market for Slingshot even more.

The essential problem we are facing is that large companies and the departments in them already have a lot of technology and a lot of processes in place. This increases the potential barriers to entry. They ask, "Why try a new software, no matter how much better it might be?"

In addition, Slingshot's competitive advantage is truly evident when an *entire* company uses it. For large companies this is difficult because they have to make widespread organizational adjustments. Further, I have found that if a company is reasonably profitable, the resistance to change is even stronger.

Ultimately, we reached a consensus that we had to segment the marketplace even more than we initially planned. We decided to focus on smaller companies because they usually don't have as much embedded technology or as many processes in place—which means they're more likely to experience the benefits of a company-wide software solution.

Moreover, we could target our sales efforts on small-company owners or CEOs who make much quicker decisions and are always concerned about how to generate efficiencies that lead to increased cash flow.

We thus developed a new hypothesis: Slingshot is the best team software for small companies with two hundred or fewer employees.

This still might not be the right hypothesis. We might have to conduct focus groups with people who fit our target audience profile and find out their needs and wants. Or we might have to test our messages to determine which communication speaks to our target audience about their likes and dislikes with their current collaboration software. Or we might also have to change Slingshot's onboarding experience. We might have to get from customers the information that would enable us to set up all their dashboards and organize all their digital workspaces.

There are other areas we may need to explore. We will have to assess and reassess—and then reassess again.

In any project we undertake, we have lots of data and lots of signals, but finding the cause and effect of any business situation is always difficult. Sometimes we can make a decision within an hour-long meeting because cause and effect are fairly clear. For example, we recently took out the "Hello" bar on our website. Shortly thereafter, our leads dropped off 10 percent. Since we hadn't altered anything else on the website, the conclusion was obvious: Put the "Hello" bar back! It worked—our leads shot up 10 percent.

But most situations are more complex, and care must be taken with any decisions we make because they will involve money, people, and time to improve a business outcome. For instance, in one of our existing products, our leads based on our organic channel (content, SEO, etc.) went down significantly year over year. One cause might have been that we shifted resources to a new product. But there could be other causes. We decided to examine them over the next month before trying to reach a final conclusion.

We are constantly asking: Why? We are always searching for the truth of a situation. We are always generating hypotheses and testing them. We are always engaged in conversations about how we can improve our products and have better and longer relationships with our customers. Like true scientists, we find no greater satisfaction than when we finally find the answer to our tireless efforts to ask why.

And like all great scientists—those who search for years for a cure to cancer, or those who are trying to understand the origins of the universe, or those who are seeking solutions to climate change—we have come to enjoy the journey and the learning that comes with it.

I can't wait to celebrate with my fellow scientists when we reach our goals. I know the answers exist, and we will find them together.

KEY POINTS FOR CREATING A VNEXT BUSINESS

1. Use the scientific method of getting better business outcomes and collaborate with your team to define experiments. Many times, data alone will not tell you why something is happening.

2. Examine the data and signals you are receiving from the market and customers. Then ask *why* these circumstances occur.

3. Formulate hypotheses about the causes and effects of the signals and data you are observing.

4. Choose which hypothesis to test based on cost and anticipated outcomes.

5. Define what you want to learn and decide on the metrics to assess those goals from the experiments.

6. Devote more resources to an experiment if it worked. If it only partially worked, modify the experiment and try again. If it did not work, pivot and implement a new one.

7. Constantly ask *why* something is happening. Always search for the truth of a situation. Keep generating hypotheses and testing them. Continually engage in conversations about how to improve your product or service to have better and longer relationships with your customers.

5

DATA-DRIVEN BUSINESSES

Being a part-time resident of Tampa Bay, Florida, I am a huge fan of the Tampa Bay Lightning, winners of the Stanley Cup in 2020 and 2021. They are a great team, and hockey is a tremendously exciting game, one that I have enjoyed for many years.

Until very recently, the analytic revolution that swept through sports had bypassed hockey. Big data now drives baseball managers to execute defensive shifts for every hitter and to pull starters as soon as they throw one hundred pitches. Analytics tell football coaches to pass on fourth down when their team only needs a yard for a first down. And it turns NBA basketball games into three-point shooting contests.

But in hockey, few organizations have focused on deeper analysis. The Lightning were different. Over a decade ago they hired mathematician Michael Peterson to be their director of analytics. Tampa Bay then began to rely heavily on data, moving away from pure statistical data and subjective evaluation of players to analytics.[1]

When Tampa Bay hired Peterson, maybe three or four NHL teams were utilizing analytics. These clubs had begun to try to find statistics that weren't just measurable but were meaningful. Statistics such as "Tampa wins 72 percent of games played on Thursdays" are measurable, but they are not particularly meaningful, except if the team only played on that day. What all these teams wanted was information that could be used to create a repeatable formula for winning.

For example, sensor data collected from hockey pucks can indicate player fatigue based on shot speed, pass speed, and more. This enables coaches to make timely substitutions to rest their players more effectively. Data analysis also helps with training and schematics, leading to better tactics, game plans, and team play.

"For an analyst to suggest a metric has value, we need to be able to explain how or why it relates to outcomes we desire, most generally goals for or against," says Sportsnet analytics writer Stephen Burtch. "Once we can identify how it relates to winning, we need to be able to show that it describes something meaningful, that it relates relatively strongly to goals/wins."[2]

> *For an analyst to suggest a metric has value, we need to be able to explain how or why it relates to outcomes we desire.*

The same goes for your business. No business can remain profitable and win in the marketplace without becoming data driven and its employees becoming skilled at assessing data and using statistical analysis. Those businesses that succeed the most are the ones that can spot the diamond in the rough, pulling a compelling, meaningful, data-driven narrative, product, or marketing strategy from the numbers.

THE DATA SURGE

When I founded Infragistics more than thirty-five years ago, we were not focused on data. We made the best decisions we could relying on our instincts as market experts and whatever research, however scarce, we could muster.

But the world was changing rapidly around us. In 1989, software and computer systems started being used extensively to analyze back-office functions such as accounting and operations. Two years later, computer scientist Tim Berners-Lee announced the birth of the internet, setting out the specifications for a worldwide, interconnected web of data, accessible to anyone from anywhere. By 1997, Google Search debuted, spurred by the company's mission to organize all the world's information and make it universally accessible, useful, and searchable.[3]

At the end of the twentieth century, business commentators were using the term big data to describe the mountain of information becoming available for analysis. At the same time, they were proclaiming an Internet of Things to chronicle the growing number of online devices with the potential to communicate with each other.[4]

In 2005, the notion of a Web 2.0 was born to identify a world where the majority of internet content was being provided by users of services, rather than by service providers.[5] Finally, by 2014, when more people were using mobile devices rather than office or home computers to access digital data, the amount of data being generated exploded.[6]

How great was this explosion? At a conference only four years earlier, Eric Schmidt, then executive chairman of Google, declared that there was as much data being generated every two days as was created from the beginning of human civilization up to the year 2003.[7] As startling as Schmidt's comparison was at that time, it seems quaint now. In 2023, people create 1.7 megabytes (MB) of data *every second*, or 3.5 quintillion bytes per day (there are eighteen zeros in a quintillion).[8]

The flood of information will only increase. More and more people around the world are tapping into the internet. There were 4.6 billion active internet users in 2023, which is close to 66 percent of the world population. (There were 2.5 billion internet users in 2013.) Access to data is becoming faster, cheaper, and easier every day.[9]

A NEW BUSINESS WORLD

This is the world we all live in now. As Emanuel Younanzadeh, vice president of marketing at the Modern Data Company, puts it succinctly when

Intensive users of customer analytics are

19x
as likely to be profitable
as nonintensive users

23x
more likely to outperform
in customer acquisition

Figure 5.1. Statistics on intensive users of customer analytics

describing the reality of business today: "It is data or die."[10] Yet according to a 2021 NewVantage survey, only 24 percent of companies have developed into data-driven businesses.[11] And even those that are focused on being data driven are experiencing problems—according to Forrester, only 32 percent of business executives could create measurable value from their data, and only 27 percent said their data and analytical products produce actionable insights. Even more startling is that between 60 percent and 73 percent of all enterprise data is never analyzed![12]

I believe companies that choose not to adopt this new data-driven approach to business are prone to inaccurate forecasting, missing revenue goals, poor decision-making, misguided marketing, and unnecessary costs.

On the other hand, the competitive advantage of being data driven can be significant. According to a McKinsey study, intensive users of customer analytics are nineteen times as likely to be profitable as nonintensive users and twenty-three times more likely to outperform in customer acquisition (see Figure 5.1).[13]

A DATA-DRIVEN BUSINESS

Being data driven puts information and analytics at the center of the decision-making process. At Infragistics, our executives and employees use their years of experience with statistical information to either prove or refute assumptions.

We have found that using data provides us with a variety of advantages in the following areas.

Launching New Products and/or Services

Trying to launch a successful new product or service activates every aspect of Infragistics—marketing, financing, development, design, sales, and more. All Infragistics departments optimize their decision-making process through data because it shines a searchlight on what customers want, like, and expect.

Monitoring and Beating the Competition

Using accurate and timely data allows us to monitor and analyze our competitors' actions. And more importantly, it allows us to be proactive rather than reactive to rapidly shifting marketplace trends.

Improving Collaboration

Data provides our teams with real-time information about needed changes and new opportunities. It's critical to interdepartmental collaboration, but it also drives horizontal innovation at Infragistics. For example, sometimes a team member in product development can propose a new and imaginative solution to a problem that marketing is struggling with. Data illuminates new ways for what we should do next.

Optimization of Costs

By following profit and loss data, we find patterns that help us make informed decisions and optimize our finances. Data also shows us critical trends. A report filled with financial data provides a snapshot of where Infragistics is at any given moment. It allows me and everyone in the company to see how that situation changes over time.

Targeting the Right Audience

Our marketing efforts, like those of all businesses, should be targeted at different audiences. Using data allows us to create the best strategy for getting the right product or service to the right customer. This is particularly important in a world with so many media channels. Without data, we are engaged in guesswork. With data, we can know whether we are succeeding or failing, whether we should sustain our strategy or pivot to a new approach.

ANSWERING *WHY?*

From my viewpoint as a CEO, the most important use for data is that it helps me get answers to the question I repeatedly ask: Why is something happening? Without answers to that question, we can't experiment and learn.

At a recent monthly meeting, our marketing team described a decrease in leads for one of our product lines. After hearing their insights on why this was happening, I continued to probe by asking them multiple questions about their assumptions as to causation. Lacking answers, the team said they'd come back with more data.

Upon further analysis, they concluded the web page needed to be redesigned, which would involve determining where to place the "Download Now" button, as well as rethinking its color. After a series of A/B tests, the team argued that the "Download Now" button should return to its original position. The data showed the button's new location had created fewer clicks and, thus, fewer leads.

A simple example, I agree. But it illustrates how being data driven must occur from the strategic level (What is the purpose of our business?) all the way down to the tactical level (Where do we put buttons on a website?).

Let me give you another, more complex example. We established a goal of three thousand leads a month. We hit our target on average every month for twelve months, with our average monthly spend being $97,000 for a conversion rate of 25 percent. During a review meeting, we noticed a dramatic drop in leads, all the way down to 1,270 because of an error in spend, which went from $97,000 to $61,000. At the same time, we introduced a new sales effort to prospects. Even with a lower spend and fewer leads, our conversion rate jumped to 50 percent. This showed us just tracking the volume of leads by itself yielded the wrong business outcome.

This data helped us change our perspective, our approach, and our goals. We decided we didn't want or need as many leads as we initially thought. The sales team pivoted to spending more time following up on fewer yet higher-quality leads. *Quality*—not quantity—became our mantra.

Then we carefully watched data on our close ratio and cost per leads. We experimented and tracked these numbers every day. The marketing team soon generated half the number of leads while the sales team closed on many more of them, which substantially increased our profitability.

Marketing made a change in the spend (inadvertently), while sales introduced a new outreach program. Measured independently, we may not have achieved the same analysis. Measured together, with all the other data points we were tracking, this approach proved meaningful. All this happened because of powerful data analysis!

SHERLOCK HOLMES'S OLDER BROTHER

Most of us are familiar with Sherlock Holmes, the still immensely popular fictional detective created by Sir Arthur Conan Doyle. Not as well known is the character of Mycroft Holmes, his older brother.[14] Mycroft possesses even greater deductive and observational powers than his younger brother, but instead of solving crimes, he works for Great Britain's Foreign Office. As Doyle writes, Mycroft would

> *get separate advice from various departments upon each, but only Mycroft can focus them all, and say offhand how each factor would affect the other. They began by using him as a*

short-cut, a convenience; now he has made himself an essen-
tial. In that great brain of his everything is pigeon-holed and
can be handed out in an instant.[15]

Figuratively, Mycroft is a computer.

More than one hundred years ago when Doyle was writing, one brilliant real person could have analyzed all the information involving Britain's overseas empire and made sound recommendations for specific actions. But that is no longer possible. However, each of us needs to think a little like Mycroft Holmes.

This is possible if we learn to utilize data and statistics. In fact, working in collaboration with others, we can create data-driven organizations that exceed the capacities of that fictional genius.

SEVEN STEPS TO MASTERING A DATA-FILLED WORLD

I think there are seven steps to mastering this data-filled world (see Figure 5.2). They include:

1. Leadership building a data-driven culture

2. Trusting the data and the tools

3. Commitment from the entire organization

4. Creating agreed-on metrics and OKRs

5. Building data literacy programs

6. Cataloging and socializing data sources

7. Encouraging a company of citizen data scientists

Let's examine each one in turn.

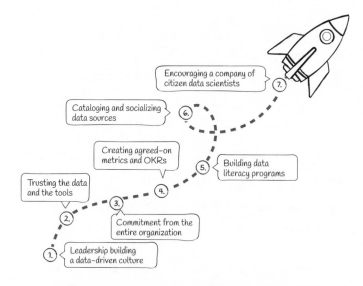

Figure 5.2. Seven steps to mastering a data-filled world

Leadership Building a Data-Driven Culture

Building a data-driven culture starts at the top of your company. Because it is a major cultural change for your organization, you need to shift your enterprise's mindset so individuals embrace data and learn to alter the way they approach decision-making.

At Infragistics, we made this a top priority. It started with me, my executive team, and our managers. To make this shift a reality, we focused on:

- Eliminating data silos and making data accessible as well as easy to use: Everyone on my team and my team's teams learned to understand how to access, read, and operationalize data without being data or IT experts. Data now helps them think about the problems they want to solve.

- Using data in any meeting where decisions were being made: Asking for data prior to making decisions at meetings and circulating this data at least two days before these meetings. If data wasn't available, we would postpone the decision until the next meeting to allow time to get and review the data.

- Communicating OKRs and KPIs (key performance indicators) through different channels, such as email, presentations, meetings, and so on, when discussing issues and topics

- Removing the tendency to listen to the loudest person in the room by asking for data to back everything up

- Displaying metrics digitally throughout our office and company web pages to keep data at the forefront of everyone's thinking

- Setting aside time for training yourself as an executive to learn new data skills

If you are feeling a little nervous about how large this task is, don't worry—you are not alone. In a recent *Harvard Business Review* survey, 91.9 percent of executives cited "cultural obstacles as the greatest barrier to becoming data driven."[16] So follow the above steps, and you and your organization will be on your way to a big cultural change.

Trusting the Data and the Tools

Gartner states that in 2020, 90 percent of corporate strategies explicitly mentioned information as a critical enterprise asset and analytics as an essential competency.[17] While this is impressive, it doesn't highlight the most important issue—the cultural shift of trusting data and believing a single source of truth can drive business decisions.

To promote trust, we did the following:

- We made datasets, databases, and SaaS system application programming interfaces (APIs) available to anyone who needed data to create dashboards. Prior to this, such data was provided to only a few members of Infragistics. It seemed risky when we did it, but it has proved tremendously important in making us a data-driven company.

- We used the Slingshot Data Catalog feature to certify that a data source or dashboard is approved and correct for broad use. Anyone in the company searching for data sets or dashboards can filter them by certification level. This ensures they are using data approved by the owner of the data. Searching a catalog makes it easy to find data across all functions of the company.

- We expanded insights across departments by allowing managers and team leaders to use data and dashboards in their meetings.

Creating trust kick-started data literacy for many key individuals in the company. This fostered better cross-departmental and team collaboration. Everyone was looking at the same metrics.

Conversations that were once based on hunches and personal assumptions now were filled with data to make decisions.

Commitment from the Entire Organization

Creating a data-driven culture relies on long-term commitment from everyone in the organization. This requires a big initiative. To ensure this level of commitment, we have had to:

- Tie analytics to critical business efforts: We cover this extensively in Chapter 3, on OKRs, and Chapter 14, on strategic planning.

- Keep data at the forefront of employee coaching: This becomes particularly evident during one-to-one meetings. After a few meetings with data as a focus, most managers and employees see its benefits.

- Make sure team OKRs and organizational OKRs are used to gauge team and company performance: We do this by having our IT teams and citizen data scientists create dashboards that are certified and used at the department and team levels.

Coaching is a key aspect of this transition. For example, Phil Dinsmore, vice president of worldwide sales, pushes our data-driven culture down to his regional directors across the globe. Phil leads by example. He runs meetings using dashboards, spreadsheets, and other analytics tools, which make these meetings meaningful and efficient.

In the past, these meetings used data to describe recent sales but utilized anecdotes to discuss future sales. Now, Phil drives conversations using prescriptive analytics and machine learning so we can create informed models. If you achieve this level of adoption in your teams, you are really succeeding in designing a data-driven culture.

Creating Agreed-On Metrics and OKRs

In Chapter 3, I delve deeply into how to create metrics and OKRs. For the time being, it is important to know that this process is top-down and bottom-up. A manager's job is to empower teams to execute their tasks effectively to achieve their goals. Using agreed-on metrics and OKRs is key to creating team unity and efficiency.

To ensure your organization can do this, you should choose the right OKRs and KPIs to measure success. As you learn in Chapter 3, this is not easy, and it takes practice. But once you start, the process will get easier over time as you and your team learn and adapt.

You should also research and look at historical data to set realistic goals as well as industry best practices for metrics. For example, what is a marketing-industry-accepted bounce rate on email campaigns? What is a sales-accepted lead-to-customer conversion timeframe? What is reasonable for days outstanding for invoices in accounting?

You might be surprised by looking at accepted norms and comparing them to your company's historical data on how you've been performing.

Building Data Literacy Programs

Gartner, the consulting firm, says in 2023, data literacy will become an explicit and necessary driver of business value, as it will be included in more than 80 percent of data and analytics strategies and change-management programs.[18]

Adjusting to this new reality means all businesses must alter how we operate in our day-to-day activities. We must develop a data literacy plan that:

- Ensures employees understand what data means

- Creates an understanding of basic statistics and statistical vocabulary

- Helps employees learn how to read business charts and graphs

- Teaches employees how to use visualizations with data

- Educates employees on how to draw correct conclusions from reading data and applying it to visualizations

- Aids employees in recognizing when data is being used to mislead or when it promotes data bias

As an engineer by training, I am familiar with many statistical concepts. More than half of Infragistics employees have computer science degrees, a field of study that has a heavy dose of statistics. However, in areas such as marketing and sales, employees are by educational background not as familiar with statistical concepts. Working with data to understand statistics and align with meaningful discussions is a necessary part of a data literacy program. In addition, employees need to learn such concepts as:

- *Hypothesis testing:* This is the use of statistics to determine the probability that a given hypothesis is true. At Infragistics, we are constantly generating hypotheses about all aspects of our business and then testing them to see if they work. You might know this process as growth hacking (see Chapter 4).

- *Correlation and causation:* Correlation is any statistical relationship, whether causal or not, between two random variables. Establishing correlation is important, but it should not be confused with causation. For example, a correlation may occur when a company decreases its marketing expenditure and experiences a decline in sales. But this decline may not be caused by fewer dollars being spent on marketing. It might be caused by the company's product not performing well or result from poor performance by the company's salespeople. Or all three. Causal inference typically requires not only good data but also subject-matter expertise to interpret the findings.

- *Bias:* A statistical estimate is biased if, on average, it provides an answer that differs from the truth. The bias is the average expected difference between the measurement and the truth. This problem occurs if you are using incomplete data sets, or if the data sets skew in a certain direction, or the data sets were created with biased intent. This kind of bias, for instance, is found in data derived from leading survey questions, or data designed to fit a specific narrative before the questions are even created or asked.

As you train your teams in the concepts I've described so far, you must continue to remember what Stephen Burtch from Sportsnet said about identifying the right data: "We need to be able to show that it describes something meaningful, that it relates relatively strongly to goals/wins."[19]

That is where understanding data analysis comes in.

The process of analyzing data typically moves through five key phases (see Figure 5.3):

1. *Ask the question:* What problem do you want to solve?

2. *Collect the data:* Identify which data points matter to solving the problem you've identified.

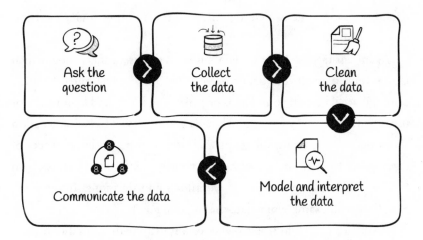

Figure 5.3. The five phases of data analysis

3. *Clean the data:* A data set is complete when you have accounted for any potential biases, assumptions, or other sources of error.

4. *Model and interpret the data:* Analysis can only occur once you apply the data to real-world situations. Does it fit with reality? What trends, patterns, or outliers reveal themselves?

5. *Communicate the data:* Communicating and sharing the data by visualizing the results and seeking feedback is probably the most important step in this process. It helps provide actionable insight on what to do next and ensures that whole teams understand why actions are necessary.

Remember—a data-driven decision isn't a true decision unless it's communicated effectively to those who will execute it.

Cataloging and Socializing Data Sources

Employees need to quickly unlock data's full potential. An IT or data analyst expert typically wastes weeks trying to find, understand, and validate data. Even more time is spent determining the meaning, logic, and business use case for it.

At Infragistics, we believe a vital business tool is a data catalog, which is an inventory of all your data sets, visualizations, and dashboards. It is a central place where all your data is organized, indexed, and kept ready for use. The catalog uses metadata, which is a summary of basic information about data that makes finding and working with particular instances of data easier. It is combined with data management and search tools to help organizations manage their workflows and decisions. Infragistics's Slingshot is an example of a data catalog (see Figure 5.4).

If you are a small-business owner or a startup with limited resources, you can use the Slingshot premium version and start cataloging the data that matters to drive better business performance. Slingshot helps support

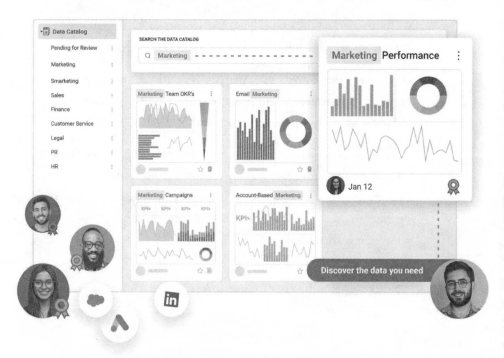

Figure 5.4. Slingshot Data Catalog enables everyday business users to easily see what data their organization possesses, to access and analyze it the moment they need it, and to use it to guide informed business decisions.

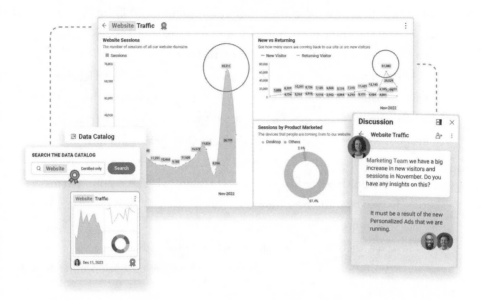

Figure 5.5. An example of how Slingshot enables users to discover data through the Data Catalog, visualize it, create a discussion around seeking insight, and create a task or work back plan to take action from that insight

a data-driven decision culture through its digital collaboration features of combining dashboards, task, and chat (see Figure 5.5).

Now you have an inexpensive way of tracking data. And you can use this data to improve your decision-making ability and to align your employees with your strategic goals. You can also examine changes in your sales and expenses and stimulate conversations about what is causing these issues. Then you can generate hypotheses and try new approaches.

Encouraging a Company of Citizen Data Scientists

In the past, business analysts relied on their insight and understanding of the marketplace to make and guide decisions. As organizations increasingly use analytics to optimize every aspect of their businesses, from pricing decisions to hiring strategies, they found their IT departments couldn't keep up with the demand to incorporate analytics into day-to-day operations. In fact, one survey found a shortage of 140,000 trained data scientists. Citizen data scientists fill that gap.[20]

A citizen data scientist is a power user who performs lightweight data science activities outside of their main job. This is someone who builds departmental business apps but is not a software developer by trade. It is a business role that has emerged in the last half-dozen or so years.[21]

Citizen data scientists do not need to be trained in analytics or mathematics; nor do they need to have deep IT knowledge about the systems used. They do have to know what results are reasonable, and they can ask for help when needed.[22]

However, there are skills that one or more individuals on a team or in an organization should learn to contribute to the data science needs of the group:

- *Data collection:* They need to know where to get data. Who is the data owner? How can you access data? What data is important to the outcomes you require?

- *Data exploration:* They need to know basic data exploration techniques. This can be as simple as Pivot Tables in Excel, or as complex as SQL Queries or basic Python and R scripting.

- *Data cleansing:* They need to understand how to create clean and consistent data to report on. ETL (for extract, transform, and load) is how data scientists combine data from multiple systems into a data source for data aggregation and analysis. Tools like Microsoft Excel Power Query are excellent data-cleansing and ETL tools.

- *Data modeling:* Here data scientists have to use their statistical background or what they learned from data literacy programs so they can apply statistical formulas to data for modeling purposes. Many business intelligence and analytics tools can perform this task. You can get started with Microsoft Excel, which can model data for most business requirements.

- *Data presentation:* They need to understand charts and graphs to create dashboards that can be shared across their team and organization.

We use Slingshot for most of the above items, but you can use Google Sheets, Microsoft Excel, or a host of other free and open-source tools to achieve most of what you need to get started with citizen data science tasks. Citizen data scientists are usually not expected to build elaborate models, but with knowledge of basic statistics, they can tackle this more complex aspect of data science.

Since the citizen data scientist position is relatively new, it often occurs organically in an organization. When there's a shortage of data science talent and a scarcity of talent in general, "citizen roles" are created. They are filled by individuals who have a passion or interest in data or by people with a math and statistics background. And employees can take data science courses if they want to fill this organizational need.

At Infragistics, our resident citizen data scientist success story is Casey McGuigan. She has a bachelor's degree in mathematics plus a master's degree in business administration. Her primary role is product management, as well as running teams in our marketing department. Casey's experience in math and her analytical mind made her a perfect fit as a citizen data scientist. She started out being the go-to person in the organization to help others with creating dashboards. Over the years, she turned into a real citizen data scientist, doing almost every aspect of what I've just described to help our teams drive better decisions.

When I first started to watch hockey, it was a game of great speed, tremendous skill, hard hits, and usually two or three fights a night. Now it is all these things, but it is also a sport that deeply believes in the power of analytics to improve every player's performance and give the teams that master it a competitive edge.

When Infragistics began, there was no need for dashboards, complex statistical analysis, or predictive analytics. But there is now. Without these tools and others outlined in this chapter, Infragistics and other businesses cannot win in the marketplace. But if they are added to your set of skills and practices, you will find a sure path to success.

 ## KEY POINTS FOR CREATING A VNEXT BUSINESS

1. Using analytics may be the single most powerful thing you can do to grow your business. We live in a new world; the reality of business today is data or die.

2. From my viewpoint as a CEO, the most important advantage to using data is that it helps me get answers to the question I repeatedly ask: Why is something happening? Without answers to that question, companies can't experiment and learn.

3. Building a data-driven culture starts at the top of your company because it involves a major cultural change for your organization.

4. If you tie analytics to critical business efforts, it drives commitment from the entire organization to be a data-driven culture.

5. To set realistic goals, do research and look at historical data as well as industry best practices for metrics.

6. Build a data literacy program in your organization. Catalog and socialize data sources.

6

LEARNING
ORGANIZATIONS

Economies dive and tumble and surge. Marketplaces are increasingly volatile. If I have learned one thing for sure, it's this: Companies and businesses that survive and prosper are all vNext *learning organizations.*

Being a learning organization means being agile enough to respond to increased competition or the disruptive effects of new technologies. It's a way of life and one of the foundations of your company culture. If companies fail to become learning organizations, they risk losing market share or even going out of business entirely.

I, like every other CEO, do not have all the answers to running a successful business and winning in the marketplace. But I can say without a doubt that the company I have built *will* be successful. It *will* overcome challenges. It *will* adapt to the next era of business. And this is because we're a learning organization—it is in our DNA.

In this chapter, I show you the benefits of transforming your company into a learning organization along with some proven strategies for instilling this way of being into your company culture.

As the late Harvard Business School professor David A. Garvin explained in a seminal *Harvard Business Review* article published almost thirty years ago:

> *How, after all, can an organization improve without first learning something new? Solving a problem, introducing a product, and reengineering a process all require seeing the world in a new light and acting accordingly. In the absence of learning, companies—and individuals—simply repeat old practices. Change remains cosmetic, and improvements are either fortuitous or short-lived.*[1]

At around this same time, MIT professor Peter Senge popularized the idea of learning organizations in his book *The Fifth Discipline.* He described them as places "where people continually expand their capacity to create the results they truly desire, where new and expansive patterns of thinking are nurtured, where collective aspiration is set free, and where people are continually learning how to learn together."[2]

At Infragistics, from our company's purpose to our one-to-one meetings, from our strategic, annual and go-to-market plans to our use of the scientific method to find the *why* of a situation, and the many other elements described in this book—all these embody what it means to be a vNext learning organization.

The process of becoming a learning organization starts with whom you hire. At Infragistics, we seek people who are curious and inquisitive and who wish to expand their knowledge of a variety of subjects, as well as improve the skills they bring to our company.

We determine a potential employee's personal drive to learn through such thoughtful interview questions as: What books have you read in the last six months? What podcasts have you listened to in the last six months? What webinars have you attended in the same time? What do you want to learn in the next year?

In addition, we ask potential employees: What do you know about Infragistics and our products? This question is designed to determine how committed they are to understanding our company and what we are doing. If they didn't take the time to learn about us, most likely they don't really want to join us and, in almost all cases, are not self-starters.

Another way to determine if potential employees are a good fit for your company is to ask them if they have any questions for you. If they mumble, "No, I'm good," they are not engaged in the interview process. I recommend moving on to another candidate. (For more on the hiring process, see Chapter 8.)

Once we hire growth-minded employees, the next step is to encourage further learning through our coaching process. After receiving feedback from managers and team members, we ask employees to create a personal development plan. This plan identifies and describes four skills they need to learn or improve during the next twelve months. (For more on the coaching process, see Chapter 11.)

We also provide financial support to help employees "skill up." This opens opportunities for them to advance their careers, whether with us or another company. These monetary resources allow them to attend relevant conferences, purchase needed books, or pursue professional education. We have gladly provided scholarships of $5,000 to $10,000 for individuals seeking a master's degree and anywhere from $2,000 to $3,000 for specific stand-alone courses.

We supply this level of support because their becoming and remaining lifelong learners helps us do our work better. It helps Infragistics stay nimble and responsive to the unforeseeable future.

It may sound altruistic, but I'll let you in on a secret: It's not. It's pragmatic. I like to win. So does everyone at Infragistics. Building a learning culture within Infragistics helps us win over and over again.

Aside from the issues of whom to hire and how to expand their knowledge, all companies, including Infragistics, face three critical challenges when designing a learning organization:

1. Creating a clear definition of what type of learning organization they want to be—a definition that should be actionable and easy to apply

2. Developing clear guidelines of day-to-day practices to help achieve that goal

3. Establishing tools to measure their company's rate and level of learning to ensure it is making gains

Let's look at each one in turn.

WHAT IS A LEARNING ORGANIZATION?

The definition that I like is an organization skilled at creating, acquiring, and transferring knowledge and at modifying its behavior to reflect new knowledge and insights. Simple. Clear. Actionable.

With this focus in mind, learning organizations should focus on five practices (see Figure 6.1):

1. Systematic problem-solving

2. Experimenting with new approaches

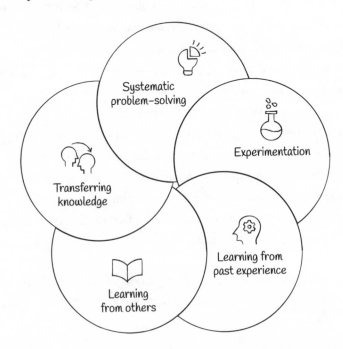

Figure 6.1. Five key practices for building a learning organization

3. Learning from past experience

4. Gaining knowledge from the best practices of other companies

5. Transferring new knowledge quickly and efficiently across the organization[3]

Let's look at each activity.

Systematic Problem-Solving

This involves:

- Relying on the scientific method (generating hypotheses and testing techniques) rather than guesswork for solving problems

- Being data driven when making decisions rather than using untested assumptions or gut instinct (see Chapter 5 for more details)

Note: Even the best systematic approach can fall apart if the process, approach, and results of each attempt at a problem are not carefully recorded and analyzed.

At Infragistics being data driven gets employees to talk to each other and to share their thoughts, experiences, and intuition about whatever problem we are dealing with. Systematic problem-solving allows you to surface different points of view. This, in turn, helps in formulating a hypothesis about what the data means and what you need to do differently. These discussions also involve determining how you will measure the hypothesis. Once a consensus is reached, the next step involves experimentation.

Here is a useful way to systematically solve problems with others. Tell the group you are leading that one-half to two-thirds of the meeting will be spent discussing the problem. During this *discovery* phase, attempts at solutions are not allowed. You are in discovery mode. Just keep asking questions. Everyone needs to be heard. When you finish, the last part of the meeting should be devoted to formulating solutions.

Experimenting with New Approaches

Learning organizations search for and test new knowledge using the scientific method, or its business variation, growth hacking (see Chapter 4). Experimentation is motivated by marketplace opportunities and takes two forms: ongoing programs and one-of-a-kind demonstration projects.

Ongoing Programs

These small experiments produce incremental gains in knowledge and are the mainstay of continuous improvement programs. Such experiments share several characteristics.

- They generate new ideas.

- Teams are encouraged to take risks, but they must remain accountable to achieve the company's goals.

- Managers and employees sometimes need training in new skills to perform these experiments.

- They are evaluated using statistical analysis.

These kinds of experiments go on daily at Infragistics. Every aspect of our company is geared to generating new ideas for how to solve problems. All our employees are encouraged to take reasonable risks when they experiment, while always being mindful that they are responsible for meeting the goals established in our strategic, annual, and go-to-market plans. If they need new training or have to purchase new software to conduct these experiments, they have to make the case, and we will back them up. And they are always required to evaluate their experiments by analyzing the results so we can come to a conclusion about what direction we should be going.

Demonstration Projects

Larger and more complex than ongoing experiments, these projects consist of company-wide initiatives, with the goal of learning how to develop new organizational capabilities. These demonstration projects:

- Involve considerable learning by doing, as well as common and necessary midcourse corrections

- Influence the rest of the organization if they are successful by changing how we do what we do

- Are developed by cross-functional teams reporting directly to senior management

For us, Slingshot exemplifies such a demonstration project. It took a number of years to develop, ultimately set Infragistics in a new direction, involved different teams in the company, and caused us to constantly learn. All our efforts were undergirded by statistical analysis.

Learning from Past Experience

Learning organizations see the value of past difficulties or even failures. These situations lead to new insights and understandings if employees and managers repeatedly ask why, analyze data, and try to improve with new approaches.

Here is a problem that we faced that could only be solved by trying to learn from one of our failures. We examined data that showed we were losing 75 percent of the people who came onto our website to look at one of our products. When we met to discuss this data, a consensus arose that we needed to change the user interface or customer experience. I didn't think we could reach that conclusion just based on the data. My experience and my intuition told me a lot of other things could be causing this reaction. For instance, the wrong customer might be coming to try the product. Was that the result of our advertising? Or our SEO? Or our special events? Or how our salespeople were interacting with our customers? Or other factors? We had to take a deeper look and do multiple experiments and then evaluate them.

You can't start making changes in processes and procedures without examining all dimensions of a problem. But you can't solve a problem if you don't see that you are failing and then take corrective measures.

Gaining Knowledge from the Best Practices of Other Companies

Two ways for companies to do this are benchmarking and talking with customers.

Benchmarking

Examining other leading companies or comparing how you are doing against industry standards is a wonderful source of new ideas and a catalyst for creative thinking and innovation.

We benchmark by studying our competitors to see how they behave and react. Before launching Slingshot, we looked at Slack and Dropbox, because they were very successful in the B-to-B product space. We read magazines, newspapers, and books about them. We examined who invested in them and how they spent this money.

Infragistics buys lots of SaaS products. So another way we benchmark against companies is by studying our suppliers. We observed their customer and sales success people and how they engaged with us. Some of them did really well, and that changed our processes and investments.

We also benchmark against our industry. We use Culture App to test our company's culture, and we benchmark our score against other companies in our industry and in our region in terms of engagement and culture.

In addition, we benchmark by industry metrics. For example: What is the industry's retention rate for a SaaS company? What is the cost per click? What is the percentage of employee retention?

If we are following behind where the industry is, then we carefully explore what processes and procedures need to change to help us catch up or even exceed industry standards. We create a set of recommendations and then implement them.

You can use benchmarking as artists have always used a muse—to inspire your team's creative thinkers. It can get you and your team out of your collective heads so they can explore the variable context of your marketplace.

Talking with Customers

Customers stimulate learning by providing reactions to your products and services, insightful comments about your competitors, and general feedback. For feedback to be impactful, organizations must be open to criticism. It's not personal, right? It's all about finding and implementing useful ideas from one of your most informed partners—your customers.

Here are some of the ways we listen to our customers.

Each year we do dozens of webinars and live digital events that involve our products. During these sessions, we ask the audience anywhere from five to fifteen questions ranging from how they use the product to what they'd like to see in the product, and if they'd allow us to follow up with them directly. This is a great source of data that enables us to track changes over time and gather analytics on how behavior and needs are changing as products evolve.

We also conduct surveys of around thirty questions regarding how customers feel about our products currently and what they expect of these products in the future. These surveys always provide us with great insights into our customers. We finish the surveys with the same six questions, which tell us if we are performing well or if we need to focus in other specific areas. We use the benchmark from 2003 (when we began the survey), and we track it every year. Some key questions from surveys from 2003 to 2021 include:

1. How would you rate the quality of your Infragistics product?

2. How would you rate the quality of service that you have received?

3. How would you rate the value of your Infragistics product?

4. Do you believe we will deliver future value?

5. Would you recommend Infragistics products to others?

6. Will you recommend renewal of your Infragistics product?

Also, customers often make feature requests during the year. We post these ideas digitally and ask our customers to vote on the features they would like to see us create. When the results are in, it affects our list of priorities.

We have a coaching app that listens to every sales conversation and reviews every email exchange between our customers and salespeople. The app is based on real-time reviews, and it helps us in our sales discussions. We can tell how much the customer was talking and how much the salesperson was talking. It allows us to review the conversations with our salespeople and, through coaching, increases their ability to listen and to ask good questions of our customers.

Our frontline people, customer support, salespeople, and sales consultants need a pipeline to our product managers and product teams. They need to keep asking: Why are we losing sales? Why are we winning sales? There has to be a constant dialogue of learning and getting signals about what is happening.

Finally, we conduct research on target customers and then create a prototype of how to solve problems they are having. Next, we have the target customers try the prototype and give us feedback. We continue our learning by asking them: Did it solve the problem? Was it easy to use?

We need to constantly change our product designs based on the customer experience and the new learning we achieve through feedback so we can create new software. We use our own Indigo Design product to do this—a digital design platform for prototyping, automated usability testing, and production code generation to build an application.

Measuring Learning

As companies engage in experiments and launch new initiatives, they assess their success by examining results using data-driven techniques and statistical tools (see Chapter 5).

But in assessing how Infragistics is doing as a learning company, we don't use statistical methods. Rather, what we observe provides the best evidence that learning is taking place on ever higher levels in Infragistics.

I can see it in a variety of ways. For instance, we are constantly finding new software systems and technology to help us run new processes so we can improve the company.

I can hear learning in our conversations and discussions at work. When I look at the exchanges in Slingshot, I can see employees and managers sharing data and taking actions to improve outcomes. People are exchanging books they have read and talking about webinars they have attended.

I can see it in our new SaaS systems. We did not have many of them three years ago or even one year ago.

I can even observe learning in myself. I recently read a book by Andrew Chen called *The Cold Start Problem: How to Start and Scale Network Effects*.[4] I was told about the book by Sean Ellis, creator of the growth hacking model and a friend. I ordered the book. I thought it was excellent and then bought it for my executive team and ten other key people at Infragistics. We all started to refer to it and have dialogues about it. We began to use the same vocabulary and metrics from the book. Even the Gartner analysts I talk with on a regular basis were reading it. Suddenly, we formed a learning community around *Cold Start*.

So I am surrounded within the company and without by constant enthusiasm about learning.

Transferring Knowledge

In a learning organization, new knowledge, insights, and best practices must be spread quickly and efficiently throughout the company. At Infragistics, we send out emails, hold company-wide meetings, invite relevant authors to speak, and buy their books for employees. In addition, because we have built an open culture, we are constantly engaged in free-flowing conversations to exchange ideas in a relaxed, safe, and open environment.

The new knowledge we acquire is also embedded in how we construct our strategic, annual, and go-to-market plans.

A learning organization is not built overnight. That was true of Infragistics. The new processes and insights we develop accrue slowly and steadily. This is because organizational learning has three distinct stages (see Figure 6.2).[5]

1. *Cognitive:* Even though we utilize multiple approaches to spread new knowledge, it takes time for employees to begin to think differently.

2. *Behavioral:* Employees internalize new insights and alter their ways of acting or approaches to solving a problem.

3. *Performative:* We begin to see results like improved quality of products, an increase in market share, or other tangible signs that our organization is growing, adapting, and thriving.

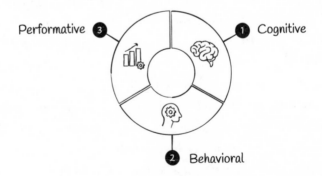

Figure 6.2. The three stages of a learning organization

So take a breath when you decide you want to become a vNext learning organization. With patience and hard work, you will ultimately emerge with a company that is precision-primed to win in our complex, ever-changing world.

 ## KEY POINTS FOR CREATING A VNEXT BUSINESS

1. To build a learning organization, start by hiring people who are lifelong learners.

2. Invest in coaching, sending people to conferences, buying books, listening to podcasts, and continuing education.

3. Share new knowledge and invest in having authors come to your company to present new ways of thinking or doing something.

4. Actively use data and the scientific method of driving better business outcomes.

5. Ask a lot of questions and find the why of outcomes.

6. Have an open mindset, continue to be in learning mode, seek out new information, and be curious.

7. Have agile process and rhythm of the business to allow for adjustments in execution as you continue to learn new information.

7

ALIGNMENT

There is an old adage that sums up what happens when an unexpected or nearly impossible event takes place, usually because of pure luck or divine intervention—it is said that the "stars align."

The meaning of the phrase suggests that stars aligning happens haphazardly, or randomly, or without any sense that we have control of the issue. Some businesses *wait* for alignment. The stars align sometimes for these companies when the economy surges, or a competitor goes under, or when one of their products or services gets gobbled up by customers. But this is rare. And worse, it's not replicable.

A vNext Business must go further. If a business wants to compete in today's markets, it must make its own luck. And that starts from the inside out. It must create alignment that is *internal and intentional,* driven by a deep understanding of what makes companies work effectively, from the smallest startups to the largest global companies.

I believe alignment is something every vNext Business needs to deliberately create. The more a company grows, the more complex its organization becomes and the more difficult it is to attain alignment toward an agreed-on mission and vision on a consistent basis.

At Infragistics, it is a daily challenge. We have more than 250 employees spread across six offices in the United States and around the world. When our alignment falters, it is experienced through the entire enterprise. An unaligned team feels like a rudderless boat, at the mercy of the currents, headed whichever way the marketplace decides to flow. Conversely, when a vNext Business like Infragistics designs its own alignment, we put our oars into that current and not only navigate our route but also begin to affect the currents themselves.

Strategy, purpose, and organizational capabilities must be in sync to ensure the alignment that every vNext Business needs.

BENEFITS OF ALIGNMENT

Alignment brings with it many key benefits, including promoting collaboration, stimulating more efficient decision-making, optimizing roles, facilitating teamwork, and developing a positive company culture.

Promoting Collaboration

Alignment encourages the easy interchange of ideas across an entire organization. When collaboration and teamwork improve, productivity, agility, and efficiency closely follow. This helps us achieve our objectives and leads to more creativity and innovation.

Stimulating More Efficient Decision-Making

Alignment provides greater clarity regarding team members' responsibilities and authority, leading to quicker decision-making.

Optimizing Roles

Alignment empowers employees to work to their highest potential because they clearly understand their roles and the roles of others. They know where their work starts and stops—but more importantly, they know how their work contributes to the overall mission of the company.

Facilitating Interdepartmental Teamwork

Alignment can help remove the pitfalls of a segmented organization structure. Too often, departments don't have visibility into what their counterparts are doing. This causes confusion, redundant work, and the "too-many-cooks-in-the-kitchen" syndrome. True alignment acts as a counterbalance, increasing individual departments' abilities to share resources and information and to work more seamlessly across the company.

Developing a Positive Company Culture

Culture is a social pact. It's hard to have a social agreement if no one knows what the end goals are. That's why alignment is one of the foundations of a solid company culture. As common goals are achieved through efficient collaborative efforts, morale increases and employee satisfaction rises. All of this helps in retaining the best employees.

—

Alignment can be defined as the processes that ensure all members of a company share a common purpose, which allows them to work together, communicate openly, and be held accountable.

In a *Harvard Business Review* article titled "How Aligned Is Your Organization?," associate professor of management practice Jonathan Trevor and associate fellow Barry Varcoe, both at Oxford University's Saïd Business School, describe alignment specifically as a

> *value chain that connects an enterprise's purpose (what we do and why we do it) to its business strategy (what we are trying to win at to fulfill our purpose), organizational capability (what we need to be good at to win), resource architecture (what makes us good), and, finally, management systems (what delivers the winning performance).*[1]

The authors then delineate four types of corporate alignment:

1. *Strategic alignment:* Your company's goals and efforts are aligned to achieve the company's long-term strategy and purpose.

2. *Personal alignment:* Your employees are aligned to your company's culture and understand completely their part in the enterprise's strategic vision.

3. *Vertical alignment:* Departments align their efforts to achieve your firm's goals.

4. *Horizontal alignment:* Departments align with each other on sharing resources and on cross-functional projects.[2]

At Infragistics we seek alignment in all four areas to achieve its maximum effects.

CREATING STRATEGIC ALIGNMENT

How can you create strategic alignment in your company? Some business experts argue that it begins by establishing and articulating a purpose, a vision, and a mission.

In an article in *Inc.*, Brent Gleeson, founder and CEO of Taking Point Leadership, says, "Without establishing the 'why' it is difficult to build and protect a great organizational culture. . . . If everyone isn't totally aligned, the employees will eventually receive mixed messaging and start to lose faith in the mission."[3]

When we first attempted to bolster alignment at Infragistics, we spent a considerable amount of time and effort developing statements about our mission, our vision, and our purpose. When we were done, I thought they were excellent summaries of what we were trying to accomplish together as an organization.

Unfortunately, we found that our employees couldn't remember all three of them; they overlapped in some ways and were too complex for the other leaders and me to communicate easily and consistently. If these statements are not used, believed, and put into practice, they will not affect business outcomes.

Statement of Purpose

Given this reality, we merged them into one statement of purpose—Create simplicity, beauty, and happiness in the world, one app at a time.

We have developed specific processes and actions to make this statement concrete and actionable to our employees and managers.

- We delineated the Infragistics Way (see Chapter 1), which is a clear and practical execution of our company values.

- We defined and articulated two main North Star goals for the company every year, which can be thought of as our mission. (For example, our goals for 2022 were (1) to be the number-one company in software tools for user-interface components sold to professional development teams and (2) to have one million active users for Slingshot, our new collaboration software product, within twenty-four months of shipping.)

- We developed OKRs to provide a strategic framework to align our teams toward accomplishing these main goals (see Chapter 3) and embedded our purpose throughout our strategic, annual, and go-to-market plans (see Chapters 14, 15, and 16, respectively, for details).

- I and other leaders repeat our purpose at every company meeting.

All these efforts have shown real results. I hear employees mentioning our purpose in their conversations. I can see it in the improvements we make to our products. It is also evident in our branding and marketing efforts. Customers and colleagues even reference our purpose statement when talking with us.

This kind of alignment exists only in a learning organization (see Chapter 6). It can't—and won't—work in a command-and-control organization.

If your teams use OKRs and execute against them while measuring results, alignment occurs naturally. Your teams get new information, which drives them to understand problems differently and to discover new solutions. Learning thus goes on all the time, as does continuous alignment.

The processes needed to create alignment are discussed in "Finding the Why" (Chapter 4) and "Data-Driven Businesses" (Chapter 5), along with later chapters on coaching (Chapter 11), running effective meetings (Chapter 12), and scrums and one-to-one meetings (Chapter 13).

Hiring the Right People

When the job of creating a framework for strategic alignment is finished, the next step is to hire the right people. Incorporate your purpose statement into your hiring practice. See if your candidates react to it, if they naturally align with it, and if they can identify how their core skills and talents are a match to your company's goals (see Chapter 3).

Once you have the right team in place, your vNext Business needs to establish personal, vertical, and horizontal alignment.

Personal Alignment

Personal alignment starts with my executive team. If I can't get them to align, the entire company won't align. Besides direct communication at our weekly meetings, processes such as our strategic plan, annual plan, and go-to-market plan, along with OKRs, enable team members to be heard and to feel that their concerns are being addressed, which in turn helps align them.

Even if you have the most inclusive process for establishing OKRs and strategic, annual, and go-to-market plans, some people might not agree with them. They can destabilize or sabotage your efforts. If your alignment becomes frayed or undone, employees won't be executing in the direction you want them to go or at the level you want them to achieve.

Aligning the Unaligned

Here are some places where I've identified unaligned people, along with some strategies for dealing with them.

Lack of Participation in Meetings

One of my pet peeves is a quiet meeting. Meetings are supposed to be vibrant exchanges of unique ideas. Which is why I notice when participants remain quiet and don't contribute to the discussion. Especially when this is new behavior for a participant, it can be a sign of a disengaged or unaligned team member.

When this happens, I ask direct questions to uncover their opinions and ideas. If the behavior persists through the course of a few meetings, I try to schedule a one-to-one conversation to discuss the behavior and let them know that I have acknowledged their disengagement. This can be useful in uncovering all manner of roadblocks to employee engagement and misalignment.

Direct Opposition to Goals

When determining how best to market some of our new offerings, Infragistics decided to become more focused on product-led growth as a mechanism to acquire new customers. Almost our entire company was aligned behind this new strategy except one key manager, who sabotaged our efforts by refusing to hold meetings about the topic with his direct reports.

At this point, I reflected on the situation with an open mind. I decided that if he was right in his opposition, I would work with him to change our direction. Upon examination, however, I was more convinced than ever that our strategy of product-led growth was headed in the correct direction. Once I realized that, I couldn't simply order him to align with us. You can't change someone's mind by edict. And that is not how change occurs at a learning organization. I needed to respect his agency and try to educate him again about the new organizational direction.

So I held a one-to-one meeting with him to review all the steps we had taken to reach our conclusion and to find out where a breakdown or misunderstanding may have occurred. Since we are a data-driven firm, I used data to back up my thinking toward the new approach. Using data helped the discussion to be more objective, moving it away from subjective points of view or emotions that either one of us might have held. As we talked, he finally expressed an issue that he had never before surfaced—he didn't think we had allocated enough money and resources for his department. We continued to talk and worked out a solution that addressed his issues. By the end of our meeting, he had agreed to align with us.

Leaders and Hidden Influencers

Getting buy-in from managers, directors, and hidden influencers is also vital. They help immeasurably in creating alignment down through the organization.

For example, let's look at hidden influencers. According to an article titled "Tapping the Power of Hidden Influencers" in the *McKinsey Quarterly* by Lili Duan, Emily Sheeren, and Leigh M. Weiss, hidden influencers have a big impact on organizational efforts such as alignment. These influencers, who in most cases lack a formal title, are found in every company and at every level. Other employees look to them for input, advice, and ideas about initiatives in a business.[4]

The authors provide four ideas about how best to use these leaders.

- *Think broad, not deep:* Look throughout your company for them in every department and division. They are there. You need to find them.

- *Trust but verify:* You want to make them feel trusted. The best way is to invite them to participate in all company-wide efforts such as alignment.

- *Don't dictate, cocreate:* Engage with them as thought partners in the company-wide effort. Their influence will dwindle if they are seen as following orders from executives and managers.

- *Connect the dots:* Try imaginative ways to encourage influencers to meet and support each other, such as a digital channel like Slingshot to converse.[5]

ALIGNING GOALS AND PROCESSES

Aligning departments with a company's overall strategic goals and with each other involves a number of processes. Such aligning is a big issue in large companies but also in small companies.

The strategic plan, the annual plan, the go-to-market plan, along with OKRs, help us achieve departmental alignment with our strategy. In addition, particularly when departments read our annual plan, they can see what they and other departments are doing and how they need to support each other. Weekly and monthly departmental meetings at Infragistics also support alignment. These are opportunities to keep everyone in the know and to communicate laterally. That way the departments can review the metrics they are following and the new information they are receiving and decide if they need to shift resources *across* departments.

You don't want employees and managers continuously communicating up and down the organization. At Infragistics we encourage them, if they see a problem, to talk to each other within a department to solve the issue instead of asking up the management chain to seek a solution. However, if they cannot reach a conclusion, they should speak to their manager. Many times the issue can be resolved by discussing their priorities and how to change deliverables timelines. Timeboxing deliverables helps the situation. If departments don't do this, projects get delayed and fall through the cracks.

Let's look at a specific example of an issue that arose between two Infragistics departments and threw them out of alignment. We had an annual sales target we were attempting to meet. The production team had decided to sell our software in the Google store. They finished their work but were waiting on the internal systems team to tie the product into our commerce system and finance system. The internal systems team was delayed because they were entangled with another product. So we timeboxed when the product had to be delivered to the Google store and reset priorities. That got the internal systems team moving and they accomplished their tasks on time.

Alignment as a major company goal needs to be communicated constantly. You can do this through email blasts, a newsletter, company-wide meetings, and small meetings with your direct reports.

You can stimulate conversations about alignment by asking questions in meetings such as:

- In what areas is our company well aligned?

- In what areas does our firm's alignment need to be improved?

- Do we or our department directly benefit from alignment?

- What practices do we need to implement to increase alignment?

Once you have the answers to these questions, identify and remove any barriers in your business that may prevent alignment, including current policies and procedures, communication issues, employee habits, organizational structures, and aspects of company culture.

Finally, celebrate your accomplishments across the company. This will increase company morale and motivate employees and managers to continue to improve alignment throughout the organization.

As with all organizational changes, practice patience. Alignment isn't achieved overnight, and it is often a slow process. As you adjust your goals and respond to both internal and external changes, continue to reexamine your alignment initiatives.

Alignment takes intentional work. You will hit multiple bumps in the road as the process unfolds. But don't wait for chance or until the stars are just right. Start today to implement greater alignment in your company. Alignment is the essential tool of managing a vNext Business.

 KEY POINTS FOR CREATING A VNEXT BUSINESS

1. To use resources effectively and focus on achieving goals and your strategic plan, you need alignment across your organization.

2. Allow the entire team to participate at different levels in the process of creating your strategic plans, annual plans, go-to-market plans, and OKRs. This will help align all who participate.

3. Communicate your purpose and two to three company goals several times a month. Use your monthly company meeting, weekly emails, and discussion posts in your digital workplace software to keep them top of mind.

4. Seek feedback on alignment through meetings and one-to-one communications to see who is aligned and who is not. Take the time to understand other points of view and if they're right, change direction.

5. Seek out hidden influencers in the company to get their assistance in creating alignment throughout the organization.

6. Over-communicate to those working in remote offices, international offices, and work-from-home offices.

7. Change direction and realign when market conditions change, new information becomes available, or signals from customers, competitors, and staff show a new direction.

8

HIRING

The process of building a great team begins with hiring stellar talent. In the last few years, this task has increased in complexity as social media, job posting sites, and networking applications have greatly expanded candidates' ability to seek new jobs. People shift from one job to another with increasing frequency.

At the same time, the first two years of the COVID-19 pandemic caused many Americans to reconsider their careers, their aspirations, and their professional goals, leading to what has become known as the Great Resignation. By May 2022, the number of current job openings (10.9 million) exceeded the number of new hires (6.3 million) by more than 4 million.[1] Research by the US Chamber of Commerce shows burnout and stress, the demands of family care, and the meaningfulness of their work played major roles in why numerous workers left their companies without even another job in hand. I cannot think of one company that has not been affected.[2]

During the pandemic many companies created a new worker "benefit" in the form of remote work. Recent studies have shown that a clearly communicated remote work policy (for applicable positions) is now necessary for attracting and retaining the best talent.[3]

Fortunately, at Infragistics, we have developed an outstanding and comprehensive recruitment process. In our early years, we relied on third-party staffing agencies. Although this worked reasonably well, it became increasingly expensive and, over time, ineffective in supplying us with the talent we needed to grow and adapt. Now we rely on our HR team and the hiring managers.

THE ROLE OF HUMAN RESOURCES

Our process begins when a hiring manager reaches out to our human resources (HR) department with a new hiring need. If a senior software developer position opens up, for instance, a hiring manager contacts HR and provides them with a job description.

Infragistics HR professionals see themselves as trusted consultants to the hiring managers. After reviewing the job description, they contact the hiring manager and begin an ongoing conversation. They refine the hiring manager's requirements and expectations for the position, which enables HR to deliver a candidate who is a good fit for the team, as well as for our culture.

They ask the hiring manager specific questions, such as:

- Does the job description you gave us make sense to prospective employees?

- Are we using internal jargon or terms that might not show up in job posting searches?

- Is the job description up to date and relevant to the types of skills necessary to accomplish the objectives of the position?

- What are the must-haves from a recruiting perspective?

- What are nice-to-haves?

In this last question, HR is looking for experiences with certain technology platforms or experiences in dealing with a certain type of problem relevant to the team's current task. Having these experiences will shorten the learning curve for the new employee.

The Job Description

HR then gives the job description a marketing flare. Job recruitment has become so competitive that the era of listing a job's requirements along with specifics such as education level and compensation won't attract top talent. At Infragistics, we think about how we market ourselves to fill a position. Here is an Infragistics job description for a senior software developer:

SENIOR SOFTWARE DEVELOPER—.NET

Infragistics is a global leader in user experience and UI design and development tools, trusted by over a million developers across all industries and company sizes, from single development shops up to the largest enterprises in the world.

At Infragistics, you get to work with other passionate, motivated colleagues to produce world-class developer tools. We prioritize developer productivity, great design and usability, and enterprise-grade reliability in everything we make. We are all about delighting customers and fostering a fun, healthy work environment with transparency, mutual trust, and innovation at the heart of our activities.

While being a member of a cross-functional team, many team members specialize in key areas such as testing, support, and docs. We are currently looking for a senior software developer who will be a key driver of innovation and excellence in developing custom UI components and libraries for desktop, tablet, and mobile devices.

You will collaborate with stakeholders in breaking down requirements into API design and concepts, team up with UX architects to ensure great user experience, participate in testing to maintain and improve quality, work on documentation, and create samples to showcase the components. You will also interact directly with our customers.

Your primary responsibilities:

- Design, develop, and test commercial user interface components and frameworks that developers use to create applications

- Participate in code reviews, debugging, testing, support, and documentation to ensure your product team's success

- Collaborate effectively and professionally with other teams within the company

- Mentor less experienced team members

- Stay on top of emerging best practices and tools for your development platforms

- Actively work on team and personal professional development plans for ongoing improvement

Qualifications:
Education/Technical Expertise:

- Have typically five-plus years of software development experience

- Formal education in computer science, software engineering, or related, or equivalent on-the-job experience

- Prior experience supporting and debugging software

- Experienced in C# with a focus on user-interface development

- Demonstrable working knowledge of software and UI/UX design patterns

- Experience with Visual Studio and Team Foundation Server and/or GitHub

Characteristics:

- Desire to build the highest level of quality into all products through relentless attention to detail

- Ability to prioritize, multitask, and organize work and set clear expectations

- Ability to effectively communicate with team members of a global organization

Nice to Have:

- Experience in at least one other language/platform besides C#/.NET/VB.NET, such as JavaScript/Web, ObjectiveC/Swift/iOS, or Java/Android

- Experience with automated testing and SpecFlow/ Cucumber a big plus

We Offer:

- Open, friendly, collaborative working environment with cutting-edge technologies

- Learn and improve top-notch, commercial software development practices through on-the-job experience and ongoing professional development programs

- Work with many other skilled developers all over the world

- Additional health insurance

- Company-provided food and beverages program

- Food vouchers

- Flexible working time

- Office massages

- Sport and relaxing activities—Xbox, table tennis, foosball in the office

- Open PTO (paid time off) policy—unlimited days over 20 with manager's approval

Interested? Send us a recent resume!

Your application will be treated with respect and confidentiality. Only shortlisted candidates will be contacted.

Finding the Right Candidates

The next step involves listing the job on the Infragistics website and on LinkedIn, which normally yields many great candidates. LinkedIn is a valuable tool because it lets us filter people by skills and/or experience so we can build up a database of qualified prospects.

Unfortunately, well-qualified candidates receive a great many offers. Sometimes they respond to our posts and sometimes they don't. It depends on whether our sales pitch gets the candidate's attention.

Networking is also an important part of recruiting. Our HR department has a deep, broad network of potential candidates whom they have worked with in the past. They contact these individuals to determine their interest in a particular job.

We ask our own employees if they know potential candidates. *Referrals* have worked very well at Infragistics, and they continue to do so. They have produced qualified candidates and are a retention tool for our current talent. People enjoy working with others they know and appreciate building a team of strong professionals who also have social bonds. This makes work a more fulfilling experience.

If we hire someone based on one of our employees' references, we give that Infragistics employee a bonus.

In general, HR screens resumes without involving the hiring manager. Based on the information they gather during the kickoff meeting with the manager, they try to identify which resumes are promising and which ones aren't.

Candidate Interviews

HR then sets up initial video calls with the candidates and asks them three to five questions to see if they are qualified to be interviewed by the hiring manager. This initial screening usually discards numerous candidates that looked promising at first glance.

Candidates are often disqualified because they don't have the right experience or knowledge, or what the candidate is looking for is not what the team needs currently. For example, HR might be looking for an individual contributor position, but the candidate aspires to become a team leader. Or the candidate is applying for a sales job but really wants to go into marketing. If hired, this person will start looking for another position shortly and the team will be forced to search for a new member.

The questions HR asks of these candidates vary based on the department, the role, and the team's specific needs. If some teams are stretched thin, HR has to hire candidates who are strong in terms of autonomy and ownership. At the same time, HR wants to know if candidates can identify when they need to involve others before making a decision. To determine this, HR typically asks: How do you like to be managed? This question is probing to see if any of the characteristics we're seeking appear in the response. If they do, HR asks the candidate to provide examples of how they dealt with situations where their team was at a very demanding point in terms of deliverables and they encountered a challenging issue that needed to be solved.

Then, HR asks the candidates to tell them:

- What was the issue?

- Why was it critical?

- What did they do?

- How did they involve others?

- What happened in the end?

HR doesn't expect perfect answers but rather realistic ones that show how the candidates make decisions, helping them visualize how these candidates will fit into teams at Infragistics.

HR also digs into how much a candidate is a lifelong learner by asking a series of open-ended questions, including:

- What books are you reading?

- What are some of your favorite business books?

- What have you learned in the past year?

- What would you like to learn in the next year?

Upper-Level Hiring

Our process is different for higher-level positions. Not long ago, I told HR we needed a new vice president of talent management. At our meeting, I detailed the kind of responsibilities the position involved and the compensation that was available. HR followed the same process described previously, but they focused more on finding candidates through their networks.

Another difference in a high-level executive process is how candidates are interviewed. HR asked many more behavioral and open-ended questions to determine the candidate's values and ethics, such as:

- Do you share information openly?

- How do you make decisions?

- Would you say you are transparent in your management style?

- How do you deal with transparency and confidentiality/managing information?

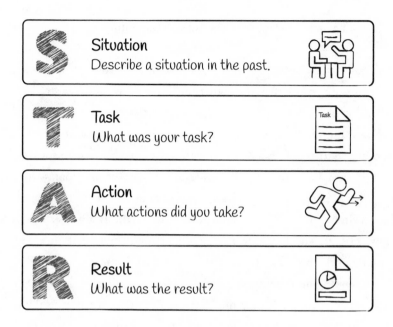

Figure 8.1. The STAR method

A strategy to elicit good responses from candidates is described by the acronym STAR. HR asks candidates to describe a situation (S) in the past, what their task (T) was, what action (A) they took, and what the result (R) of that action was (see Figure 8.1).

HR might ask:

- Give me an example of a goal at work and how you achieved it.

- While working on your goal, did you come across a difficulty?

- What happened?

- What did you do about it?

Other questions asked were:

- Give me an example of how you worked under pressure.

- What did you do?

- What was your input and what was the result?

Finally, this question: Tell me about a time at your company when a decision was made that you didn't fully agree with but you still had to support it and follow through on it.

These questions forced candidates to draw on their actual experiences (as opposed to hypothesizing on how things should be done or solved). In the first sets of questions, HR wanted to see how the candidates worked toward achieving a goal (planning, prioritizing) and how they handled the inevitable difficulties they encountered. In the second set of questions, HR aimed at having the candidates illustrate what they see as working under pressure and how they manage pressure.

Depending on the responses, HR could determine if a candidate is a good collaborator, or if they might try to get their own way to the detriment of team members. One candidate, for instance, told them that because of time pressure, he completely rewrote a report his team had drafted. Such behavior could wind up destroying a team. Candidates have to fit in with our culture and our way of management.

After HR had interviewed a small number of executives, they scheduled a meeting with me. They shared their impressions of the candidates in Slingshot but followed with an in-person conversation before proceeding with interviews.

At the meeting, they reported on how these people answered the open-ended questions, and together we narrowed down the number of candidates to one or two who appeared to be a good fit. They had also already discussed with the candidates their compensation, benefits, short- and long-term incentives, and whether they would accept this position. At the eleventh hour, HR doesn't expect a candidate to reject an offer, which rarely happens.

In my interviews with the final candidates, I am always authentic and transparent because this is the best way to build a meaningful relationship. I will be working with them, hopefully for a long time, and I don't want them to say I misled them in any way.

I also ask candidates: What do you know about Infragistics? I am looking to see if they have done some research on their own to learn about the company and are serious about joining us. I also ask them to explain what our products do, and if they see competitive advantage in them. How they answer tells me how well they understand our business and if they believe in Infragistics and our products.

Onboarding the New Hire

Just as the HR department serves as consultants to hiring managers, they play the same role with new hires. Onboarding begins with the first contact they have with a candidate, whether it is through an email, a phone call, or a Zoom meeting.

Onboarding continues after the decision is made to hire the individual. HR does behind-the-scenes coordination and facilitation to ensure the new hire has a smooth transition. They work with IT to provide the person with all the equipment they need, which can be difficult because we have both regional and international offices.

They also work with the hiring manager on the 30/60/90-days document. This is an overview of what the new hire is going to be learning over these different time periods and what is expected of them in terms of tasks and what needs to be learned by the ninetieth day.

HR conducts the first meeting with the new hire. They walk them through the general aspects of the company: information about our mission and vision, our divisions, and overview of our products, offices, and company values and programs (IGGI Awards Recognition Program), and the systems we use.

The 30/60/90-Day Plan

Then the hiring manager presents them with a 30/60/90-day plan, shown in Table 8.1. This plan is presented to the new hire by their manager, who is responsible for designing it. HR ensures the manager creates one.

Table 8.1. 30/60/90-day plan

WELCOME TO INFRAGISTICS

EMPLOYEE NAME		
MANAGER/TL		
SUGGESTED ACTION PLAN		
OVERVIEW	**ITEM**	**SPECIFICS**
In your first 30 days, you will	Learn the basics of Infragistics business processes and how the systems are used in it	Go through the complete process of trialing a product; purchasing the product; assigning users; submitting support cases; renewing the product; processing an opportunity, quote, and order; and fulfilling an order
	Set up development environment	Set up main websites, IS cloud services, customer portal to run locally
	Learn the IS/web systems architecture and applications/related technologies	Attend meetings with team to gain knowledge
		Review documents available
		Get familiar with the architecture of customer portal and IS cloud services
	Get familiar with Angular	Work with the customer portal to learn working with an Angular application
	Get familiar with newer technologies	Get familiar with basics of Azure Service Fabric and IdentityServer
	Get familiar with team processes	Get familiar with sprint planning, scrum, Azure dev ops process, ISRequests, etc. used within the team
	Deep-dive into IS business processes	Deep-dive into IS business processes, subscriptions, the different aspects of IS apps, Salesforce
	Contribute to sprint and support	Resolve at least 3 support requests and 3 sprint tasks
Your next 30 days will focus on	Deep-dive into systems	Deep-dive into main website, customer portal, IS services, and Salesforce CRM
	Begin contributing to IS projects	Complete at least 10 sprint tasks
	Continuing contribution to sprint and support	Handle at least 5 support requests and 5 sprint tasks
In your next 30 days, you should	Fully contribute to projects	Be a full-time member of IS/web sprints and contribute to major projects under guidance from senior members

Onboarding Survey

About a month and a half after a new employee joins, HR sends the new hire an onboarding survey. This is vital in obtaining feedback that allows us to alter the job experience for the new hire.

We use the Culture Amp Onboarding Survey, which contains twenty-two questions and checklist items that cover the following areas:

- The decision to join the company (sample question: Why did you join the company?)

- The hiring process (sample question: How long did the hiring process take from your first application/contact until you accepted the offer?)

- The onboarding checklist (sample checklist item: I have been introduced to my team.)

- "Feeling welcome" checklist (sample checklist item: I am feeling productive.)

- The onboarding experience (sample question: What are the three things you have most enjoyed so far about working at Infragistics?)

- "Role perceptions" checklist (sample checklist item: My role so far matches the role description provided to me.)

- Organizational alignment (sample checklist item: I know what the organizational values of Infragistics are.)

If the survey indicates that everything is good, then no further action is taken. On the other hand, if someone says that their role isn't what they expected, or if there are other issues, HR holds a short meeting with the new hire to find out why this has happened, because the new hire may not be confident enough yet to bring up a major concern with their manager. HR shares this information with the manager to resolve any issues that have arisen.

Sometimes at the beginning of their employment, an individual needs more handholding by the manager. A manager may not be aware of this because the new hire has been doing a good job. Sometimes the new hire says they didn't have enough time to learn the technology necessary for the job. HR helps facilitate more time.

The Continuing Role of HR

HR checks in periodically with the employee throughout their career at Infragistics and asks how everything is going. This builds their relationship with that person, which, in turn, helps in our retention efforts.

HR is always available to facilitate communication between managers and employees. They recognize breakdowns in this area occur over time. They have found, however, that when issues are surfaced and communication is reignited, a shared understanding occurs and bonds strengthen.

HR is also there to help when an employee has a major illness or if there is a death or illness in the family, which may require an extended absence from work. We provide them with paid time off (PTO) to sustain them financially and work with their team members to carry out assignments until they return.

Recently, for example, an employee's mother had a heart attack, and his father almost lost his life to the COVID virus. His team divided up his tasks and collaborated on getting his work done while he was away. At one point, however, the team could not accomplish one task without his assistance. HR contacted him and asked if he could help. The employee was quick to jump in to unblock the team. He recognized the team was being very supportive of his situation and they now needed his help.

In a learning-driven culture like Infragistics, people get to know each other and are used to assisting one another. This time was no different. When he returned a few weeks later, he was greeted warmly by his colleagues and the company.

Despite all these efforts, some people leave Infragistics for other jobs. When that happens, we don't take it personally. We tell them we will miss them and wish them well. Infragistics has supported them throughout their career at the company and it supports them now that they are departing.

We believe the way you treat people going out the door is as important as the way you greeted them when they came in the door. In some cases, employees have come back after leaving and we welcome them as old friends.

The Infragistics hiring process is effective, humane, well thought through, and consistent with a marketplace that is ever changing and relentlessly competitive when looking for talent. It is well worth emulating when you think about how you hire your next candidates.

 ## KEY POINTS FOR CREATING A VNEXT BUSINESS

1. The process of building a great team and company begins with hiring stellar talent.

2. Managers should team up with recruiters and HR to calibrate job descriptions.

3. Hire for the ability to work autonomously, alignment with the company's culture and values, and the desire to be a lifelong learner.

4. HR can elicit good responses from candidates by asking STAR questions: describe a situation (S) in the past, what was their task (T), what action (A) did they take, and what was the result (R) of that action.

5. Design a 30/60/90-day plan of what success looks like for a candidate. This should be done before their interview to tell them what is expected and then again once when a candidate starts so those expectations are reaffirmed.

6. Act swiftly once high-quality candidates are in the interview process, as they will have many other offers.

7. Ensure your new employees have a great first day and all the equipment and software they need is available.

TOUGH CONVERSATIONS

My heart beats faster, there is an uptick in my blood pressure, my mouth dries, and beads of sweat sometimes cross my forehead. They are all the physical signs that I am about to have what is commonly called a tough conversation.

In a learning organization such as Infragistics where feedback is constant and check-ins, coaching, and one-to-one meetings are commonplace, tough conversations are vital to maintain the innovation, creativity, and productivity needed to compete in the software industry. I and other managers must have discussions to correct behavior that is unproductive and possibly destructive to the full engagement of our employees and teams (see Figure 9.1).

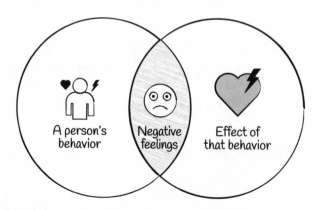

Figure 9.1. Factors that contribute to tough conversations

Two recent surveys support the need for tough conversations. Culture Amp, an employee engagement company, conducted a survey of 150 companies involving more than sixty thousand employees. They determined there are ten drivers of engagement, one of which is effective communication: "The things that really set the highly engaged employees and great managers apart are things that relate to communication."[1]

A second study highlighted why great internal communication is needed to drive external business outcomes. Gallup surveyed 198,514 employees across 36 companies in 21 industries and found that "those in the top quartile of engagement realize substantially better customer engagement, higher productivity, better retention, fewer accidents, and 21 percent higher profitability."[2]

A number of authors champion the need for tough conversations but use other labels. Susan Scott, a leading business consultant, describes them as "fierce" conversations.[3] Harvard Business School Professor Michael Beer calls them "honest" conversations.[4] Former Google and Apple executive Kim Scott labels it "radical candor."[5] Famed investor Ray Dalio calls it "radical truth."[6] And Julie Musilek, a director at Great Place to Work, characterizes them as "courageous" conversations.[7]

There's no shortage of sources affirming that tough conversations are needed and helpful within an organization. But before we look into how to have these productive conversations, let me describe from my personal experience the negative impact of failing to undertake them within an organization.

Impact on individuals: If a manager or team doesn't have tough conversations, employees who engage in bad or unproductive behavior may:

- Take silence as de facto approval and keep doing their unproductive behavior

- See their career advancement blocked

- Stop achieving pay increases

- Eventually lose their job if this unproductive behavior persists

Impact on managers: If a manager opts to avoid productive conflict, they may experience negative effects as well, such as:

- Having to work harder to cover work that is not being accomplished by direct reports with unproductive behavior

- Having to spend time with other team members to mollify their anger and resentment

- Having difficulty keeping the team aligned around the goals of the company

Impact on teams: If unproductive and bad behavior persists because it is not correctly addressed, teams might:

- Experience an erosion of cohesion, destroying trust and lowering respect for the manager

- Become demotivated, causing a loss in productivity and creativity

- Have a decreased sense of ownership and accountability

Impact on a company: Obviously, unproductive and bad behavior will directly affect a company's results, having negative, tangential effects on:

- Retention, as star performers leave because they don't want to be around others who engage in unproductive behavior

- Morale, as attrition issues arise with other employees

- Reputation, lowering the company's standing with customers, the industry, and stakeholders

I get it. Very few people *enjoy* conflict. It's definitely easier to turn a blind eye or to assume that problem behavior will work itself out. But when you have these tough conversations, you clear the air, making it possible to change behavior and improve the situation. Efficiency, alignment, and achieving goals becomes possible.

So, what is a tough conversation?

THE SBI METHOD FOR TOUGH CONVERSATIONS

I learned many new approaches to business when I attended the Center for Creative Leadership in 2003. One of the most important lessons was the Situation-Behavior-Impact method for delivering feedback. In this model, a manager captures and clarifies the *situation*, describes the specific *behaviors* observed, and explains the *impact* the person's behavior is having on the manager and other members of a team.

Over time, I have added two more elements. Managers need to *listen* to the other party, because the manager may have made assumptions about a situation that are wrong. These assumptions need to be examined based on facts. And at the end of the conversation, there needs to be a *resolution*. Both parties must come to an agreement. If they cannot, the manager should set a timetable of a couple days if more facts are needed to clarify a situation. By the end of that time, however, a resolution must be found. Letting things drag on too long will only make matters worse.

Learning to Take Feedback: Dean's Journey

Let's take a look at how this framework applies to me. From the Center for Creative Leadership, I learned about my strengths and weaknesses. Through one of their exercises, I discovered I was very focused on wanting to get things done and was very impatient with others. I was all about work and tasks. At the same time, I liked people and didn't want to hurt their feelings. When I was rated on a scale of five as to how much I cared about others, I got a two. I was shocked.

Over the years, through additional coaching, meditation, and things not going well, I became even more aware of Impatient Dean. Unfortunately, he still shows up at meetings. Sometimes I catch him and replace him with Empathetic Dean, Focused Dean, and Listening Dean. Sometimes I don't. That is where feedback comes in handy, but that can be difficult to get when you're the "boss." Fortunately, my executive team has learned how to give me feedback straight.

A short time ago, I was in an executive meeting, and I was in a grumpy mood. I had not been getting enough sleep for weeks, as I was kept up worrying about a variety of issues concerning Infragistics. I was snapping at the team and cutting members off when they tried to make points or give honest reactions to what I was proposing.

They called me on it using a tough conversation. Bullying my colleagues was not how I want to behave. Shutting down others was not the impact I wanted to have. I apologized and thanked them for bringing it to my attention. That cleared the air, and we moved on. I felt good. So did they.

Know Yourself to Understand Others

It is important to understand how your own personal proclivities may be unproductive at work and how important it is to alter them through feedback. In addition, it will help you be empathetic with the persons you must have tough conversations with because you will be conscious of how hard it is to be self-aware.

There are other strategies I use in addition to the framework of situation, behavior, and impact. The most important of these additions is to *not make assumptions about anyone.*

Ask the Right Questions

You can't get into anyone's mind and know what they are thinking. You have to ask. So don't pass judgment on an individual's behavior until you've had a productive conversation with them. There are two sides to every situation. Find out the other party's intent before jumping to conclusions.

I try to transition my *why* questions to *what* or *how* questions. When I ask people *why* they did something, they usually answer from a defensive posture. It's no longer about an explanation of circumstances but justifying their actions or thought process. While a powerful framing for some types of conversations, *why* questions often start off tough conversations with a conflict mindset.

Rather, a one-word transition to your question can make all the difference. Instead of "Why did you do [insert specific action]?" try "What circumstances led you to do [insert specific action]?" This motivates the other party to describe the facts of the situation rather than to simply defend their own personal interaction with the situation.

Listening to Understand (Not to Win)

Another element of tough conversations is ensuring you go in with an open mind. These are conversations, after all! Don't ask for the other party's thoughts or opinions without *really* being open to hearing them.

This is difficult to do. I think about it as the difference between listening to understand versus listening to win. When you are listening to understand, you enter the conversation with the idea that you might not have the right perception of a situation, and you are willing to learn and receive new information. With this approach, the conversation shifts from a one-way to a two-way exchange of perceptions and ideas. On the other hand, when you are merely listening to win, you are already forming your response or retort before the other party finishes speaking.

Listening to win is about getting ready to contradict the feedback you are getting from the other party. Listening to understand is about trying to incorporate the feedback you are getting from the other party.

From a manager's point of view, the goal of tough conversations is to help the other party reflect on their behavior and begin the process of changing it. Some people will listen, and the conversation will go well. Others will be contentious during the conversation but, upon reflecting on a manager's observations, might become more responsive over time. For still others, there may have to be more conversations before their unproductive behavior changes.

Tough Conversations Happen in Many Ways

Having effective tough conversations is a skill. It takes practice, courage, honesty, and leadership by the manager. But unproductive behavior *has* to be confronted.

Learning How to Have a Tough Conversation

Recently an Infragistics senior manager came to me to discuss a situation she was facing. She had been conducting a meeting and following our company's process of having check-ins. As I detail in Chapter 12 (on running great meetings), check-ins are very helpful to build team morale, to set the tone for a meeting, and to help with team cohesion. They're *part of* the meeting.

The check-ins were well underway, and the conversation was flowing freely, with everyone being open and contributing. Then another executive entered and questioned why everyone was wasting time. He proclaimed, "Why are we discussing this nonsense? We need to be talking about sales leads!" Ah, shades of Impatient Dean!

The manager was taken aback by his hostility and didn't know what to say. The team members immediately stopped talking, the good feelings that had been generated ended, and potential creative ideas of how to deal with business issues ceased.

Knowing the manager was not as familiar with the process of tough conversations as I was, I walked her through it. First, I said she needed to find out if he had any awareness of how dramatically he had altered the tone of the meeting and how unproductive it had become as a result of his behavior.

Then I emphasized that she had to be careful not to make him defensive as the conversation unfolded. The strategy for doing this involves the following:

1. First, describe the *situation*: A free-flowing conversation designed to build team bonding and to spur creativity was underway.

2. Then point out the *behavior*: He interrupted the check-in process and characterized it in a negative way.

3. Indicate the *impact*: The conversation shut down, and there was an abrupt change in the meeting's emotional tone and the sharing of problems.

4. Next, *listen* carefully to understand his point of view.

5. Finally, determine how to *resolve* this situation going forward.

I also counseled her to *pause* after delivering these pieces of information to give the other party time to respond. A conversation to understand, rather than to win, must ensure the other party has time to offer their opinions. A pause also lessens the potential for defensiveness.

Also, I told her to verify—check with the executive to see if he now understood how his behavior had affected the meeting. If they agreed on the impact of his behavior, the tough conversation should continue. If, however, the executive disputed the description of the events, she should try to understand his point of view by asking a *what* question: "What circumstances made you think the team was wasting its time?" That would motivate him to describe the facts of the situation, rather than having to defend his reaction to them.

The last bit of coaching I gave her was that tough conversations eventually need to end, otherwise they become unproductive. I told her to timebox the conversation and declare it as the talk begins. If the discussion goes on and on, simply say, "I have given you my feedback, and I hope you will reflect on it."

The tough conversation went well. The executive admitted he was unaware of the effect he had on the meeting, and he was not familiar with the intentional reasons for meeting check-ins. He agreed to spend more time learning about the importance of check-ins.

Tough Conversations Are Part of Growth

Another tough conversation involved addressing a skill deficiency. We hired a senior writer who could translate software development into exciting written materials. The job title required managing other writers, which was not her strength. I received feedback about this situation and discovered several employees would be on the verge of leaving if I didn't address this problem.

I had two options.

- I could fire her. That would require us to start a search for another senior writer, which takes time and money and reduces productivity during the process. In addition, I don't think anyone should be fired without being given a chance to reflect on their behavior and then try to improve the situation.

- I could have a tough conversation with her and explain that although she was an excellent writer, a senior writer at Infragistics needs to manage others, a skill she had not yet demonstrated. I could tell her that I would work with her to develop her leadership skills and encourage her to take leadership courses.

The tough conversation made the most sense. I explained the situation to her from my point of view and told her the other writers were considering leaving. Then I paused.

She hesitated for a few moments and then acknowledged that she had been overwhelmed managing the writers in a tech company, a more complex environment than she had ever imagined. She also said that, having been at Infragistics for a relatively short time, she worried about expressing her concerns.

As with any tough conversation, the recipient of feedback must trust that the person providing the feedback has no ulterior motivation. I affirmed my faith in her and suggested that she take courses on leadership to improve her skills in this area. I explained that if she did, it would not affect her title or salary. I did not want to in any way demotivate her or undermine her efforts at improvement.

We talked a little more, and she agreed with this course of action.

I informed her direct reports about her decision, and they agreed they would take on some of her responsibilities while she ramped up her skill level. The courses she took had an impact. The team became productive again, and they again enjoyed their work. By the end of the year, she was getting high grades on how she managed her team.

The situation, behavior, and impact of the senior writer had a relatively straightforward solution, which was facilitated by her buying in quickly to the course of action I proposed.

Many other situations are more emotionally complex, and solutions are more difficult to achieve. These are the ones that really make the heart beat faster, the blood pressure rise rapidly, and sweat bead on the forehead.

A Tough Conversation about a Tough Conversation

In one company I know of, a sales manager refused to discuss performance with a particular salesperson who had been with the company more than twenty years and had always been an excellent performer. Recently, however, his performance had slipped. The salesperson was meeting the company's yearly *overall* sales goals, but his contribution consisted almost entirely of renewals of existing clients. The company's best performers acquired seventy-five *new* seats per month, with the average for the entire sales team being forty-five new seats per month. By contrast, this salesperson picked up only ten new seats.

The sales manager was reluctant to have a tough conversation because he felt the salesperson would eventually return to form. An emotional element was also at play—they were close friends.

The company's CEO had a tough conversation with the manager in which he indicated that the manager wasn't helping the salesperson by delaying the conversation. His continuing not to acquire new seats would eventually lead to his being fired.

The CEO added that the salesperson's lack of production was having negative effects on the rest of the team, who would say, "Why do we have company sales goals if everyone is not held accountable for a certain level of performance? How can the team hit its goals with him on it?" If that happened, the CEO feared the entire company would be in trouble.

The CEO now asked several clarifying questions: "Do you understand why hitting the quota on renewals without bringing in new customers hurts the long-term health of the business?" And "Is there something that is preventing him from achieving a baseline quota of new seats each month?"

With these questions, the CEO acknowledged that something must be preventing him from hitting his new seat quota and that he was open to understanding what it was. When having a tough conversation, it's best to be open to another viewpoint. It builds trust in the sincerity of the person giving the feedback.

At first, the sales manager repeated his belief that the salesperson would regain his former effectiveness. "He's always done it before. He's a great salesperson." As the conversation continued, he slowly heard the CEO's concerns and realized that his friendship with the salesperson might be clouding his responsibilities as a manager. He agreed to have the tough conversation with him.

At their meeting, the sales manager described the situation, the behavior, and the impact his friend—the salesperson—was having on the company, other salespeople, and himself. Then he listened. His frankness, honesty, and courage enabled a resolution. The salesperson admitted to slacking off because he was burned out. He was ashamed to discuss this with the sales manager, since he had always been such a high achiever. In turn, the manager admitted that their personal closeness had kept him from having a talk about poor performance earlier.

The manager suggested that the salesperson take two weeks off so he could get counseling for his feelings of burnout. The manager also said he would inform the other salespeople about the absence without getting into personal details and ask them to assume some of his responsibilities.

The salesperson would be paid during this time. At the end of the month, they would discuss if he wanted to return and if he was ready to improve on his new client quota.

At the end of fourteen days, the salesperson decided to return. The counseling began to help his emotional state, and he continued it on a regular basis. His new client acquisitions began to increase over the next few months. It would take more than a year, but he finally returned to being the star performer he had once been. As this process unfolded, the manager felt that he had taken the right course of action, and he had a new appreciation for how important it was to have tough conversations.

Powerful and productive outcomes occur when managers engage in tough conversations with their employees and fellow executives. I have given you a tool kit for conducting these conversations. Without them, other efforts at constant communication and feedback will be in jeopardy. With them, the alignment, innovation, and productivity that every learning organization seeks will become a reality.

 ## KEY POINTS FOR CREATING A VNEXT BUSINESS

1. Give feedback as close as possible to the situation that is of concern to you.

2. Conduct the feedback in a one-to-one conversation.

3. Don't avoid tough conversations. Without them, people do not have the opportunity to improve.

4. Remember SBILR—situation, behavior, impact, listening, resolution—which is a technique to communicate in a less judgmental way and helps the other party to understand the feedback.

5. In situations where you are the receiver of tough feedback, even if you do not agree with it, you may want to take it as a challenge to change the perception of the person giving you the feedback.

6. Having tough conversations will strengthen your leadership and will increase respect for you from your team and from the individual to whom you are giving feedback.

7. Building trust with people before having to have a tough conversation is very important, even if it's not always possible.

8. Attitude and tone are very important in these conversations. Having empathy and the person's best interests in mind helps ensure you have the proper attitude and tone in the conversation.

10

LEADERSHIP STYLE

Effective leadership is a big part of the Infragistics culture.

As the late Warren Bennis, professor of business administration at the University of Southern California, said, "Effective leaders allow great people to do the work they were born to do."[1] Such leadership helps create an environment where people love to work, support each other, and learn how to complement each other's skills. This helps everyone collaborate, innovate, and create.

> *Effective leaders allow great people to do the work they were born to do.*

At Infragistics, leadership starts with me but extends to our board members, our vice presidents, and our managers. We have all become aware of the importance of how we communicate—not just the words we speak but the *tone* of what we say and the *way* we say it through our mannerisms and body language. Effective leadership builds trust between Infragistics leaders and our employees; it is the glue that enables all our efforts to succeed.

When I began Infragistics, I was not aware of all these dimensions of communication. At that time, my focus was on the words I spoke, whether at executive meetings, in company-wide directives, or in one-to-one interactions with our customers.

Then I had an eye-opening experience while attending a communications seminar at Vistage, a leading executive coaching company.

MANNER AND MANNERISMS

After being split into small groups, a Vistage leader launched an interesting exercise: One executive would have to convey a message to another executive, and that executive, in turn, would relay a different message back to the first person. We had to use the tone of our voice, our facial gestures, our hands, and our body to express the meaning of the words. The message would have nothing to do with business.

The leader handed me my message. I glanced down and saw the familiar words of Sarah Josepha Hale's classic children's poem "Mary Had a Little Lamb":

> Mary had a little lamb,
> Its fleece was white as snow;
> And everywhere that Mary went
> The lamb was sure to go.
> It followed her to school one day,
> Which was against the rule;
> It made the children laugh and play
> To see a lamb at school . . .

I hesitated: What should I do? Then I thought: How would I proceed if I were reading this to a child? I began slowly and softly saying the words, staring directly into the eyes of my partner. When I came to the lines "It made the children laugh and play to see a lamb at school," my face brightened, and my eyes sparkled in delight to convey that joyous sight. My partner returned my smile. I realized I had correctly expressed the poem's emotional subtext, which gave meaning and resonance to the words.

Since that experience, whenever I speak with either a group or an individual, I think about my tone of voice, how I am saying something, my mannerisms, and my body language. They are all important in being an effective leader.

COMMAND PRESENCE

Over the years, I also became aware of another dimension of leadership communication, which some have called "executive presence" and others call "command presence," a military term.

John Beeson, a principal of management at Beeson Consulting, defines executive presence as the "ability to project mature self-confidence, a sense that you can take control of difficult, unpredictable situations; make tough decisions in a timely way[;] and hold your own with other talented and strong-willed members of the executive team."[2]

Fortune 500 leadership adviser Mike Myatt defines "command presence" as "someone whose demeanor . . . leaves no doubt that they are someone to be respected."[3] Think Ukrainian president Volodymyr Zelensky as he leads his country in its war against Russia. Gone are the suit and tie, replaced by a military T-shirt and boots. While on camera, he walks the bombed-out streets of his nation, unafraid, rallying his country and the world with his tone of voice, his expressions, and his words.

I, too, have to be as aware as Zelensky as to how I present myself. Like most business leaders, I have hundreds of interpersonal interactions every day—with my executive team and my employees, as well as with customers, partners, suppliers, vendors, and other stakeholders. I bring my executive/command presence to all of them.

AUTHENTICITY

In all these interactions, I strive to be authentic, which can be defined as "being true to who you are—your values, beliefs and feelings—and expressing yourself."[4] With collaborative, learning-based companies such as Infragistics, authenticity is essential. However, as Professor Lisa Rosh of Yeshiva University and Professor Lynn Offerman of George

Washington University wrote in their *Harvard Business Review* article "Be Yourself, but Carefully," being authentic can be a double-edged sword if it is "hastily conceived, poorly timed, or inconsistent with cultural or organizational norms—hurting your reputation, alienating employees, fostering distrust, and hindering teamwork. Getting it right takes a deft touch for leaders."[5] They contend a leader's authenticity must rest on a foundation of self-knowledge, derived from honest feedback and effective coaching.

That is the basis for my authenticity and that of other leaders at Infragistics. As I describe in earlier chapters, feedback and coaching are built into our culture. These consistent interactions greatly expand my self-knowledge, which, in turn, leads me to make statements and take actions I truly believe in and that are consistent with who I am.

In addition, authenticity is also found in our business practices. Through our daily exchanges and feedback opportunities, company leaders constantly seek to build trust and maintain credibility with our employees. Authenticity is also essential as we develop our OKRs, as well as our strategic, annual, and go-to-market plans (see Chapters 14, 15, and 16).

FAIRNESS

Let me add one more quality of leadership—fairness. Everyone wants to be treated fairly. When leaders make an effort to be fair, they maintain the effort and passion of their direct reports and their team members. If they act unfairly, favoring certain employees or not correcting inappropriate behavior by individuals, they risk demotivating talented team members and, eventually, losing them. Fairness is a commonsense element of leadership, but many leaders unfortunately aren't aware of its importance.

A final thought: Some people are natural leaders, born with an awareness of all the dimensions discussed here. However, those leaders are rare. Most of us, including me, have to *learn* how to be effective leaders.

TRY THE POWER POSE

Harvard Business School professor Amy Cuddy's 2012 TED Talk provided millions of leaders with a technique that dramatically increases their sense of power and confidence.[6]

She asked TED conference attendees to adopt the "Wonder Woman" stance used by actor Lynda Carter in the 1980s television series. This "power pose" involves putting hands on your hips, planting your feet firmly, and lifting your chin.[7]

Based on her research, Professor Cuddy contends your body can profoundly influence your mind. When her research subjects assumed a power pose posture, their testosterone levels (dominance hormone) increased 20 percent while their cortisol levels (stress hormone) declined 25 percent. This little exercise can make any person more assertive, confident, calm, and optimistic—all characteristics of effective leadership.[8]

How influential was her presentation? It is the second-most-watched TED Talk in history,[9] with more than 68 million views on YouTube.

I have used this exercise multiple times. It has helped me immeasurably increase my energy and confidence when I faced a difficult meeting or when I needed to boost my executive/command presence. I also use music to boost my positive energy. My favorite is "Thunderstruck" by AC/DC. There is nothing like Angus Young to energize me and help me focus on whatever I must deal with next.

Taken together, the elements of leadership and communication I outline can help you be a much more effective leader. This will dramatically improve your ability to bring out the best qualities and abilities of your team members and company employees, helping sustain the success of your business for many years.

KEY POINTS FOR CREATING A VNEXT BUSINESS

1. Be mindful of how your body language, tone, and energy affect your ability to communicate—positively or negatively.

2. Build trust by being authentic.

3. Treat everyone fairly to maintain the effort and passion of all team members.

4. Become a more effective leader by seeking out executive coaching and listening to feedback. This will help improve your communication skills and uncover your blind spots.

5. When you're a leader, everyone is watching you, and the way you bring energy into a room, meeting, or conversation matters. Learn to adopt command presence, which is vital in achieving mature self-confidence.

6. Use power posing and/or uplifting music to give yourself the positive energy and proper attitude so you can express yourself best.

11

COACHING

Almost all of us have had some type of coach. You might have had a team sports coach in Little League or soccer as a kid. Maybe you received individual swimming, dance, or piano instruction. You might have had a teacher, guidance counselor, or mentor as your educational or life coach. You might even have had friends coach you before your first date, your prom, or any of the other immensely awkward social interactions of your adolescence.

Whatever the circumstances, a good coach guides our personal development and teaches us necessary and useful skills we can draw on throughout our lives.

A good coach is invaluable—especially for a vNext Business leader.

The coaching process at Infragistics has a huge effect on our ability to win in the marketplace. Effective coaching is integral to creating a true learning organization. It transforms employees into smarter, more skilled, and more adaptive team members. It empowers employees and managers to make better decisions on a more consistent basis.

But I want to be clear about what I mean by "effective coaching." Like many things in a vNext Business, it may be a bit different from what you're used to.

The old "command and control" management style is *not* effective coaching. Fear doesn't work in today's business environment. A company now must respond rapidly to changes in the marketplace, foster resilience in its employees and managers, leverage creativity in its workforce, and stimulate individual effort and performance. Old management styles can't come close to doing any of that. But effective coaching can help you and your vNext Business achieve these extraordinary results.

Here's another distinction. Effective coaching isn't just about providing feedback to employees. It offers the level of support needed to develop the professional and personal habits that help employees become more focused, more efficient, and more productive.

WHAT EFFECTIVE COACHING CAN DO

At Infragistics, we're a team and we have a coaching culture to guide us toward success. Some of its benefits are outlined in the following sections.

More-Engaged Employees

When our leadership went beyond simply providing feedback to our team and began truly coaching them, everyone became more motivated. Just as a skilled coach can inspire their team to a late-fourth-quarter touchdown on the football field, skilled workplace coaches can motivate your team to bring their absolute best every day—especially when the stakes are high.

The more motivated and engaged your team is, the more your organization will thrive. Gallup studied what effects more engaged employees might have on a business. Its research showed that with a motivated team, companies can achieve 10 percent to 19 percent increased sales, and 14 percent to 29 percent increased profit while at the same time lowering absenteeism by 41 percent (see Figure 11.1).[1]

Decreased Employee Turnover

Employee retention is one of the greatest challenges facing many organizations today. To keep top talent and maintain productivity, a vNext

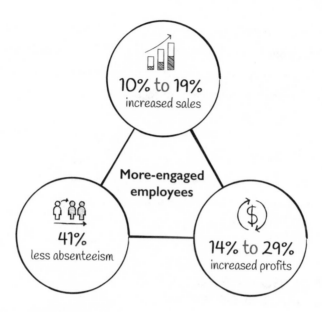

Figure 11.1. The impact of employee engagement on sales, profit, and productivity

Business should focus on measuring and improving job satisfaction, engagement, and loyalty.

And how can you improve those three metrics? You guessed it—coaching.

Coaching makes employees feel more connected to the company by illuminating how their work directly affects the team's overarching goals and mission. Employees feel that having leaders who coach rather than manage them is a sign that they are cared for—that their opinions really matter. Coached employees feel valued and necessary in the organization. Managed employees feel like a cog in the machine without direction and with limited agency and purpose.[2]

Increased Productivity

It's easy to draw a straight line from engaged employees and lower turn-over rates directly to increased productivity, both individually and for the company.

Coaching aligns your team. It gives them direction and insight into how they're progressing. Employees become more confident as coaches help them reach their goals. Similarly, employees who stay with an organization become more competent in their roles through coaching.

Stronger Bonds

Workplace coaching helps create stronger bonds within teams. Employees become more comfortable with their managers and speak up or ask for assistance when they encounter problems.

HOW DOES EFFECTIVE BUSINESS COACHING WORK?

I've described why you might want to employ effective coaching in your company. But what does that look like? What is effective business coaching?

For me it is the process of equipping employees with the knowledge, tools, skills, opportunities, and agency needed for them to take ownership of their work and be more effective at achieving the goals of an organization.

The Infragistics coaching process involves a number of steps. But before I describe them to you, there are two things you should keep in mind.

First, the coaching process should not be tied to salary or compensation negotiations. Doing so distorts the goal of achieving professional growth. There's a time and a place for a formal review process and performance improvement plans. Coaching is about connecting on a deeper level.

Second, although coaching involves feedback, it is different from the continuous feedback that employees need throughout the year. Coaching feedback should be offered immediately after a personal issue arises, a management decision is disputed, or a problem occurs.

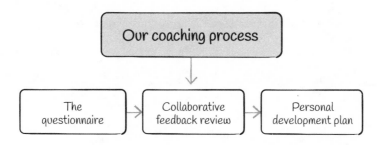

Figure 11.2. Steps for an effective coaching process

Infragistics coaching is a *process* that is part of a *coaching season*. It provides management and team members' feedback to employees so they can self-reflect and improve their performance over time.

OUR COACHING PROCESS

At Infragistics, we time-bound the coaching process so we don't unnecessarily interfere with different teams who are responsible for delivering different products on different schedules. Managers must complete the coaching process within three weeks for their direct reports during the three-month period we allot for the process. Our HR department works to ensure that managers meet their self-imposed deadlines and that the company achieves its overall deadline. Our coaching process involves a questionnaire, collaborative feedback review, and a personal development plan (see Figure 11.2).

The Questionnaire

The Infragistics coaching process helps employees design an asynchronous, digital personal development plan. An online guided questionnaire is sent out to each employee's peers and teammates to illicit honest feedback anonymously. Another separate guided questionnaire link is dispatched to the employee's manager. Before employees receive any of this feedback, they complete a questionnaire that helps them engage in

What do you believe are your biggest opportunities to improve that could make a real difference?
Please select up to 3.

☐ APPROACHABLE: Being easy to approach and talk openly to

☐ CARING: Demonstrating that I genuinely care about others

☐ COLLABORATING: Working well with a range of people from across the business

☐ COMMUNICATION: Communicating information, ideas, and concepts clearly

☐ FOCUS: Focusing my efforts wisely; strategically choosing where I spend my time

☐ GETTING FEEDBACK: Actively seeking and responding positively to thoughtful feedback

☐ LISTENING: Listening and allowing others sufficient time and opportunity to speak

☐ ORGANIZED: Prioritizing work and managing my time well; balancing my schedule

☐ OWNERSHIP: Being accountable; taking the lead and showing ownership of issues

☐ PROBLEM-SOLVING: Providing practical solutions to problems; being analytical

☐ PRODUCTIVE: Producing high-quality work (in the context of time constraints)

☐ RESILIENCE: Remaining composed and productive under pressure/stress

Figure 11.3. An example of the questionnaire to help
the employee self-reflect on areas for improvement

genuine self-reflection focused on their top four strengths and four areas for growth (see Figure 11.3).

Collaborative Feedback Review

Once these steps are completed, the manager and the employee hold a collaboration session to review the feedback. I emphasize the word *review*. The manager's job is to talk through the feedback *with* the employee, not to dictate the results to the employee.

Personal Development Plan

After this session, the employee creates a personal development plan for the next year. In the plan, the employee lists four areas where they need improvement.

An employee and a manager might disagree about what should be included in a personal development plan. Let's look at software coders. These employees may think they have increased their individual knowledge about a particular concept—for example, artificial intelligence (AI)—in the past year and might not believe they need to improve more in this specific area. But their manager may conclude that while the effort was made, so many new AI developments have occurred that the coders must continue to learn more about the concept.

The last step in the process is to review the plan with the manager. This plan will identify up to four areas of professional development with SMART goals on how to achieve these new skills and learnings. Every vNext company should have a budget to support the plan and give employees time to learn and/or have experiential learning on projects.

To ensure accountability, employees and their managers reexamine their plans every quarter. Are the employees making headway toward improving in their chosen areas for growth? Does the manager have suggestions on how to change the employees' course or a strategy for them to be more effective? These coaching sessions should be learning experiences for both parties. Otherwise, compliance with the process will diminish.

What Is Good Feedback?

Coaching I describe works well in theory. But every employee, every manager, and every circumstance is different. Conflict can arise if an employee thinks a manager does not have their best interests at heart. The employee may thus perceive feedback as inaccurate or even hurtful. When this happens, a manager should reflect on how they have given feedback. It should always contain concrete examples.

This is not good feedback: "Joe does not collaborate well with certain team members, and this hurts overall team camaraderie."

Better feedback is this: "At our last meeting, Joe interrupted Sally a number of times as he tried to prove his point of view. Sally eventually stopped talking, and the other team members remained silent. Intimidation replaced camaraderie among team members."

During their coaching session, a manager should suggest to Joe how to improve in an area where he is causing an adverse reaction, such as by saying, "You need to work on listening to other team members' viewpoints before expressing your own opinion."

Feedback is hard to hear sometimes. But the only path to improving an employee's performance and behavior is to be as direct as possible, removing the chance a coaching session becomes a debate.

Despite a manager's best efforts, an employee might still feel the feedback is unfair. If this occurs, remind the employee that these are *your* observations, and then provide the employee the opportunity to ask clarifying questions, such as:

- Can you give me a specific example of what concerns you?

- How long have you been aware of this behavior?

While our formal coaching process happens on a yearly cycle, managers should always be coaching. In their one-to-one meetings with their direct reports, they should continuously bring up issues that are potentially detrimental to an individual's and the team's performance.

MY COACHING EXPERIENCE

I have been coaching others for thirty years. I currently coach my six direct reports. My board of directors, my direct reports, my CEO group, and an executive coach all provide me with feedback. I also do a ton of self-review. After all the feedback is completed, like everyone at Infragistics, I create my own personal development plan for the year.

Coaching can be an unbelievably eye-opening experience. "I didn't know that my team thought that way about me" and "I didn't know I was doing that" were *both* frequent thoughts I had after going through our coaching process. All of us have blind spots. Isn't it refreshing for someone to spot them so we can improve?

This year, my personal development plan consisted of two areas:

- Skills improvement

- Behavioral improvement—curtailing my aggressive manner

Skills improvement involves increasing my sales and marketing abilities, an ongoing project for the last ten years. No matter how good you think you are, there's always a better approach, a better solution, a better strategy. I improve my skills by listening to talks by experts, reading books, and attending conferences on marketing and sales. Ultimately all this work makes me better at my job.

Behavioral improvement has been a continuing challenge for me. Despite all the years of feedback, I still tend to become too aggressive when championing my ideas. I get too "in the zone." This has caused hurt feelings among my team members and employees. It never leads to good outcomes, and it doesn't help achieve what I want.

My aggressive side flares when I am under pressure or feeling stressed, or when the company is going through tough times.

The feedback I receive, although hard to hear, helps me become more mindful of how I am affecting others. Plus, it forces me to focus more on my daily meditation practice and forms of self-care, such as taking breaks during the day or even just taking a random day off (see Chapter 17 for more on self-care).

If I have harmed someone, I see it as an opportunity to build a better relationship. I try to apologize to individuals I have hurt when I have become too aggressive in pursuing my goals. Being the CEO and a business leader doesn't excuse me from my responsibility to respect others.

Business coaching is mutually rewarding to the managers, the employees, and the entire company. Remember the good feeling you had when you finally hit the baseball for a double, hugged your teammates after scoring a goal, or glided across the dance floor with your partner? Remember the look on your coach's face when you finally accomplished what you had both been working to achieve? That is the same feeling that employees at Infragistics get when our coaching process is effective. And it is the feeling every vNext Business needs to achieve to stay adaptable and competitive.

KEY POINTS FOR CREATING A VNEXT BUSINESS

1. Investing in your people is critical to compete in the ever-changing market and to have a learning organization, and coaching is an important tool to achieve this.

2. Timebox your coaching season and assign a leader to oversee that coaching is occurring throughout the organization.

3. Be thoughtful and have empathy as you are coaching your team.

4. Have a budget to help each manager invest in learning new skills.

5. Encourage your managers to give employees the right projects and work so they can have the experiences to grow with the proper amount of risk mitigation.

6. Put the time in for your team and yourself to work on new skills and learning.

7. Follow up with your team quarterly on their personal development plans. Too many people don't invest the time to build new skills because of the daily pressures of the work and deadlines.

12

HIGHLY EFFECTIVE MEETINGS

As the laughter subsided, I looked around at my direct reports during the first phase of our weekly two-hour meeting and thought about how the years of hard work figuring out how to make meetings highly effective was paying off.

Phil Dinsmore, our vice president of worldwide sales, had just cracked a joke, sending a ripple of laughter through the room. We had begun checking in, which is always our first agenda item. This takes up to forty-five minutes of our weekly two-hour meeting. During this time, we discuss the personal and professional issues affecting our lives.

Phil is our resident comedian, and his sense of humor is part of what makes coming to meetings so enjoyable. Meetings should be a place where everyone feels comfortable and relaxed so they can be their authentic selves, which leads to doing their best work. Far from wasting time, moments of levity help solidify the bond between us. Our personal and professional discussions build relationships, cultivate team empathy, and communicate that we care deeply about the individuals there. Spending time with each other as people is an investment in our team's cohesion and, ultimately, in the productivity of our company.

At this meeting, besides Phil, were Chris Rogers, chief financial officer; Jason Beres, senior vice president of development; and Holly Fee, vice president of marketing. Collectively, they bring world-class skills and experiences. But more than that, each checks their ego at the door and fully participates with an open mind and open heart as we solve problems and collaborate. We trust each other implicitly to always seek the best idea or solution for Infragistics.

Phil, Jason, Holly, Chris, and I always meet in the conference room next to my office, the largest room in the Infragistics building. It is filled with sunlight and has a window that looks out on the bustling café and the tranquil green, open spaces behind our building. In the room is a three-hundred-gallon fish tank, a long conference table, and numerous plugs for everyone's laptops. We project our weekly agenda on a large screen. Another big screen, if needed, can slide down from the ceiling. In addition, old-school flip boards are available for writing down items. Yes, we still find them useful and effective.

My assistant, Diane, has placed on the table bowls of trail mix and M&Ms, plain and peanut. They make the room feel like part of a home. Little touches help a lot when creating a communal sensibility.

Our CFO, Chris Rogers, and I go back to Infragistics's startup days. Prior to Chris, we had never had a CFO, just a bookkeeper. When I interviewed him for the position, I was frank—I said we had $618 in the bank and a $580,000-a-month expense structure. He replied, "Sign me up." I responded, "You're crazy! Did you hear what I just said?" He laughed heartedly. That's when I knew that Chris and I were going to get along just fine. Chris came aboard because he loved what we were doing and believed in our vision for the future. He is that kind of guy—someone you want in a foxhole with you. If a person sticks with you as you try to turn around such a difficult financial situation, they are really invested. Chris is smart, loves to talk, enjoys overcoming obstacles, and has an intricate knowledge of finance and running a global operation.

I met Jason at a Microsoft technology conference in Buenos Aires some years ago, where we were both speakers on software development. I really enjoyed his talk, and over breakfast the next day we hit it off immediately. By the end of the meal, I offered him a job as an Infragistics evangelist, which is someone who promotes our products to the world. Jason would also serve as an executive team member, giving him a view of how our software company ran from the inside. He had always wanted to be a hands-on guy. Jason accepted my offer even though it meant moving from the lovely, year-round weather of Boca Raton, Florida, to the some-times-endless cold of Cranbury, New Jersey. I'll never understand how I convinced him to do that or how he convinced his wife! I am so glad he signed on, as he is one of the top players who has helped build Infragistics and maintain our top performance over the decades.

In addition to connecting with potential customers and being fully engaged in sales, Jason became the director of a team of nearly 250 people. Besides his formidable intelligence and leadership qualities, Jason always steps up to a challenge, gives maximum effort, and gets things done.

Holly Fee was a design major in college—a background that dif-fers vastly from the rest of the folks in the room but gave her a solid foundation for joining the creative team at Infragistics. Her "steel spine" propelled her to become director of marketing. She is unafraid to have tough conversations with her direct reports, which are sometimes needed to focus and align everyone with the company's goals. She also has rapidly mastered the analytics and strategic marketing expertise required for her new role. Loyal and imaginative, Holly fights hard for what she thinks is the right direction for Infragistics.

Phil Dinsmore came to Infragistics with extensive experience in business. He has an MBA, worked for many years in financial sales and enterprise sales, and has an excellent grasp of macroeconomic issues. Phil is articulate, confident, intelligent, and analytical. Besides his sense of humor, he has a unique ability to understand our clients' needs, along with the capacity to dissect the strengths and weaknesses of the positions we might take in the marketplace.

The only way to compete and win in today's business environment is for *all* employees and managers to be fully involved. Weekly meetings keep Infragistics agile, so we can pivot quickly when the market changes. We discuss problems and issues, we make decisions quickly, and we align our efforts so that things are achieved between meetings. We are united in constantly seeking new ways to create simple, beautiful products for our customers.

THE FUNDAMENTALS OF MEETINGS

Meetings can be a powerful tool for accomplishing goals and implementing projects, or they can be a complete waste of time, leading to organizational breakdowns and creating hostility among team members.

How a leader approaches a meeting is vital. Will there be strategy, goals, an agenda, and accountability? Or will chaos dictate the course of the conversation?

Before we learned the best practices of conducting meetings, we suffered from an acute lack of accountability. We often left a meeting without clear commitments and without specifics: What are the next steps? Who is responsible for them? And when are key action items to be completed? This created enormous frustration for the team, held us back in terms of productivity, and decreased the efficiency of our business.

The best book I have read on the fundamentals of meetings is *The Team Handbook* by Peter R. Scholtes, Brian L. Joiner, and Barbara J. Streibel.[1] It was named one of the one hundred best business books of all time by authors Jack Covert and Todd Sattersten.[2]

The authors of *The Team Handbook* were heavily influenced by Edwin Demings, the so-called father of total quality management. He proposes continual improvement to help increase quality while decreasing costs. Quality is achieved by giving customer concerns top priority and by studying and constantly improving key work processes. As processes improve, productivity goes up and inefficiencies go down.[3]

In their book, Scholtes, Joiner, and Streibel describe how meetings are like other processes in business, and thus they can be improved. Their insights form the fundamentals for our meetings at Infragistics. They give particular focus to the structure of meetings and to key roles such as facilitator, scribe, and timekeeper.[4]

Figure 12.1. Dimensions of effective meetings

Over the years I have learned there are many dimensions of a highly effective meeting, including the importance of where you meet, how you meet, and times for meetings, among other considerations (see Figure 12.1).

Where You Meet

As I mentioned, our meeting room for our weekly gathering, like many other rooms at Infragistics, is designed to relax people and make them comfortable. We even have some rooms at Infragistics where you can write on the walls!

Each company makes its own decisions about how to create relaxation. You can spend a lot of money on this, or you can devise less expensive methods. The idea is to enjoy being in the place where you meet.

How You Meet

Usually when I enter the room, Phil, Holly, Jason, and Chris are engaged in small talk and are near the middle of the table. I always look each one in the eye, say their names, and smile. Dale Carnegie's teachings reinforce our friendship and respect.

Sometimes I sit in front of the fish tank, while at other times I sit across from it. Sometimes I ask my colleagues to change where they sit. Shaking up seating makes things more interesting. Most important, we stay physically close and greet each other with affection.

Times for Meetings

How many times have you heard someone say, "I have a 12:05 meeting"?

Scheduling meetings *not* on the exact hours or half hours is essential. We start and end all our meetings on the fives. When meetings are scheduled back-to-back-to-back, participants get no breaks, no chances to rest, no time to even go to the bathroom or grab a bottle of water. For productive meetings, schedule them for five after the hour or end them five or ten minutes early.

That said, meetings should *always* begin within a few minutes of the scheduled time, whether or not all have arrived. Late members can be briefed later.

When meetings are longer than one hour, take a five-minute comfort break if one is not officially scheduled. Everyone always appreciates this!

These are small things, but attention to details adds up to more productive time and increasing harmony in a team.

The Purpose of the Meeting

Always identify a meeting's purpose. A team leader must ask two questions: What do I want to accomplish? And whom do I need at the meeting to accomplish this purpose?

How does this work? At a recent meeting, Jason wanted to discuss changing our website search from Google to an open-source solution. He knew our team would be helpful in reaching a decision, but he also realized we needed to hear other opinions before reaching a conclusion. Jason invited our coworkers J.Z., Pete, Sathya, and Pam. Pete and Sathya are both familiar with open source. Pam and J.Z. are both experts in implementing such a program. Their insights helped us reach a quick decision.

Once you have determined a meeting's purpose, put it in writing at the top of the agenda.

Creating an Agenda

An agenda should sequence the activities and the topics that need to be addressed to accomplish a meeting's objectives.

It should be sent out in advance with all the supporting content needed for each agenda item. This helps participants understand the meeting's purpose and gives presenters sufficient time to prepare. It also allows other participants to prep so they can contribute meaningfully.

Think about this: How many times have you been in a meeting where someone brings up a new idea or topic and immediately asks for feedback? This will happen, but it should not be the norm. Participants aren't given enough time to fully process the new information. They're being asked for feedback while still trying to form opinions.

If participants are prepared and information is previewed, they come to the meeting with more fully developed ideas and responses. An agenda dramatically increases your meeting's productivity. Jason was well aware of this when he discussed our website search. He provided us with loads of relevant material to digest before our meeting.

Our team goes one step further—we develop our agendas in Slingshot. Any team member can concurrently edit and add items to the agenda, along with supporting information for the discussion. This technology empowers our team to plan, inform, and collaborate simultaneously.

Having a digital record of every meeting helps us if we want to check action items, recall how a vote was reconciled, or review the facts that led to an informed decision.

In addition to these considerations, Scholtes, Joiner, and Streibel recommend that agendas should include:

- Names of the facilitator, the scribe, and the timekeeper

- Critical topics and optional topics—along with a sentence or two that defines each item and why it is being discussed

- The person who will direct the conversation about each topic

- Time allotted for each topic

- Review of action items, including what the key next steps are, who's doing them, and when they're due (usually, five to ten minutes is enough)

- Optional: discussion of the pluses/deltas (good and bad parts) of the meeting, giving members the opportunity to bring up viewpoints that were missed (five minutes should suffice)[5]

Our agenda is projected on the large screen in the conference room. If the small talk doesn't die down a few minutes after I enter, I kick off the meeting by reviewing the agenda and the purpose and desired outcome of the meeting. The review is a ritual that focuses everyone and gets us going.

First Agenda Item

As mentioned, the first forty-five minutes of our meeting is devoted to personal and professional check-ins, each one about nine minutes, so we all know how everyone is doing in their life and in their work. Each of us can then get or give help. It makes us "real" and generates the empathy needed to assist each other throughout the rest of the week. When a team is connected in this way, better business results occur, including increases in productivity, efficiency, and alignment.

If an executive team member discusses a professional issue that relates to our agenda, I allow it to speed up the meeting and perhaps eliminate the agenda item. This combines format, agility, and flow to get work done. But normally, the professional discussion relates to other issues.

As the meeting facilitator, I pick who goes first, next, and last. I change the order from week to week. On one particular week, Chris began the discussion.

Chris spoke about a great conversation he had with his son regarding memories of the house he and his wife were selling. Each of us was touched by what he was saying. We all understood the emotional difficulty of leaving a home after many years, particularly one in which you raised your children.

For his professional discussion, Chris reviewed the impact a congressional debate over new taxes might have on individuals and on Infragistics. His expertise in this area has helped us all weather numerous changes in federal tax policy.

Holly sketched out some of the conflicts she had been having with her husband, who is an expert tiler and a union member. Since he never knows when he'll receive an assignment, his work schedules vary considerably. Clashes between couples over schedules are something we all share.

Holly's professional discussion centered on her efforts to improve the customer journey through her various outreach efforts. She told us about two webinars she just held for one of our products, each one drawing more than five hundred participants. We praised Holly for doing such a good job and acknowledged all the hard work needed to make these webinars a success.

Like Holly, Phil talked about an issue he was having with his spouse, Patty, an elementary school principal. Her job often requires Patty to work nights meeting with parents and on weekends attending various sporting events. This leaves her little time to see their daughter and new grandson. Compounding this situation, their daughter had recently moved to Philadelphia. Patty had been talking with Phil about relocating to be nearer to their daughter and grandson. I said to Phil that we could accommodate such a change if that was the decision he and his wife reached.

Phil also told us about a terrific present his son gave him—a trip to Pebble Beach for a weekend of golf. Phil suffered from chronic back issues for years until a recent surgery brought him relief. Now he enjoys golfing pain-free.

Professionally, Phil informed us he was making progress in hiring fifteen new salespeople in the United States and Europe. He admitted to doing a lot of coaching to assist these new people in getting up to speed.

Jason, like Chris, just moved. He returned to Michigan, where he grew up and where his family still lives. He told us he was helping his daughter, who is a brilliant student, adjust to a big public high school after attending a much smaller school in New Jersey. He complained about the difficulties he was having in selling his old house.

Professionally, Jason explained the issues he was facing in improving our new business app builder development products. He told us he needs to increase the speed of delivering new code generation capabilities.

As we hear these personal and professional updates, sometimes we can provide ideas on how to deal with issues; sometimes we just listen and support one another, which is often what helps the most. With each conversation, our team becomes more bonded to each other, which translates to increased productivity, efficiency, and alignment as we go about our tasks and handle our responsibilities during the week. We will be there for each other, no matter what challenges we face.

KEY MEETING ROLES

Our meetings at Infragistics changed for the better once we implemented a structure and assigned fundamental roles to participants within the meeting. In each meeting we have a facilitator, a scribe, and a timekeeper (see Figure 12.2). I often act as both facilitator and timekeeper.

Figure 12.2. Meeting roles

Facilitator

As the facilitator, I open the meeting and review the agenda and our purpose. From then on, I keep the meeting focused and moving forward. With help from Chris, I manage the time allotted to each agenda item. Sometimes I ask Holly, Jason, or Phil to facilitate, since they are all experienced in the role. Rotating the facilitator role helps others gain experience and creates the opportunity for everyone to discuss the agenda items. Chris is excellent at multitasking—he can participate and still perform the role of scribe. For the rest of us, we hand off the role to another team member, so we can speak freely.

I have two other major responsibilities as a facilitator. First, I must ensure I put together items for the next meeting's agenda. This includes capturing "parking lot" issues—important topics that need to be discussed but are not among the agenda items of the current meeting. And second, I have to close the meeting on time. If the meeting must exceed the allotted time, I ask everyone if they can stay to complete the discussion. I am specific with my time request, such as thirty minutes. If they cannot stay that long, I schedule a follow-up meeting to complete the discussion.

To achieve the level of efficiency, intimacy, and creativity I experience with Phil, Jason, Holly, and Chris, a facilitator should be aware of several subtle factors that can become obstacles.

As a founder and the CEO of Infragistics, I am aware of a power differential between me and the other members when I act as a facilitator. They have less power and authority than I do and may keep quiet out of fear of offending me or because they believe speaking out will jeopardize their job.

To deal with this issue at meetings, I often repeat my desire for participants to express their ideas, concerns, and comments. I support my statements by being open and inviting in my words and in my body language. I don't want to intimidate anyone. I tell them we are there to solve problems and allocate resources, not to massage my ego.

Additionally, I praise any team member who vigorously challenges my viewpoint. Not long ago, a young employee we asked to attend because of her expertise argued passionately for a software design. I didn't agree with her, and the team voted to support me. I still lauded her for opposing me with such conviction. In this way, I showed her respect and sent the message to the others that they could also be frank and open with their opinions.

Drawing ideas from participants who are introverts is another challenge. Being keen observers, introverts often have great insights, but they tend to keep their thoughts to themselves. To counteract this, I ask for their opinions continuously. Over time, they usually become full participants as they realize I want to hear what they're thinking and I value their opinions.

You also have to pay attention to those members who don't participate. Sometimes they don't align with the team's direction. You must get them to share their point of view because doing so avoids outside meeting conversations that can derail execution. Plus, their point of view may change the direction of the plan or modify it in important ways. Once a decision is made, all team members must support and execute it.

Finally, I involve team members I call influential leaders, particularly if they are from outside our core group. They may not be top managers, but they carry a lot of weight in the organization and are widely respected. I always ask for their ideas and opinions. When we reach a decision, I will try to align them with this outcome so they can help implement it throughout Infragistics.

Scribe

The scribe may be one of the most important roles to rotate.

Have you ever had to keep detailed notes about other people's ideas as they're being stated and still have enough brain power to contribute your own ideas to the conversation? It's difficult. And as a result, many scribes can't contribute to the topics discussed at the meeting.

Here are two solutions. Rotate the scribe role so the burden is spread. Or find someone really good at multitasking, which, on my team, is Chris. He accurately records our conversations and still makes important and insightful contributions. I'm in awe of his ability; it directly contributes to our team's efficiency and effectiveness.

Scribe responsibilities include:

- Posting ideas on a flipchart, whiteboard, or digital note-taking software (again, we use Slingshot) as the discussion unfolds so that everyone can see them. This helps the team stay focused and prevents the team's "memory" from changing as the discussion unfolds. It also shows team members their ideas have been captured for consideration and acknowledgment, which stimulates participation.

- Writing legibly and large enough so all can see. A shared and continuously updated collaboration space like Slingshot or Google Docs can make this a nonissue.

- Serving as historian for the team by recording key topics, points raised during the discussions, decisions made, action items (who will do what by when), and items to be discussed at future meetings. Meeting minutes also help managers and others to understand the issues and challenges facing the team.

- Using a standard form for meeting minutes with space for key items. This helps ensure that the most useful information is easy to locate.

- Compiling action items into Slingshot, which assigns and sends out a notification of the people who must do the work.

- Capturing issues that do not directly relate to the topic but deserve future consideration—the so-called "parking lot" issues.

At the end of a meeting, Chris asks us if he missed anything. If he has, he adds it immediately. Chris' excellence as a CFO is repeated when he acts as scribe. He is as proficient at taking notes as he is at manipulating numbers.

Timekeeper

I usually serve as the timekeeper with an assist from Chris. Some companies separate the timekeeper and facilitator roles. Either way works.

As the timekeeper, I move the meeting along by keeping track of time allocated for each of the items. During the meeting, I alert the team when the time for an item is almost up, so Chris, Holly, Phil, and Jason can decide whether to continue the discussion or to cut it short.

A timekeeper plays a vital role in achieving an agreeable pace to the meeting, what I call the meeting's cadence. If the meeting is too slow and some members get bogged down discussing a particular item, other members will check out, leading to frustration on their part. This makes it more difficult to obtain their full participation at the next meeting because they anticipate another tedious gathering.

Moving too fast through the agenda items is also a danger. Members will feel they are not being given sufficient time to make their points and express themselves.

Being an effective facilitator and timekeeper involves learning the right pace and rhythm of a meeting.

As team members become more skilled in the different meeting roles, they can take turns as scribe, timekeeper, and facilitator.

DETAILS OF A RECENT INFRAGISTICS MEETING

Following our personal and professional check-ins at a recent meeting, we began to talk about the agenda items. I acted as facilitator and timekeeper, and Chris acted as scribe. Also in attendance were Holly, Jason, and Phil.

Holly led the first discussion for fifteen minutes, which involved thinking about upsell pricing after we added Indigo Design. She was looking for help in terms of clarity and alignment with other company needs and issues. The team's opinion was that we should think through what the next steps are based on buyers' needs now and in the future, and go from there. In addition, the team thought we shouldn't rush this decision. A change could be targeted for 2022. They suggested Holly could use $20,000 to get designers to create multiple templates for app builders for each market.

As her discussion ended, Holly was clear on the necessary action steps. She would identify where in the budget to find the $20,000 to build templates. In addition, she would do A/B testing on different offerings and upsell opportunities. Jason would help Holly by working on identifying and building templates for app builders.

The second discussion involved the pricing point for our customers for using Indigo Design. Jason led the discussion and talked for fifteen minutes. The team thought each deal was unique based on a customer's needs and would involve a high-level sales process. It was decided that Holly would ask customers to contact sales regarding Indigo Design pricing, and she would follow up with customers via links after purchase. In addition, Phil would package up sales content and send it to me for review.

For the next thirty minutes, Jason led a discussion of whether we should leave Google Enterprise Search for an open-source alternative. Jason had sent a significant number of materials to review before the meeting, which was very helpful. He also invited four members of Infragistics to share their viewpoints, including: Pete, director of information technology; Sathya, director of information systems, the department that writes the software to support our business; J.Z., a team leader involved in the software that runs our website; and Pam, director of product development, in charge of two-thirds of our product teams. Each one provided the team with their experience and their thoughts about making this switch.

A consensus emerged that although some savings might occur by making a change, the open-source options were problematic. The team decided that J.Z. and Sathya would work together to identify what actions were needed to improve our use of Google Enterprise Search.

We moved swiftly and efficiently through the meeting in only an hour. We made three decisions and detailed action items to be accomplished and by whom. This occurred because our structure was effective, and because we are so closely bonded as a team, we can handle complex issues with speed, skill, and insight.

By all these measures, it was a most successful meeting. But another marker of its success could be found in the minutes after the meeting formally finished. Team members were still talking with each other, adding some points they wanted to make or providing a suggestion that had just occurred to them. Energy, enthusiasm, and warmth were still ongoing. We ended as we began, a team fully engaged in making our best effort to improve daily as well as to help one another in any way we could.

 ## KEY POINTS FOR CREATING A VNEXT BUSINESS

1. Hold meetings in a welcoming space; use food and a pleasant environment to maximize comfort, engagement, and collaboration by the participants.

2. Remember, personal check-ins at the beginning of meetings, along with laughter and fun throughout, improve team performance and create social connection.

3. Begin and end meetings on the fives (9:05–9:55, for example). This allows participants to have enough time to get to the next meeting. If a meeting is to last longer than an hour, take a five-minute break in the middle.

4. For every meeting, have an agenda, a purpose, and a time allocated for each agenda item. Always send out the agenda and any related content in advance of the meeting.

5. Make sure you invite subject matter experts from the company to participate—those who may be affected by decisions made at the meeting.

6. Designate the scribe in advance. They should capture all the relevant points, as well as the decisions and the action items made at the meeting. Remember to assign to members the action items they are responsible for and when the action items are to be completed.

7. Pick the facilitator in advance. They should keep the meeting focused on the agenda items, ensure all opinions are heard and discussed, and capture important items that should be processed at a subsequent meeting.

8. Consensus decisions are a preferred outcome of meetings but, in some cases, consultative decisions are needed. If possible, let participants know in advance how decisions will be made.

9. Meeting notes and action items should be digitally recorded so all participants can view them in real time. This helps ensure that by the end of the meeting, everything is captured and agreed on, and it serves as a reference for all members in the future.

13

RHYTHM OF
THE BUSINESS

As your organization matures, certain practices occur organically. Checking on inventory, viewing daily sales, dealing with product backlogs, and so on. This is the *rhythm of the business* (RoB), so vital for any company that aspires to be a vNext Business. You need to keep tabs of the *metrics that matter* (derived from OKRs created by your planning process) for your area of the organization. You need to have a handle on what is working and what is not working. Once you determine what is not working, you can adapt and adjust and get back on track. Before I describe in detail what a successful RoB is, I need to talk more about OKRs.

OKRS AND ACTION PLANS

Infragistics OKRs have their origins in our strategic and annual plans, whose purpose is to align everyone around our goals, from the board of directors to the executive team to individual teams—marketing, sales, design, product development, and so on. Members of the executive team then communicate and execute the annual plan and the OKRs through their respective teams. At the individual team level, members create *action plans*, which are granular actions (sub-OKRs) that support

Figure 13.1. Action plan OKRs are derived from higher-level strategic planning.

the key results of the objectives created in the strategic planning process (see Figure 13.1).

Two key elements to the line items in your action plans are:

- They can't be created in isolation; all goals are cross-functional, just like your organization.

- Being agile is what makes this entire rhythm work. If you are not constantly learning, adjusting, adapting, and making improvements, you will miss out on potential successes.

Depending on what your team's role is, you'll have different rhythms to track how your team is performing against the goals in your OKRs. You might even use different terminology to describe this rhythm, but the result is the same—to hit your goals. Many software development teams use a methodology called *scrum* to ensure they are on track and hitting goals. This aligns perfectly with how you approach running your agile business.

SCRUM AND AGILE SOFTWARE TEAMS

The term "scrum" comes from rugby. It is a method of restarting a play that involves players packing closely together, their heads down and their arms linked while pushing against each other in a furious attempt to gain possession of the ball.[1]

The business use of the term is based on a 1986 *Harvard Business Review* article, "The New New Product Development Game" by Professors Hirotaka Takeuchi and Ikujiro Nonaka, in which the authors compare high-performing, cross-functional product development teams to rugby team huddles.[2]

Several years later, Jeff Sutherland and his colleagues at the Easel Corporation, a software developer, began to use the term. Sutherland was trying to develop a framework that would create greater business agility across an entire organization to generate larger productivity gains.[3]

This was a radical idea in that era. Traditionally, a new product would start in one department and be worked on by a single team. Then that team would pass the product to another department, where this new team would work on another piece of the project. The passing from one department to another would continue until the product was completed.[4]

Think of this process as an assembly line. But while this might work for assembling a car, where each piece has a unique place (like in a puzzle), it's highly inefficient for developing products, when each piece isn't yet fully formed. This process was so time-consuming that the final result, in many cases, would no longer match the needs of a rapidly changing marketplace.

A scrum team, on the other hand, develops a product utilizing a *sprint* framework—a short, timeboxed period of usually two to four weeks to complete a set amount of work. Important to scrum rhythm are scrum team roles and scrum meetings.[5]

Roles at Scrum Team Meetings

Several defined scrum roles drive the success of the scrum process (see Figure 13.2).[6]

- *Product owner:* Owns the product backlog, sets prioritization, and is the conduit between the product team and its

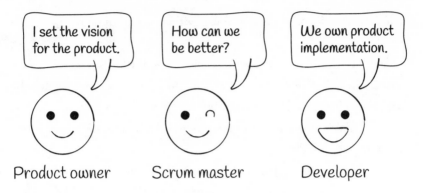

Figure 13.2. Key players in a high-performing scrum team

stakeholders. The product owner has a clear understanding of the product road map, product strategy, and OKRs.

- *Scrum master:* Owns the scrum process, keeps meetings on track, and ensures no barriers affect the development team's ability to complete the sprint goals.

- *Development team member:* Owns the product implementation. A team is a collection of architects, developers, designers, product marketing, and others who are responsible for clearly understanding the backlog item(s) and building them in a sprint or a series of sprints.

In smaller companies with fewer teams, the product owner and the scrum master are often the same person. At Infragistics, we started with just product managers, team leads, and developers, but we made it work. We believed the process and rhythm was important to keeping on track to deliver the product backlog.

Meetings in the Scrum Process

The scrum process includes "ceremonies" (meetings) that foster collaboration, communication, and transparency. Its elements consist of:

- *Sprint planning:* The product owner meets with the scrum team to discuss the sprint's deliverables. At this meeting, the product owner explains the most important product backlog items and decides what items can be developed within a sprint, which becomes the sprint backlog.

- *Daily standups/scrums:* These daily meetings are fifteen minutes long. Each team member answers three questions: What did you do yesterday? What are you doing today? Is anything in your way?

- *Sprint review:* Team members demonstrate features that were completed during the sprint and discuss what was not completed.

- *Sprint retrospective:* Team members review issues in the sprint and then adjust and adapt for the next sprint planning meeting.[7]

With this meeting rhythm, team members are "in the know" and are completely transparent with each other. This agile rhythm's purpose is to adapt and adjust to changing conditions. Did a critical bug come in from a customer that derailed delivery on a sprint backlog item? Was a team member unexpectedly out of the office? Was there stakeholder feedback regarding a feature in a previous sprint that needed to be addressed? In an agile framework, team members can respond quickly to issues that arise.

The communication path from high-level strategic plan and vision to detailed, granular deliverable in the sprint backlog item, along with the communication handoff to the development team, is illustrated in Figure 13.3.

Software development teams have used scrums for many years. The scrum team is cross-functional and contains all the skills and personnel necessary to bring the product from idea to delivery. But this process is equally effective for teams in any business. Scrums increase communication and alignment, keep everyone informed, and provide teams with the agility to change direction based on market and business needs. The outcome for any business is improved accountability and performance.

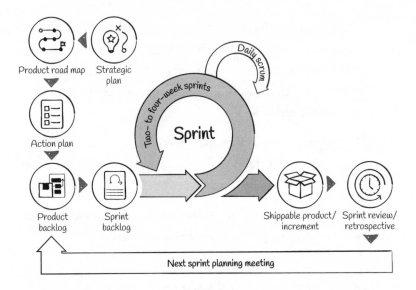

Figure 13.3. From strategic planning to sprint backlog to shipping product

Scrum and Running an Agile Business

As you can see, running your organization and/or your team(s) is no different than running a software development team scrum process. The primary goal of a scrum team's meeting is alignment on each step of a specific project. This applies equally to business scrums and running an agile business. Let's compare the typical scrum role on a software development team with how your teams might be organized (see Table 13.1).

Just like a scrum process, there are roles for team members and meetings at a certain cadence or rhythm based on your needs and goals. You are always iterating on "what's next" in terms of your team's OKRs based on your action plans. This is the rhythm of the business, or RoB.

RHYTHM OF THE BUSINESS

Just like your business, and just like a software development team, Infragistics has a rhythm to what we do. This rhythm runs the business—it is how we organize, act, and execute as a team. Without a consistent, known rhythm, no business can succeed. In a profitable, agile business, creating an RoB

Table 13.1. Agile business roles and software scrum roles

SOFTWARE SCRUM	AGILE BUSINESS	AGILE BUSINESS ROLE
Product owner	Director/manager	Owns the OKRs for their department/team, fully in sync and aligned with upper management on strategic vision and strategic plan
Scrum master	Team lead	Reports to director/manager of department, owns key deliverables from the action plans and creates backlogs/project plans for the team members
Development team member	Team member	Executes the backlog/project plan with other cross-functional team members

enables a regular series of data-driven conversations, decisions, and actions. As you implement this with your own team, you will notice:

- Improved orchestration and collaboration

- Greater transparency and accountability regarding OKR performance

- Deeper, data-driven business insights

- Increased ability to proactively identify and respond to threats and opportunities

At Infragistics, we have improved how we execute RoB. In our early days, when we were much smaller, my rhythm looked like this:

- Biweekly 60-minute one-to-one meetings with direct reports

- Weekly 60-minute meeting with department heads (product, quality assurance, marketing, etc.)

- Weekly 120-minute meeting with my executive team

During this time, we followed the strategic plan process outlined in Chapter 14. Although we weren't yet aware of agile scrums, we did have a regular cadence of meetings to discuss progress on our action plans and deliverables.

Today, Infragistics is more complex, with more teams, more product lines, and more employees spread out around the globe. Our rhythm has adapted as we grew and as we learned how to run the business more efficiently. We incorporated OKRs along with the strategic planning and action plan process, getting smarter in a data-driven way at what to track, how to measure, and how to report across the organization.

MEETING CADENCE

Nobody wants to add more meetings to their calendars, but a successful RoB is anchored by a regular cadence of predictable cross-company meetings where managers and teams review and track the progress of your OKRs. See Table 13.2 for an example.

While this may seem daunting, not everyone attends every meeting. If you are a director or above, you can expect to be in more meetings than others. For the most part, a typical team member will have daily check-ins, weekly status meetings, and on-demand/ad hoc meetings as necessary. No matter what level you are at in the organization, with an RoB process, you will have more clarity on OKRs, how your team(s) and organization are performing against OKRs, and where you can pitch in to drive company success.

Through this frequent discussion of priorities, resources, how to drive growth and customer concerns, and assigning timeboxing goals over two-to-four-week periods, team members acquire the agility to respond to marketplace changes. They then can realign goals and priorities to take advantage of new market opportunities. At the same time, team members still have long-term assignment of resources available to them.

Table 13.2. Examples of an organization's RoB meetings

MEETING NAME	FREQUENCY	PURPOSE	PARTICIPANTS	LENGTH
Check-in	Daily	Check-in: What did you accomplish yesterday? What is on tap for today?	Departmental	< 15 minutes
Executive team meeting	Weekly	• Executive personal/business check-in • Sales review • Discuss key topics	Executive team	120 minutes
Department status meeting	Weekly	• OKR review • Break logjams • Identify and mitigate risks • Information and insights	Department members, led by manager/team lead	60 minutes
Sales forecast meeting	Weekly	• Review quarter-to-date and month-to-date sales • Review of next quarter forecast • Highlight outliers (big deals, lost deals, deals in progress)	Sales VP and regional sales directors	60 minutes
One-to-one	Biweekly or monthly	• Discuss issues • Agenda set by direct report	Manager and direct report	60 minutes
GTM review	Monthly	• This is a deep-dive reporting and analytics meeting on OKR status; critical in the RoB process • Sales OKR update • Marketing OKR update • OKR review/insights • Review marketing spend • Update plans/OKRs as necessary	Executives, department heads, and team leads per division	90/120 minutes
Board meeting	Quarterly	• OKR reviews across all departments • Issue processing per agenda	Board of directors, CEO, and key executives as needed	6 hours

The Daily Check-In

At Infragistics, we use Slingshot, our digital workplace product, to run almost every aspect of the business. From daily check-ins, detailed project planning, and data analysis and dashboards, Slingshot brings together people and processes to create transparency, trust, and reporting.

The daily check-in is an important part of this transparency for my executive team and me. While we have lengthy meetings to deep-dive into and analyze every aspect of sales and OKRs, the daily check-in gives every team member a sense of the whole. We write down one or two sentences about what we did yesterday and one or two sentences about what we are doing today. That's all.

This short exercise keeps everyone informed of what is going on, as well as focusing on what we should be doing going forward. It also allows other departments and teams to align on goals and head in the same direction quickly and efficiently. Other teams and managers can then see where time is being spent, particularly which things are taking longer.

Executive Team Meeting

Every week the executive team meets for two hours. This ritual has been happening for more than twenty-five years (see Chapter 12, on highly effective meetings). I want to highlight a few things about the executive team meeting that makes it special and important to the rhythm of the business.

It has these key benefits:

- I get a chance to see how we are working together as a team. The business and personal check-ins by each team member create key discussions as well as bring the team closer together.

- It allows all of us insight into issues and events we might not be aware of in other areas of the business.

- It lets individuals on the team put forward strategic agenda items that we process as a team.

- It gives me the chance to highlight, reinforce, and inform the executive team of what I think is most important or critical to the business at that moment.

For Infragistics to thrive, my team and I must be on the same page and aware of everything that is happening in the business at all times. This helps the executives run their teams more efficiently, and it ensures that issues from the top are pushed down, and vice versa.

If you aren't already meeting with your executive team or key managers on a *consistent* basis, you will quickly see the benefits once you start.

Department Status Meeting

Like my executive team meeting, each department head has meetings with their own managers and team leads. While every manager has a different management style and must execute a strategic directive from the strategic plan, these meetings all seek the same result—to discover the key issues that affect running the business, and as a team, figure out how to overcome the issue(s).

A manager's style usually reflects their academic background and their department. A manager with a master's degree in mathematics and a doctorate in computer science might be very analytical in running an engineering team. On the other hand, a marketing team manager with a bachelor's in the arts along with an MBA might focus on team cohesion and camaraderie as their highest priority. Each of these managers has diverse skills and oversees a very different team. Both achieve their objectives but use different approaches to getting their teams organized, engaged, and motivated.

If your team is struggling or not executing and hitting their OKRs, you need to help that manager. Ask how they are approaching managing their team and how they are keeping team members accountable. This may assist them in figuring out the cause of these issues.

At the department level, discussions become more granular because management is charged with ensuring teams are contributing to production—whether it is marketing, sales, internal systems, product development, or accounting. Besides the usual of having each team member inform the others about their project status, these meetings involve:

- Raising potential flags in current deliverables that affect overarching OKRs (reviewing OKRs at every meeting will bring this to the surface)

- Discovering if team members are encountering roadblocks on current initiatives that they need their manager's help to clear, or if they need assistance from other team members

- Discussing risks and how to mitigate them in deliverables

Sales Forecast Meeting

The sales forecast meeting is a weekly ritual that is key to running the business. Each week, for one hour, the regional sales directors give a status update on their business. The VP of global sales sets the agenda and runs the meeting, and I attend this meeting with the executive team. Obviously, sales are the most important aspect of how we are performing as a business. At the same time, we are all involved with key customers and large deals. This meeting informs everyone and creates the collaboration needed to run an agile business.

The meeting usually kicks off with updates about our largest sales region, the Americas. We then round-robin to each regional manager—Europe, Middle East, Africa (EMEA); Japan, Asia Pacific (APAC); and India—for their updates. Each regional director gives an update on:

- Monthly forecast by division (developer tools/business tools)

- Quarterly forecast by division (developer tools/business tools)

- Next quarter forecast by division (developer tools/business tools)

- A view for the remainder of the year (flags, outliers, large renewals or new business, etc.)

The update for each division includes:

- New seat sales and a forecast for the current month and the current quarter

- Discussion of this year's and last year's sales at the same time

- Risks against forecasted plan (renewals not happening, late renewals, late new seat deals)

- Large customer deals (any deal over $20,000 USD is highlighted and discussed)

- Customer or prospect issues or flags

In the past, we ran this meeting using spreadsheets created by our VP of sales and maintained by his regional directors. This worked, but it was problematic. We depended on regional managers to update and maintain the data needed to have meaningful conversations. As with any file shared across more than one person, there were accidental overwrites and merger issues, not to mention out-of-date data.

Sales Dashboards Provide Real-Time Data

Today, we run this meeting with Slingshot dashboards that directly pull data from Salesforce, Dynamics, and other systems we use to track financials, sales, and customer activity. Without this sort of automation, you can't make sound business decisions, as your data isn't current and up to date. A sales dashboard example is shown in Figure 13.4.

In a data-driven business, you'll see the benefit of real-time dashboards like this for sales meetings. The discussion focuses on real data, with drilldowns to any level of detail you need, which gives everyone more time for collaboration on real issues.

To achieve agility, don't have sales meetings with just your sales leadership. The marketing VP at the meeting can inform global sales leadership on spending, campaigns, or other relevant activity that could affect their monthly or quarterly goals. Accounting can give insights on any payment

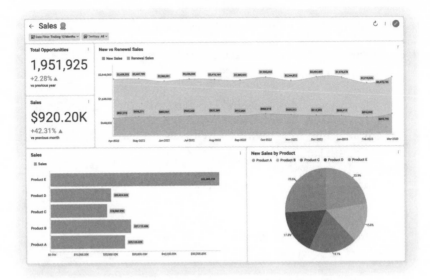

Figure 13.4. Slingshot sales dashboard

issues, collection issues with large accounts, or general economic insights for a specific region. Product leadership can highlight key updates, "hot" fixes, support trends, and general market trends that could affect a region for the month or for the quarter. Including all key players at your weekly sales meetings will improve collaboration, communication, and ultimately have a positive impact on how your agile business runs.

One-to-One Meetings

If scrums are fast and short engagements between team members, then one-to-ones are longer and deeper interactions between managers and employees. One-to-one meetings help build an agile, high-performing team culture through real-time and thoughtful feedback between managers and employees. Employees create the agenda for the meeting and discuss it in real time with their managers. These meetings should be used to ask for help and talk about issues and problem-solving.

Companies like Accenture, Adobe, Zappos, Deloitte, IBM, Gap, Goldman Sachs, Microsoft, and Netflix have all moved to this form of managing employees.[8] The rhythm of modern businesses dictates much more frequent and more profound interactions.

These meetings drive substantial improvements in productivity if facilitated correctly. Gallup's "State of the American Manager" report indicates that employees who meet regularly with their managers are almost three times more engaged and productive than employees who don't. Such meetings give managers and their direct reports uninterrupted time to discuss projects, review performance, remove blocks to success, and more. They also provide managers with the opportunity to know their team members on a more personal level.[9]

Your direct reports can prepare for their one-to-one meeting with you by using a template such as the one in Figure 13.5, which helps focus the conversation.

This template isn't something employees hand in like homework but a tool to get their minds into the meeting and to come prepared with issues, blockers they've identified, and so on.

I have found that one-to-one meetings help build trust and make being part of a team more enjoyable. Managers also become more invested in their teams, while team members feel more ownership of their work. It's a win-win.

To create a good one-to-one meeting, you should:

- *Set an agenda:* Employees, not managers, should define the agenda for one-to-one meetings, starting with the very first one. They should discuss with their managers what problems they are facing, what priorities they have, and what help they need from others in the company to achieve their goals and projects. One-to-one meetings are a great opportunity for employees and managers to get to know each other at a personal and professional level.

- *Pick a topic:* One way to keep discussions fresh is to alternate topics between the "medium-term" progress on projects and initiatives the employee is involved in and "long-term" progress toward career goals, learning, and development.

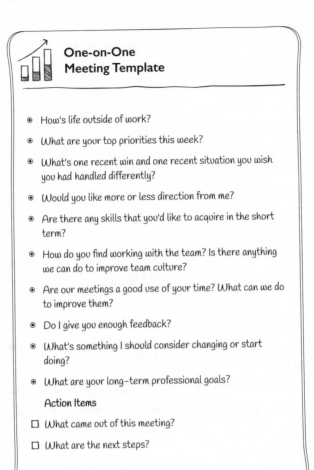

Figure 13.5. One-to-one meeting template

- *Set a meeting cadence:* When I first meet with a new direct report, I make sure to do it every week. Once we become familiar with each other, I move the meetings to every two weeks, which becomes our cadence. As you define your own meeting cadence, your goal should be to determine what works best in terms of your business and how work gets done. The Goldilocks Rule applies—not too many meetings and not too few. Just right! The definition of "just right" will depend on your culture and the individuals you work with.

- *Be consistent:* Don't skip meetings if either person becomes too busy on the day scheduled, or if either party gets sick. Just reschedule if possible.

I know too many managers and business leaders who constantly deprioritize or cancel their internal one-to-one meetings. What message does that send to your team?

GTM Review

The monthly go-to-market (GTM) review is a deep-dive meeting where every executive, manager, and team-lead reports on their OKR status. This meeting is really a roll-up or summary of the various weekly or biweekly sales, marketing, and other departmental meetings among teams, but it's different in that everyone attends. All sales, marketing, and executive leaders are in the meeting, expanding the discussion and bringing updates and issues to more of the organization's leadership. We have this meeting twice each month, one meeting for each division in the company—business tools and developer tools.

In an agile organization, continuous improvement is the ethos. In the GTM review, the outcome is informing, discussing, and debating, but ultimately its goal is continuous improvement. I need to hear directly from the team that is executing key aspects of the business. I also must ask questions, probe into key issues, and generally know how well they understand their business.

The agenda for this meeting is set by the VP of marketing. To ensure success, all slides, data, and/or dashboards are sent two days prior to the meeting. Everyone who attends is responsible for reviewing the content and coming to the meeting prepared with questions. If you don't follow this practice, the meeting can end up taking significantly longer. And you might make deep dives on one bullet point on a slide that isn't that important.

In recent years, we have moved the heavily detailed content to an appendix, where information is included at the suggestion of a team member, but it's not part of what we review during the meeting. Getting this information beforehand allows everyone to review all the data and makes the meeting efficient and focused on what's important. You discuss the content instead of information about the content.

Monthly GTM Meeting Flow with Key KPIs

The following sections outline the flow of a go-to-market meeting.

Sales

The sales VP gives an update on global sales numbers, as well as anecdotal information/stories on current issues with customers, hot topics, general concerns, or customer highlights.

IT

The IT department updates their OKRs for projects that affect marketing and sales.

Marketing Executive Overview

Marketing leadership presents an executive summary of the meeting data. This includes two to three slides that include where we are at with actuals compared to OKRs:

- Sales metrics such as total sales, new seats, renewal seats, open pipeline, and forecasted pipeline
- Month-over-month trends comparing new seats to leads, along with key accounts in each phase of the sales process with notes
- Leads and trials started, compared to overall marketing spend in a twelve-month trial
- Conversion rate of leads to trials to paying customers

- Conversation rates by channel, like PPC, organic, and direct

- Key insights that tie together all the metrics and KPIs on the summary slides

SEO Deep Dive

Our SEO (search engine optimization) team lead presents five to eight slides on every aspect of SEO performance. We look at key page performance and keyword performance, with actions on what is in process to improve SEO performance. For example, on a per-product basis, we might track ten to fifteen keywords that drive traffic to specific pages, along with "long-tail" pages that we focus on to support the main traffic pages.

We look at our page scores and page index each month, considering data from the trailing twelve months and examining how we've improved and what specific page tweaks we are making to improve. The goal for us is to be number one in search index of all our keywords that matter.

PPC Deep Dive

Our Google Ads lead presents five to eight slides on our PPC (pay per click) performance. In today's ultra-competitive world, you can't survive on SEO alone. Paid advertising gives us a boost in areas where we may not be in the number-one search result position from SEO, while giving a boost overall to brand recognition and brand keywords. Information presented includes:

- Spending versus leads

- Conversion rate versus OKR

- Bounce rate versus OKR

- Conversation rate by audience

- Total conversions by audience

- Key insights across all PPC data

Social Media Deep Dive

Social media can't be avoided in business conversations today. While B2B tools usually don't have a viral impact on social media like B2C products, it is important to track OKRs and KPIs on social media. Our social media team lead presents OKRs for:

- Follower campaign improvement

- Lead generation campaigns

- Webinar sign-up campaigns

- Reaction and engagement across Facebook, LinkedIn, and Twitter

- Insights across all social media platforms, as well as examples of the visuals that lead to the best improvements in engagement for the month

Account-Based Marketing (ABM) Deep Dive

ABM is a key part of our sales and marketing rhythm. We target our top 125 accounts across multiple channels with key messaging and content to drive sales discussions, to get webinar registrations, and to move customers to content like infographics or white papers. The OKRs for ABM are campaign and customer based:

- Page views

- Intent

- Leads

- Conversions

Public Relations Deep Dive

PR is a big part of our go-to-market efforts. At the executive level, we spend significant time working with our PR team to get placed in publications like *Fortune, Harvard Business Review,* and dozens of other online outlets.

PR is usually hard to track in terms of success, but with a good PR strategy and a good PR team, you will see results based on the quality and caliber of outlets, which leads to even bigger and better placements. This increases brand awareness, thought leadership, and eventual product engagement. Our OKRs for PR are centered around:

- Placement

- Placement in high-impact sites (like *Fortune*)

- Reach

- Engagement

Budgets Deep Dive

Reviewing budget OKRs is something the marketing VP and team do on a daily and weekly basis. At the monthly GTM meeting, this data is socialized, and it gives me a chance to further tweak the budget based on how I see us doing in certain areas of the business. When times are good, we can spend more; when times are not as good, I can adjust this spending as a lever to reduce expenses.

This was especially important in 2020, when the world was adjusting to COVID-19 and there was mass uncertainty in the global economy. In 2022, when there was high inflation and fear of a global recession, looking at marketing spend (the largest cash spend beyond salary in our company) was key to managing the business.

Final Meeting

At the end of each monthly GTM meeting, I have a thorough understanding of where we are with our business. This meeting includes the executive overview, key insights, important discussions, and the details from each key manager and team in the organization on the state of their business. As an entire team, we are current on OKR status, we know about any flags across departments, and we have insight on what the business looks like moving forward. This is the kind of information that is essential to any vNext Business succeeding in the marketplace.

Finding One's Rhythm and Making Adjustments

Every business runs on a rhythm. Tapping into this rhythm with meetings and checkpoints with your team(s) and adjusting KPIs, OKRs, and actions will make you an agile business. There is no silver bullet to success. However, taking a data-driven, collaborative, and transparent approach to running your business in an agile way will help you proactively identify and respond to threats and opportunities.

Just like scrum retrospectives, your agile business meetings should include discussion on:

- What worked well?

- What didn't go as planned?

- What did we learn?

- What can be improved for the next sprint (month, project plan, etc.)?

When software teams talk about how they implement scrum meetings, the conversation usually starts with "We do scrum, but . . ." It's what follows the "but" that is unique to their business and how they implement their process.

The same goes for the design of your rhythm of the business. Use our example as a framework but implement it based on your needs and your team skills. The important thing is to start.

 ## KEY POINTS FOR CREATING A VNEXT BUSINESS

1. Be agile. This will help you drive a successful business—if you and your team(s) are not constantly learning, adjusting, adapting, and making improvements, you will miss out on potential successes.

2. Running your organization and/or your team(s) is no different than running a scrum process as a software development team would—creating a consistent business rhythm ensures alignment on OKRs across your organization.

3. Have frequent discussions on priorities, resources, how to drive growth, customer concerns, and successes.

4. Improve the way you orchestrate and collaborate in order to bring greater transparency and accountability to OKR performance; deeper, data-driven business insights; and the ability to proactively identify and respond to threats and opportunities.

14

STRATEGIC PLANNING

I've spent years with my executive team developing a thoughtful and cohesive strategic plan for Infragistics so we can continue to be agile, efficient, and innovative. How else would we survive, let alone thrive? How could anyone?

But in numerous meetings with CEOs and other executives over the years, I have heard this reality: Most of them admit to not having a strategic plan, and those who have one do not pay much attention to it.

Based on my own experience, even if these companies may currently be profitable, they are headed for trouble.

Every business needs a strategic plan, particularly in modern times where change is constant and yet somehow always unexpected. Even without a formal strategic plan, CEOs and executives make decisions based on metrics to determine where money is coming from and what they are spending it on. That's a strategic plan—even if it is informal. What's missing is the conscious intent to analyze what a company's current assets are, what its current customer base is, and what opportunities it has to create new value.

According to research published in the *Harvard Business Review*, 85 percent of executive leadership teams spend less than *one* hour per month discussing strategy, and 50 percent spend *no time at all* (see Figure 14.1).[1]

Let that sink in. *Half* of executive leadership teams are flying blind! Or at best, building and repairing the plane midflight.

85%

of executive leadership teams spend less than one hour per month discussing strategy, and 50% spend no time at all.

Figure 14.1. Lack of focus on strategic discussions

Other research reveals additional disturbing information: On average, 95 percent of a company's employees don't *understand* its strategy, and 90 percent of businesses fail to meet their strategic targets![2] (See Figure 14.2.) Astonishing.

Such a level of failure makes me wonder how companies are even functioning—and how much better they would function if business leaders instituted the process Infragistics uses to create a strategic plan.

In this chapter, I show you the purpose and value of strategic plans, how you can create your own strategic plan, and how you can use that plan to run your company effectively and profitably.

Once you master strategic planning, you will see how it can completely transform your company's success. Running a company without a strategic plan is like going on an extended trip without a map, money, accommodations, or planned activities. While some people might relish such an adventure, long-lasting business success requires a more intentional foundation. A strategic plan acts as a built-in GPS, guiding a successful journey into the future.

95%

of a company's employees don't understand its strategy.

90%

of businesses fail to meet their strategic targets!

Figure 14.2. Lack of strategic understanding, leading to strategic failures

More than that, a sound strategic plan helps ensure your peace of mind. All responsible executives worry constantly about their companies and about taking the necessary risks that enable their growth. This creates significant and sometimes extreme stress when a company is facing multiple problems or dips into the red. A strategic plan dramatically lessens your anxiety and keeps sleepless nights to a minimum (see Chapter 17).

WHAT STRATEGIC PLANS DO

Strategic plans have several specific, positive impacts on a business.

A Strategic Plan Gives a Company Focus

Without a coherent and consistent strategic plan that is properly implemented and communicated, your company will lack the focus needed to define and achieve corporate goals. Companies often struggle to develop even the foundational objectives that can move them forward. Goals and objectives are vital for long-term growth and productivity, since they provide measurements of success. Without these benchmarks, how can you define where you are and how you want to grow?

A Strategic Plan Allocates Resources Properly

Strategic plans help allocate your financial and personnel resources into the new products, ideas, and operational efficiencies that grow a company. Without a strategic plan, or with plans that are poorly thought through or never fully executed, leaders allocate resources on a catch-as-catch-can basis. This often results in the most aggressive person in the organization accumulating the resources for their project, at the expense of other areas. Operating this way can cause a company to be short of funds for critical activities or during a crisis.

A Strategic Plan Helps Transform Insights into Decision-Making

Creating a strategic plan draws attention to biases and flaws in decisions a company may be making. The planning process forces executive teams and managers to closely observe, examine, and explain why they are making decisions and to support their choices with data, financial projections, or case studies.

A Strategic Plan Creates Transparency and Alignment across Teams

By working on a strategic plan, executives and employees can see how all the company's disparate elements work together and where the "whole" business is headed; this helps align everyone in the organization.

A Strategic Plan Improves Company Communication

A strategic plan helps establish effective lines of communication up and down an organization. Executives and employees come to see eye-to-eye on priorities and goals while correctly assessing available resources and responsibilities. Without a strategic plan, employees may focus on what they individually believe is important, which may or may not align with the company's overarching goals and priorities.

A Strategic Plan Creates a Learning Culture within an Organization

As executives and employees collaborate on and implement the plan, they have to repeatedly question whether it is working well. If it is, they should continue to execute it. If it isn't, they must collect and analyze more data to generate new hypotheses and try again.

WHY DON'T COMPANIES
HAVE STRATEGIC PLANS?

I'll be honest: I just don't get it. It's not like strategic plans are a secret. Great business thinkers from Peter Drucker to Michael Porter have written about the importance of strategic planning.[3] Almost all business schools have entry-level and advanced courses on the subject. Business publications and the internet are saturated with articles on the topic. So why do many companies not develop these formative plans? Or if they do, why don't they utilize them to meet their goals?

If your company lacks a formalized strategic plan, see if you can identify which pitfall applies to your organization.

Fear of the unknown: According to Professor Robert S. Kaplan of Harvard Business School and Dr. David P. Norton, authors of *The Balanced Scorecard: Translating Strategy into Action* and *The Strategy-Focused Organization*, the foremost reason companies do not have strategic plans is that most executives and managers have little experience in creating them, and they fear the unknown.[4] Kaplan and Norton state that many executives and managers are afraid they don't have the skills required to create such plans and are worried about how comfortable they will be in assuming the new roles described in them. Ultimately, their fear proves crippling.

Fighting fires mindset: Kaplan and Norton quote one executive who put it this way: "We have no time for strategy. If we miss our quarterly numbers, we might cease to exist. For us, the long term is the short term."[5] Many companies operate under the gun of Wall Street pressure for quarterly results. If your organization has this firefighting mentality—jumping from one crisis to another—your top managers often will not have the necessary energy or focus to engage in strategic, long-term thinking. This type of business chaos is a self-perpetuating cycle. Companies that forego strategic planning deprioritize the one solution that might lift them out of their stressful crisis-to-crisis existence.

Waste of time: Some firms view strategic planning as a waste of time. Top executives believe they can handle longer-term imperatives by doing things the way they have always done them. This is particularly true of firms that have been in business for many years. Leaders often think, "If it's not broken, don't fix it."

No good, insightful books on strategic plans: I agree with all the above explanations and want to add one more—no book provides a step-by-step, in-depth, and comprehensive guide explaining the nuances of creating a great strategic plan. Yes, there are many books on strategic planning—and I have read most of them. Unfortunately, these books contain only bits and pieces of a process that's filled with nuances and insights, the types of which I've learned through years of effort and trial and error. I hope this chapter fills this void of a step-by-step process to create a strategic plan.

STRATEGIC PLANNING AT INFRAGISTICS

In the remainder of this chapter, I describe the best process we came up with for strategic planning—ideally countering all the negative attitudes and emotions described previously. I show how it can be relatively easy to create a basic strategic plan and what the key benefits are of doing so.

Let's begin with a clear definition and then walk through the next steps.

What Is a Strategic Plan?

Simply put, a strategic plan helps you decide where to invest your time and resources over a given number of years. It is an intentional, structured process of using available knowledge and data to chart a business's direction. This process prioritizes efforts; allocates resources; aligns executives, shareholders, and employees with the organization's goals; and ensures that decisions are backed by data and sound reasoning.

Most importantly, a strategic plan is an *ongoing* process—not a once-a-year effort or an occasional meeting. It must be continually updated and adapted to moving variables in your business cycle.

As the late Harvard Business School professor Clayton Christensen noted in a study of HBS graduates who started businesses, 93 percent of those with successful strategies evolved and pivoted away from their original strategic plans.[6]

He wrote, "Most people think of strategy as an event, but that's not the way the world works. When we run into unanticipated opportunities and threats, we have to respond. Sometimes we respond successfully; sometimes we don't. But most strategies develop through this process. More often than not, the strategy that leads to success emerges through a process that's at work 24/7 in almost every industry."[7]

How Strategic Planning Developed at Infragistics

When Infragistics started thirty-five years ago, we had a vision and a set of goals, but we didn't take the next step to weave them into a feasible strategic plan. As the company grew and matured, and as the world and the market changed at ever-increasing speed, the need for a strategic plan became clear. We realized we had to articulate to employees, customers, and stakeholders our values, goals, and priorities. We also had to tell them what new products we were building, where we were investing, where our revenue was coming from, what our cash flow looked like, and what adjustments we needed to make from year to year.

Infragistics Core Strategies

Infragistics is a product-focused company, and we have four product strategies and two operational strategies that form the bedrock of our strategic plan.

A product strategy is a high-level plan developed by an executive team that describes what a business hopes to accomplish with a product. The strategy should answer key questions about whom the product serves, how the product will benefit those customers, and the company's goals for the product throughout its life cycle. One of our product strategies, for example, involves the launch of Slingshot, a digital workspace which helps create highly effective teams.

An operations strategy is a plan created by an executive team to support the strategic direction of a company. A well-developed operations strategy will result in building expertise in sales, marketing, support, and finance based on your go-to-market focus. You could invest in sales lead growth, product lead growth, and/or merger and acquisition growth. It could also include the types of technology that need to be acquired or developed in-house, and a set of suppliers from which the firm obtains goods and services.

> *One of the main reasons why companies ignore or fail to execute their strategic plans is that nobody reads them.*

For instance, one of our operational strategies is that we are a learning company. That means we create improvement through the scientific method (see Chapter 4). Always done in collaboration by a team, this process involves creating a hypothesis based on data, making assumptions, and then going to market to test it in the real world. Either the hypothesis works or it doesn't. Or it sort of works. If one of the latter two results occur, the team collects more data, analyzes it, creates an improved hypothesis, and repeats the process.

How Many Strategies in a Strategic Plan?

As Bernard Marr, a leading consultant to corporations and a columnist for *Forbes*, points out, one of the main reasons why companies ignore or fail to execute their strategic plans is that nobody reads them, or if they *do* read them, they don't *understand* them.[8]

So, what is the right number of core strategies around which to build a strategic plan?

To answer this question, a little cognitive science is required. The brain's "working memory" capacity is the amount of information it can easily process and recall in the short term. In the 1950s, psychologists determined that the limit to our working memory is around seven items, meaning the longest sequence of things we could memorize and recall is seven items long (plus or minus two, depending on the individual).[9] But there's reason to believe this number is actually decreasing. One recent study found the magic number could be as low as three or four items when people aren't using memory-boosting strategies.[10]

At Infragistics, as mentioned, we have six core strategies in our strategic plan: four product strategies and two operational strategies. We have found that six is the number for us because it allows employees to recall what they need to know and to stay focused as they execute the plan.

Marr adds that having a simple, achievable strategic plan is often one of the main things that separates a top-performing company from its weaker competition.[11] That is what we strive for when we do our planning.

First Steps in Putting Together a Strategic Plan

In this section, I discuss the many small elements that are essential for a strategic plan—how long it takes to create, who creates it, some of the subtle issues to look out for, and other concerns.

How Long Does It Take to Create a Strategic Plan from Scratch?

The Infragistics Strategic Plan is developed in eight weeks, with the most intense efforts occurring over a two-to-four-week period. (This is not actual time but calendar time.) As previously mentioned, it's always being adapted, transformed, and molded to ever-changing circumstances in our market. Throughout the year, if new data, new trends, or better ways of doing something appear, or a new competitor emerges, we add to the strategic plan at that moment rather than wait for the annual strategic planning process. What matters is that we create something that's *actionable*.

If you've never put together a strategic plan, consider that it may take longer than you expect this first time around. When you begin, the CEO and a team of leaders should give focused attention to the process and devote working hours to it.

If possible, set up a retreat around the plan's creation. Avoid hotels as they have a very structured, formal business feel to them. I recommend finding a place that combines a vacation-like experience and business functionality so you and your team can share information effectively. Such an atmosphere will directly affect your and your team's creativity, ability to collaborate, and flow of ideas. I'd advise breaking up the one to three days you will be there with nice meals and fun activities. Your mind has a chance to rest and everyone can decompress. You will work better together and produce improved outcomes.

You can't go on a retreat every time. At Infragistics, we often update our strategic plan at our headquarters or via video conference. But the first time you create your plan and intermittently throughout the years, go someplace where you can be creative, work hard, and have fun.

How Large Is the Team?

The team should consist of between three and eight people, but that may vary depending on your team's dynamics and the company's size. A much larger group is more difficult to bring to consensus.

Who Is on the Team?

You need to get the right people in the room for the discussion to be fruitful. Not everyone is good at strategic thinking. For those you have identified as having a natural ability in this area, these sessions will be enjoyable, and they will make major contributions to the vision and goals of the company.

Who Should Run the Strategic Planning Team and How?

A facilitator should run the meeting and write ideas and statements on a collaborative board. Getting the right words is difficult. The group should keep iterating on these sentences until they have achieved wording that reflects a consensus. It doesn't have to be perfect, just keep at it.

After the session ends, the team members can show the results to outsiders familiar with the company and ask for opinions. Then, they should tweak the language again. These statements can be turned over to someone at the company or to an outsider skilled at writing for final polishing.

If the conversation gets off track or breaks down, the facilitator needs to steer it back on topic. They should also manage the meeting's emotional tone, making sure everyone's viewpoint is expressed and heard. No one should attack anyone personally.

The facilitator must pay particular attention to *groupthink*—the tendency of team members to say what they believe the leader wants them to say or to agree with others on the team without expressing their true feelings and thoughts. Groupthink is anathema to strategic planning. If a key member of your planning group disagrees strongly with a strategy, there's probably something fundamental that needs to be worked through. If groupthink takes hold, you'll never unearth these differences until it's too late.

To guard against this, the facilitator should create a safe space for conversation and continually ask why members of the group agree with a line of thinking. Challenge them to back up their feelings with evidence. The facilitator should also actively seek out viewpoints from those who are remaining quiet by encouraging them to offer their expertise to the group.

In addition, all key ideas should be challenged. The US Army creates a blue team and a red team to do just that. One team defends a strategy while the other team challenges it. Try doing the same with your team.[12]

Starting the Discussion

One way to start the discussion is to have the facilitator ask: What impact do you want the company to have on the world, on a customer, on a market? Keep your company's vision and purpose in mind as your team answers this question.

After achieving some consensus on a vision and purpose, the facilitator should ask: What core strategies are needed to achieve our vision? What should our focus be to achieve our objectives? Ideas generally flow freely once the team finds a common target (vision and purpose) at which to aim the strategy.

The Outcome of the Initial Strategic Plan Meeting

At the end of the one to three days, the team should be able to describe the company's vision and purpose, agree on four to eight core strategies, and list between two and four business objectives.

You now have the basis of your first strategic plan, but it needs to be developed in collaboration with the company's other stakeholders.

Putting the Strategic Plan Together at Infragistics

This process assumes we have a strategic plan and spreadsheet modeling our business over the next three years. I discuss later in the chapter how to go about creating these documents.

In the first quarter of every year, I meet with my executive team, get their input, and align them around our key financial targets, which include sales, expenses, profits, and cash flow for the current year and the next three years, while we discuss the key strategic drivers of these numbers.

I update our spreadsheet based on the current business run rate. I get input from my executive team on the numbers and key strategic drivers of the numbers for the current year and for the next three years. We are constantly updating, discussing, and using current market conditions and data to keep up with the numbers and the drivers of the numbers. The numbers include the next year in the future, as we have a rolling plan. The strategic drivers may or may not be part of the four to eight strategies.

I next meet with the four members of the Strategic Planning Committee of the board of directors. Before this meeting, I send them a draft of the initial spreadsheet with the numbers and the strategic drivers discussed above, so they have some time to review it.

The Strategic Planning Committee meeting focuses on Infragistics's current financial picture and where the company is headed in the next three years. We also discuss the Infragistics vision, key goals, and core strategy, but these don't alter much year to year unless there has been a massive change in the marketplace.

After input from the Strategic Planning Committee, I put together a presentation for the full board that covers:

- Vision, key goals, and core strategy

- A detailed financial plan—where the money is coming from (sales and product lines)

- How much money the company will spend in development, sales, marketing, and administration

This is approved by the board at the second-quarter board meeting. Based on the members' feedback and comments, the plan can be completed at this meeting. If not, there will be a third meeting with the updates within a week of that meeting.

After the board's approval of the high-level financials and strategic drivers, our executive team and others from our company update our strategic plan for approval at the third-quarter board meeting.

In the fourth quarter, the executive team and I work on the annual plan and budget that supports the strategic plan, and this is approved by our board in the fourth quarter. (The annual plan, which is discussed in Chapter 15, is more specific and detailed than the strategic plan.)

As I said, for us the strategic plan is not a static document. We are a learning company committed to the scientific method of driving business outcomes and growth hacking, so we are constantly collaborating and exchanging feedback as we execute the strategic plan. We adjust to changes in the marketplace, customer buying habits, competitors, and other factors. We find out what works and what doesn't and change the strategic plan when appropriate. The plan allows us to run our current business effectively and still make the investments needed over the next one to three years to remain nimble enough to move where the market is going and have a competitive advantage.

Let me outline a strategic plan in detail.

OUTLINE OF A STRATEGIC PLAN

At the highest level, a strategic plan will have these seven parts:

1. Vision and purpose statement

2. Show the purpose of each major business objective (mission)

3. Core strategies

4. Financial plan

5. Sales strategies

6. Marketing strategies

7. Appendix

For each product line or division (high-level group of products or services) you need:

a. Market analysis

b. Market sizing

c. Product/service positioning—how you fit in the market and your value to a customer

d. Product/service positioning—messaging and key business outcomes for your customers

e. Pricing strategy

The appendix of your strategic plan might include:

a. Other objectives, such as experience objectives, market objectives, culture objectives, organizational objectives, and financial objectives over three years

b. Your SWOT analysis—for your whole company or one for each division, product, or service line

c. Competitive analysis for each product or service line

d. High-level product road map for each product and service over three years

Let's break down each of these elements.

Vision and Purpose

This should be a statement you don't mind saying over and over again to customers, employees, and investors. In one sentence, it should clearly describe your vision of your company while delivering a positive message to your target audience. It should also contain the impact you want to have on the world.

Many books talk about a company having a vision, purpose, and mission. In my opinion, having three concepts is too complex for employees, customers, and investors to remember.

I prefer to have one vision/purpose statement and for the mission to

Infragistics Vision/Purpose

Create simplicity, beauty, and happiness
in the world, one app at a time

Figure 14.3. Infragistics vision/purpose

be described in two to four business goals along with a purpose definition
for each. See Figure 14.3.

Major Business Objectives Showing the Purpose of Each Goal

These are the most important business goals you have for your company,
and the fewer the better. There should be between two and four goals,
which should be communicated at every company meeting or at least
once a month (see Figure 14.4).

These key goals should follow a SMART goal format (specific,
measurable, achievable, realistic, timely). They should also be stated as
affirmations—what you envision them to be. Adding a separate statement addressing purpose for each objective is very helpful. You want
definitions of the purpose of these major business objectives that will last
even after you achieve them. Some people are motivated by achieving
business goals, some are motivated by a purpose-driven focus, and some
are motivated by both.

Two major goals for Infragistics over the next one to three years

Purpose: The most innovative digital experiences and the world's best developers and designers use Ignite UI and Indigo to build simple and beautiful apps.

Business goal: We will be #1 in the web UI framework market by the end of 2022.

Purpose: Slingshot unleashes the power of the team and drives extraordinary business growth for all who use it.

Business goal: We will have over 1M active users in Slingshot by the end of 2024.

Figure 14.4. Infragistics mission/goals

Core Strategies

Your core strategies are the foundation of your strategic plan and should give your employees direction on how to make decisions and where to focus and put resources. They should give your company a competitive advantage in the market and deliver exceptional value to your customers.

Core strategies should be simply stated, and the rest of the strategic plan should support the achievement of your core strategies as well as your annual plan and go-to-market plans. Four to six core strategies is a good number to shoot for with a mix of product/service strategies and operational strategies. (See Figure 14.5.)

Financial Plan

Sales and Profits

Data is best viewed in dashboard and spreadsheet format. The data should show the aggregate percentage of growth or decline in revenue and profit for the last three years, current year plan, and the next three years. This historical perspective will show high-level trends and how your strategic plan will affect sales and profits going forward. (See Figure 14.6.)

Core Strategies

Deliver the **fastest grids and charts** on the web stack.

Deliver products from **design to code that integrate with popular tools** to produce incredible app experiences on modern UIs for web, cloud, and mobile.

In **one app**, though a digital workplace, connect everyone you work with to data analytics, projects, content, and chats to boost team and company results.

Focus on **beauty and simplicity** to help development teams embed dashboards and analytics to drive business insight on modern web and cloud technologies.

Nurture a **learning organization** to drive growth through growth hacking.

Execute a **three-prong approach to grow sales** via transactional engagements, opportunities in key accounts through ABM and ABS methodology, and a new Sales 2.0 structure to engage with Slingshot and Reveal market.

Figure 14.5. Infragistics strategies

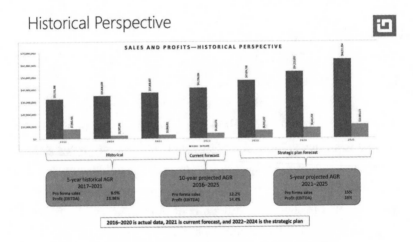

Figure 14.6. Historic and future financial projections for the plan

Service by Line

If you have more than one product line or division, be sure to show sales, expenses, and profits by each product or service line (see Figure 14.7). For the last three years, the current year, and the next three years, show the following:

- Percentage of expenses and percentage of profit

Overview by Product Line

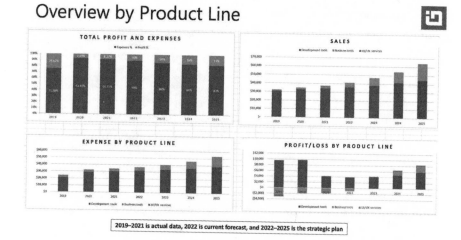

2019–2021 is actual data, 2022 is current forecast, and 2022–2025 is the strategic plan

Figure 14.7. Overview of sales, expenses, profit, and loss by product line, including past and future years of the plan

- Expense by product line

- Sales by product line

- Profit and loss by product line

All this information will demonstrate which products are receiving the most funding, driving the most sales, and generating the most profit or loss.

Profit and Loss by Product Line

This statement should show the percentage of sales, expense, and profit growth year over year for the prior three years, the current year, and the next three years (see Figure 14.8).

The statement should also indicate the percentage change in sales, expense, and profit. This information is very helpful when you have to invest in a new revenue stream from the current one that is giving you most of your sales. Readers of this statement will see in the numbers the strategic investments and actions you are taking. This data will show

Profit and Loss by Product Line

	2019	2020	2021	2022	2023	2024	2025
2 Total							
3 Sales	$32,315,288	$34,886,638	$37,308,637	$ 41,196,094	$ 47,074,749	$ 54,221,032	$ 64,221,034
4 Sales growth %	0.00%	7.96%	6.94%	10%	14%	15%	18%
5 Expense	$24,359,825	$32,379,577	$34,222,546	$ 36,913,721	$ 40,543,092	$ 45,735,574	$ 53,237,860
6 Expense %	75.38%	92.81%	91.73%	90%	86%	84%	83%
7 Profit	$7,955,463	$2,507,061	$3,086,091	$ 4,282,373	$ 6,531,657	$ 8,485,458	$ 10,983,173
8 Profit %	24.62%	7.19%	8.27%	10%	14%	16%	17%
10 Development tools							
11 Sales	$30,755,158	$32,880,927	$34,058,400	$ 35,871,234	$ 38,145,403	$ 41,669,929	$ 44,669,930
12 Sales growth %	0.00%	6.91%	3.58%	5%	6%	9%	7%
13 Expense	$21,168,095	$28,859,389	$30,302,358	$ 31,817,476	$ 33,408,350	$ 35,746,935	$ 38,249,220
14 Expense %	68.83%	87.77%	88.97%	89%	88%	86%	86%
15 Profit	$9,587,063	$4,021,538	$3,756,041	$ 4,053,758	$ 4,737,053	$ 5,922,994	$ 6,420,709
16 Profit %	31.17%	12.23%	11.03%	11%	12%	14%	14%
28 Business tools							
29 Sales	$1,310,130	$1,755,711	$3,000,237	5,074,860	8,679,346	12,301,103	19,301,104
30 Sales growth %	0.00%	34.01%	70.88%	69%	71%	42%	57%
31 Expense	$3,191,730	$3,520,188	$3,920,188	5,096,244	7,134,742	9,988,639	14,988,640
32 Expense %	243.62%	200.50%	130.66%	100%	82%	81%	78%
33 Profit	($1,881,600)	($1,764,477)	($919,951)	(21,384)	1,544,604	2,312,464	4,312,464
34 Profit %	-143.62%	-100.50%	-30.66%	0%	18%	19%	22%
47 UI/UX services							
48 Sales	$250,000	$250,000	$250,000	250,000	250,000	250,000	250,000
49 Sales growth %	0.00%	0.00%	0.00%	0%	0%	0%	0%
50 Expense	$0	$0	$0	-	-	-	-
51 Expense %	0.00%	0.00%	0.00%	0%	0%	0%	0%
52 Profit	$250,000	$250,000	$250,000	250,000	250,000	250,000	250,000
53 Profit %	100.00%	100.00%	100.00%	100%	100%	100%	100%
55 DT	95%	94%	91%	87%	81%	77%	70%
56 BT	4%	5%	8%	12%	18%	23%	30%
57 Svc	1%	1%	1%	1%	1%	0%	0%

2019–2021 is actual, 2022 is current forecast, and 2023–2025 is strategic plan

Figure 14.8. The past and future years of the profit/loss

them how you see the future unfolding and where the past and current sales, investment, cash flow, and profits are coming from.

Sales Strategies

This section explains how you will organize sales to support your core strategies and achieve your business goals and sales and profit numbers from your financial section. It is a high-level description of how you will sell, along with your key priorities and investments and maybe new investments needed to achieve your strategic plan. (See Figures 14.9 and 14.10 as examples.)

Some examples of this could be:

- Enterprise selling: Account-based selling, longer sales cycles, higher cost of sales/sales consultants (SC), and possible travel and expenses (T&E), supporting marketing systems for account-based marketing and personalized content for roles and industries.

- Transaction selling: Shorter sales cycles, can be handled by inside sales or order takers, e-commerce, selling through distributors and/or resellers, usually lower-cost products or services.

Global Sales Strategy

Improve transactional engagements focused on drive-to-trial-and-nurture and in key accounts.

- Market segmentation—segment market in US into enterprise and transactional, and redistribute staff accordingly.
- Develop transactional sales channel focusing on lower-level renewals and small incremental sales across all product lines, to be completed in summer 2021.
- Rebuild e-commerce capability with focus on easy, seamless, transactional support.
- Relook at leveraging bots and AI to enable an efficient sales process.
- Maintain partner channel in direct market coverage areas, and enhance partner channel (i.e., Korea) to leverage our available resources.
- Expand footprint in existing accounts, with a focus on building ELAs with large, longtime clients, using a combination of ABM and IG 125—face-to-face "IG Day" customer meetings.
- Focus on Indigo.Design sales through re-implementation of Challenger sales methods.

Figure 14.9. Example sales strategies for improving transactional engagements

Global Sales Strategy

Create opportunities by transitioning to an account-based marketing and sales plan for customer engagement.

- Drive new logo/new seats.
- Each geography will target key accounts for enterprise-level sales.
- Discover account maps and create account plans for ABE and IG 125.
- Leverage new technology to improve customer touch, sales, and marketing processes to advance the business (trial, purchase, sales interactions, CRM, blog, etc.).
- Better understand customer behavior and increase conversion rate.

Figure 14.10. Example sales strategies related to account-based marketing and sales

- Partner channel: Business development salespeople, partner channel managers, sales enablement, and training of partner channel. This includes the time spent getting new partners and helping existing partners sell.

- Retail channel: Products sold through retail channels, time spent on getting new retail coverage for products, promotions, and then managing the orders, along with supplying and marketing with the retail channel.

- Product lead growth (PLG): An end-user-focused growth model that relies on the product itself as the primary driver of customer acquisition, conversion, and expansion. This leads to investment in content, customer support, and design of the product.

- Hybrid sales and product-led growth: A combination of sales motion with product-led growth.

- Geography expansion and selling: Expanding into new territories. It requires business development people and salespeople to develop these new markets. In addition, it could involve investment in new technologies and processes to improve sales outcomes.

After reading this section, you should now understand how to sell your product, your go-to-market plan, and where you are investing to achieve your sales numbers.

Marketing Strategies

This section covers how you will organize marketing to support your core strategies and achieve your business goals and sales and profit numbers from your financial section. (See Figure 14.11 for an example.) Strategies could include:

- How you will align marketing and sales

- How to focus on public relations and advocacy

- Digital marketing

- Search engine optimization (SEO) and content marketing

- Account-based marketing

- How you are going to use technology like artificial intelligence (AI), analytics, and other SaaS systems to increase results

- Customer success management

Global Marketing Strategy

Leverage new team, AI tools, and sales coordination to drive transactional and enterprise account growth.

1. Increase emphasis on drive to trial with organic and paid demand-generation efforts, nurture, and aligned sales follow-up. Optimize marketing mix for the buyer-centric market, with a focus on middle-of-the-funnel efforts.

2. Align with sales to drive business growth through account-based marketing and advertising. Expand targeted account sets with personalized messaging to decision-makers on channels that they actively use.

3. Focus product marketing managers on going deep on single-product and GTM efforts.

4. PR and advocacy: Create active community influencers (IG) and leverage existing community to tell stories through our customers.

5. Create global digital destinations focused on attracting and growing audience engagement through compelling product samples, how-to content, and addressing timely/topical issues.

6. Increase our content for SEO and third-party sites to influence the buyer's journey of spending 66% of their time on deciding what to purchase outside the vendor's digital properties and personnel.

Figure 14.11. Example of marketing strategies

- Analyst relations

- Influencer marketing

The amount of detail for the sales and marketing sections should be high level. Using the annual plan and go-to-market plan, you should go into more detail (see Chapters 15 and 16).

Market Analysis, Product/Service Strategy, and Pricing

Create a section for each product, service, or division—however you group your products or services.

- Market analysis: Describe the macro and micro trends affecting your product or service.

- Market sizing: Define the total market, addressable market, and your target market share (see Figure 14.12).

- Product/service strategy: How do you fit in the market and what value are you creating for the customer? (See Figure 14.13.)

Dev Tools Market Sizing

- RMAD/MADP tools
  - Addressable market: 1.36M citizen developers, low-code IT professionals

- UX tools
  - Addressable market: 1.53M UX designers, business analysts, product managers

- UI tools
  - 11M professional developers worldwide
  - 2M professional Visual Studio developers
  - 2M professional JavaScript developers

Figure 14.12. Example of market sizing

Dev Tools UI/UX Product Strategy 2022–2024

Embrace design ecosystem

- Deliver to market UI kits/design systems and plug-ins for major visual design/UX design tools that map to our Angular and cross-platform UI controls and have 100% integration with Indigo.Design and app builder.
- Ensure we are not left out if a design team uses a specific design tool.

Accelerate design to code

- Cloud-based digital product design platform for design system management, image-based prototyping, collaboration, user testing, code markup tooling, and low-code app building.
- Ensure we can compete against point solutions like InVision, Zeplin, and others in the market on the designer side while attracting developers for app dev acceleration with a complete no-sacrifice design to code offering.

Own the modern web space

- Tooling, extensions, plug-ins for all major modern web frameworks in Visual Studio/VS code that accelerate app development
- Best-of-breed grids, charts, Excel, schedule, editors, and differentiating UI components for all modern frameworks
- Focus on turnkey solutions versus building blocks.
- Multilevel code generation options based on Indigo Studios models with a template-driven approach to app creation

Embrace the design and development process with persona-based tooling

Figure 14.13. Example of explaining product strategies

- Product/service positioning: Create messaging and key business outcomes for your customers (see Figures 14.14 and 14.15).

- Pricing strategy: What will you charge for your product or service? (See Figure 14.16.)

UX Tools: Go-to-Market Positioning

- Indigo.Design is a design-to-code digital product design platform that enables operational alignment, deep collaboration, and ongoing innovation at the product level (design ops) with complete low-code multi-experience application delivery of business apps, mobile apps, progressive web apps, conversational apps, and immersive apps.

- Indigo.Design enables enterprise UX and product delivery teams to operationalize compatibility between UX, product management, and product development.

- Using Indigo.Design design systems and plug-ins for major visual design/UX design tools means that a single source of truth can be used across enterprise teams.

- Collaboration with stakeholders, user testing with deep analytics, and image-based prototyping are built in.

- WYSIWYG low-code tooling output to modern web platforms.

- Target system integrators and partners for new license opportunities.

Figure 14.14. Example of explaining a product's go-to-market positioning

Indigo.Design Go-to-Market Messaging
Streamline app creation from design to code

- Unparalleled team flow and productivity
  - *Cloud-based digital product design platform with complete design to code for design system management, image-based prototyping, collaboration, user testing, code markup tooling, and low-code app building*
- User-friendly design, powerful backbone
  - *Designers or developers can choose how to approach app output with our design-to-code options—from our design system to the app builder in Indigo.Design, we don't restrict how a team can get hyper-productivity-delivering apps.*
- Don't hand off your designs. Generate code instead.
  - *Unlike other Sketch UI kits and libraries, the Indigo library will help you export a usable code in Angular, React, Web Components, or Blazor in project with all components generated for your team's productivity.*

- Customer Benefits
  - Fast, code-free, cloud-based prototyping and app building
  - Integration with vector design tools like Adobe XD, Figma, and Sketch
  - End-to-end design system management for a single source of truth across your team or the enterprise
  - Instant usability testing with recordings, results, and analytics
  - Collaborative review and feedback with email notifications
  - Pixel-perfect code generation for Angular, React, Web Components, or Blazor apps from app builder or Visual Studio code plug-ins
  - Application template libraries for easy app creation, duplication, and experimentation
  - Easy design system creation and management
  - On-prem container deployment with security and administration
  - Embeddable SDK of app builder with extensibility

Figure 14.15. Another example of a product's go-to-market messaging

Appendix

In the appendix to your strategic plan, you could have high-level objectives for experience objectives, market objectives, culture objectives, organization objectives, and/or financial objectives over the next three years. (See Figures 14.17, 14.18, and 14.19.)

Dev Tools Pricing Strategy

- Best-value pricing: All roads should lead to Ultimate, Professional, or Ignite UI for upsell to highest-price product choice.
- Subscription pricing model for new seat sales across dev tools products (with the exception of test automation products)
- New trial watermarks on our modern web products, including Angular, React, and Web Components
- Indigo.Design subscription
  - Essential: $39 monthly or $399 yearly
  - Indigo.Design: $99 monthly or $1,099 yearly
  - Indigo.Design on-prem: $30K yearly
  - Indigo.Design embed: $50K yearly

* License updates requiring an active subscription to access previously owned software

Figure 14.16. Example of product pricing

Experience Objectives

1. Delight the customer: Deliver exceptional end-to-end customer experiences.
2. Expand our design culture by living our brand: Create a culture that lives and breathes experience design so that this discipline is core to every aspect of our business, inwardly and externally.
3. Foster creativity: Grow an open and engaged culture that rewards curiosity, exploration, innovation, and ownership.
4. Evangelize our value: Create a culture that encourages and delivers thought leadership.
5. Deliver quality: Ingrain quality into everything we do internally and externally.

Figure 14.17. Example of experience objectives

SWOT Analysis

A SWOT (strengths, weaknesses, opportunities, threats) analysis involves our whole company. Benefits of doing the SWOT analysis begin with being able to see how each region views the company and the market. You can also assess regional issues as well through the areas of focus or results of the SWOT analysis of each region.

We have eight different SWOT sessions, including our six regions, which generate eight separate SWOT analyses. Our CFO and our head

Culture Objectives

1. **Grow trust:** Grow and protect a culture of transparency, openness, ownership, and trust.

2. **Invest in people:** Actively invest in our people to develop them to their maximum potential, with the right skills, tools, and knowledge to succeed.

3. **Collaborate broadly:** Drive results through effective collaboration across teams, departments, and regions internally and externally, with customers and partners.

4. **Multicultural view:** Take an international view, and make it a core part of our thinking, planning, and execution.

5. **Be a good citizen:** Be a socially responsible corporate citizen within each of our global communities.

Figure 14.18. Example of culture objectives

Organizational Objectives

1. **Be agile:** Grow a flexible organization that is capable of restructuring itself whenever necessary to carry out our mission.

2. **Turn data into knowledge and action:** Develop relevant and accurate data sources, and turn them into knowledge that drives actions to optimize the business.

3. **Globalize operations:** Effectively manage a geographically diverse company so as to best leverage global and local opportunities, resources, and personnel.

4. **Ensure the health of our organization:** Instill and follow a rigorous health-of-the-organization process across all departments and regions.

5. **Continuously improve operations:** Create a culture of continuous improvement, individually, regionally, technologically, and as a company.

Figure 14.19. Example of organizational objects

of human resources facilitate our SWOT analysis process. They ask everyone before the meeting to write down their top five SWOT items in each category. They put the lists on sticky notes and place them on a board, grouping the notes under each category.

The facilitator reads the lists to the members of the group. The list is culled to ten items per category. The facilitator assigns one hundred points (ten points per item) for each category to each member, and each member must use their points to vote on the ten items under each category.

The group debates and finally agrees on five top items in each category. We retain the other five items in each category for final analysis by the executive team to create a single SWOT for the company by adding and using the eight different SWOTs as input.

The easiest category to fill up is strengths. Who does not want to tell us how great Infragistics is? In the past, there have sometimes been thirty items under this category.

Trying to explore weaknesses and threats is more difficult, since people normally are reluctant to share problems. They may feel problems reflect badly on them. If problems are shared, however, more people will work on them and ultimately fix them. The quickest way to failure for a company is to have employees hide their problems and issues.

Beware of Groupthink and the Importance of Working with Indirect Leaders

Just as they did during the first phase of the strategic plan, the facilitator has to be aware of groupthink. Groupthink is the phenomenon that occurs when a group of individuals reaches consensus without critical reasoning, rather based on a common desire not to upset the balance of the group. During a SWOT analysis, indirect leaders (also called hidden influencers) can dominate. Indirect leaders are individuals who may not hold a high executive position but have considerable influence over other employees. Facilitators have to identify these individuals and pay careful attention to their willingness to participate and be aligned with the company's goals. The facilitator needs to get them to speak their mind. Their point of view (POV) must be heard, discussed, and aligned with the group's POV. It is better to have public discussions than for indirect leaders to subvert the process.

Indirect leaders can feel personally threatened during a debate over an issue, such as a price point on a product. They may try to sabotage any decision regarding their department or their position in the company.

If necessary, the facilitator should have an intense conversation with the indirect leader, either in a one-to-one meeting or in front of the group.

All the information from these meetings is sent to the executive team. We look at prior SWOTs and what was agreed on. Then we reach consensus on the top five items for the four SWOT categories for our organization and for core products within our business. We do this in two to three one-hour meetings. Our finalized SWOT is included in the strategic plan.

Once the board approves the strategic plan, I report the SWOT analysis to the company. In addition, I mention the SWOT in my communications to the company. We send out a questionnaire survey twice a year to get feedback on the SWOT. It is included in the strategic plan as an appendix.

Figure 14.20 shows the SWOT for 2021.

In this example from 2021, the SWOT analysis shows how Infragistics is facing enormous competition from well-resourced competitors, which is increasing our costs for go-to-market and talent acquisition. This requires us to pick our battles and put our resources behind those opportunities where we know we can compete. We need

SWOT: 2021 Global

Figure 14.20. Example of SWOT analysis

to stay focused on our strategy and continue to delight our customers and invest in things that always deliver competitive advantage.

When you have completed the SWOT analysis, you must communicate it. Be transparent. I report the results of last year's SWOT analysis and the current SWOT analysis to the entire company every year. I indicate how we tried to fix our weaknesses and where we succeeded. If we only had partial success, I describe what stood in the way of eradicating weaknesses and the progress we made toward our goals. I also provide the same kind of discussion of our opportunities and threats.

Don't hide your SWOT analysis. Sharing it allows teams to focus on improving their weaknesses and their alignment, so they can neutralize threats and take advantage of opportunities. How can you expect improvement if your teams don't have an accurate assessment of where things stand currently and how you'd like them to improve?

Communicating the SWOT analysis also shows that the executive team is listening to input from all employees and taking actions to address their concerns and insights. This communication increases your credibility and the credibility of the strategic planning process.

When you are transparent and honest, you engender the same qualities in your employees. They will then tell you what problems they are experiencing and what issues they are dealing with every day. This will allow everyone to fix weaknesses, find new opportunities, and reduce threats from competitors. The SWOT analysis process helps to get everyone on the same page and working together, to be more authentic, more aligned, and committed to winning as a group.

IMPLEMENTING STRATEGIC PLANS

According to Dave Norton, companies that effectively execute their strategy evidence a 50 to 150 percent increase in their stock value. At the same time, his research with Robert Kaplan indicates that between 80 and 90 percent of companies fail at strategy execution. Part of the reason Kaplan and Norton identified for this high level of execution failure is that *85 percent of executive teams spend less than an hour per month discussing strategy.*[13]

This is a recipe for failure. Once the strategic plan is formulated and approved, it must be part of the daily consciousness of executive teams and, in fact, of all employees. This is why being a learning organization is so important. In multiple conversations, feedback opportunities, and the reformulating of a hypothesis to adjust to new realities, the strategic plan is ever present, providing direction at every level of the company. Leaders must spend sufficient time in executing it, or they will lose credibility with the workforce, which will further undermine efforts to achieve company goals.

This means, of course, the strategic plan should be communicated throughout the organization. The evidence cited above indicates that only 5 percent of employees understand company strategic plans. CEOs and executive teams should constantly articulate the strategic plan at company-wide meetings, department meetings, and in a variety of company communications. Repeat, repeat, and repeat. Then repeat again.

TAKE A LEAP OF FAITH

One of the most difficult things in life is to take a leap of faith. Fear keeps us from taking such leaps. So do old habits and what social scientists call behavioral inertia.

What is true for people is true for companies. In a world of constant change, there really is no other option but to cast aside fear and ancient ways of doing things and try something new. Otherwise, catastrophe awaits.

At Infragistics we took that leap of faith a few years ago. We plunged ahead in remaking ourselves as a twenty-first-century vNext Business. It took time and patience, and we made mistakes. But we learned the importance of strategic plans in our journey.

My hope is that this chapter has given you the impetus to explore this process and see how it applies to your business. I am sure you will, in a relatively short time, gain mastery of it and see how it benefits your company. And how it benefits you—less anxiety and worry and more restful nights of sleep.

In the next two chapters, I turn to annual plans and go-to-market plans, which build on the insights and processes established by a strategic plan.

KEY POINTS FOR CREATING A VNEXT BUSINESS

1. Create and update your strategic plan. The process of creating and updating strategic plans will create strategic conversations and alignment with your executive team and key managers.

2. Communicate your vision, purpose, and core goals every chance you get. This will give your company focus, confidence, and direction, as people understand what they're working toward each day.

3. Share your strategies—at least one or two strategies every month; this helps create company alignment and aids in everyday decision-making for your company.

4. Take slides from your strategic plan and communicate them to teams in meetings where it makes sense. (The only part of the plan you may not want to share is financial numbers.)

5. Having a three-year plan will explain investment in new products and movement of resources to future products and other capabilities you may not have now.

6. Keep your plan updated as new data or ideas arise. Don't wait for your annual strategic plan update process. You may need to change direction or investment, or simply update your market analysis.

15

ANNUAL PLANS

After you have completed your strategic plan, your next challenge is creating an annual plan—that is, what you want to accomplish in the next twelve months.

Often, companies spend a great deal of time on their strategic plans only to falter when they try to implement them on a yearly basis. Old behavioral habits and traditional processes reassert themselves. Institutional inertia thwarts efforts at effective implementation.

The annual plan's purpose is to create company-wide alignment. This means everyone must understand what an annual plan does. Annual plans do the following:

- They enlighten, motivate, and engage your teams because they paint a clear picture of what has to be done quarter by quarter.

- They clarify your company's strategic intent for the year and empower employees to define what will lead to success.

- They define core priorities that facilitate your decision-making process.

- They enhance team conversations about what processes are needed to reach growth targets.

- They measure what matters through OKRs (objectives and key results), giving specificity to the plan's execution.

INFRAGISTICS'S ANNUAL PLANNING PROCESS

The annual planning process at Infragistics involves a number of steps.

1. I work with our executive team to construct a yearly sales forecast, which we break down on a monthly and a quarterly basis. In this forecast, we describe where we think we will acquire new accounts (new seats) and where we will have repeat business (renewals).

2. We agree on our sales targets for our products for the coming year. These targets should be achievable but should stretch sales, marketing, and the company, which will drive us all to work harder and more efficiently.

3. At Infragistics, like most companies, we strive for profitability by year's end, which is determined by our sales results minus our expenses. In some time periods, this may not be possible. We might project expenses of $82 million while only seeing $80 million in sales, a $2 million loss. This could be justified if we determined in our strategic plan that we had to build a new go-to-market capability or because we were launching a new product.

Our expense structure is broken down by our main departments such as sales, marketing, administration, product development, finance, human resources, and so on. We then look further at each department in terms of its payroll costs and operating expenses.

Cash Is King—Projecting Targets

After we have completed these tasks, we determine our cash flow on a monthly, quarterly, and yearly basis. Cash flow is very different from the concept of profit.

I cannot stress this enough: *Cash is king.*

If we run out of it, it's game over. So we *must* manage our cash (minus our expenses) quarterly, monthly, and for the year. When we are done, we have a rolling twelve-month profit/loss (P/L) forecast sheet and a rolling twelve-month cash flow forecast. We constantly update our spreadsheets with actual results, so we can determine if we are effectively executing our annual plan. This data tells us whether we should spend on specific items in our strategic plan. And it allows us to make informed decisions about whether to spend more or throttle expenses. These decisions are based on our sales and current spend-run rate and where we will end up at year's end based on actuals and rest-of-year forecast.

Once we have determined our sales targets, expenses, and cash flow, we provide our executive team with a budget. They then can plan their activities, taking into account what funds they can devote to their projects over the course of the year.

Sometimes, however, a department cannot completely project its needs for the next year. When we decided to implement account-based marketing capabilities from scratch, we realized the project would take one or more years to fully implement and for us to get good enough at it that we were generating more sales than spend. The first year's costs were based on assumptions made in the strategic plan. As the year unfolded, the marketing department adjusted its budget quarterly as its expenses became a reality.

After the budget is determined, the executive team and other departments meet with their teams to craft OKRs. Organizing our priorities into OKRs helps map out our objectives. They are, in essence, a one-sentence strategic plan of what will be measured at a deeper level of execution. Each department is charged with determining objectives and how they will spend their money to obtain these key results (see Chapter 3).

By the end of this exercise, our annual plan is transformed essentially into a compilation of OKRs by department (see Figures 15.1–15.4).

The budget, which includes spend, sales commission plans, raises and capital spend, and taxes, along with the action plan for cash flow, should be completed in the fourth quarter, and in our case approved by our board of directors. That way you are aligned and ready on day one of the first quarter to hit the ground running.

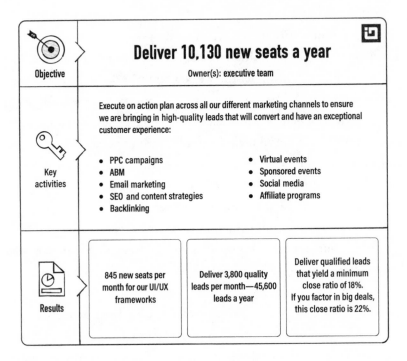

Figure 15.1. Annual plan OKRs for the new seats

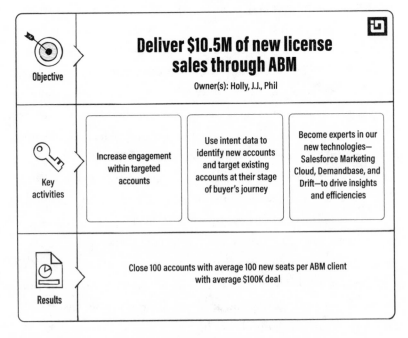

Figure 15.2. Annual plan OKRs for sales through ABM motion

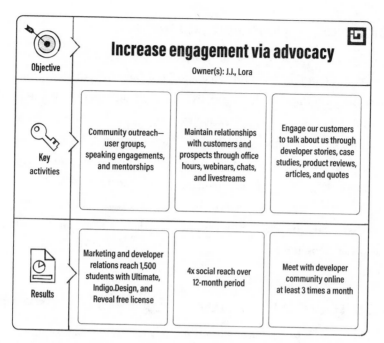

Figure 15.3. Annual plan OKRs related to increasing engagement through advocacy

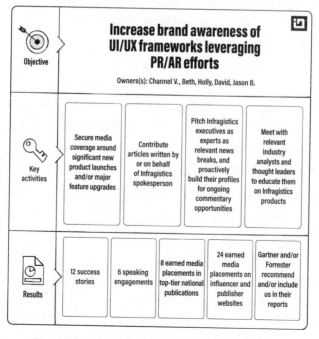

Figure 15.4. Annual plan OKRs related to increasing
brand awareness for UI/UX product line

Communication Is Key—Share the Plan

Once you have finished the annual plan, share it with everyone in the company, excluding some financial and budgetary information. This will drive the plan through the company and align managers and employees around it. For more tips on how to effectively share key internal communications like this, check out Chapter 7 and Chapter 10.

Your annual plan is also very useful for onboarding new hires. By reading it they can more quicky understand what the company is doing. And it gives them confidence in the company's leadership by providing them with step-by-step reasoning for why decisions are made and the execution steps and goals.

YOU HAVE AN ANNUAL PLAN—NOW USE IT

Too many CEOs and companies don't rely on annual plans, preferring, as the expression goes, to fly by the seat of their pants. They started their companies by running hard and have continued to do so with success.

I was like them when I started Infragistics. Through sheer hard work and personal sacrifice (I learned to love hot dogs for a couple of years, as they were all I could afford), I made a success of the company. Then one day, I realized personal drive was not enough. We were heading for trouble. The competition changes, the market turns down, the economy stumbles. Can you adapt? Perhaps. Does it feel like you're constantly putting out fires? Absolutely.

But I have a very clear message to anyone who hasn't implemented an annual plan for their business: *There is a better way.*

At some point, a CEO must deal with reality and implement processes that will continue to drive sustained success in a measured and well-thought-out way.

An annual plan provides you with a view of the future, so you can measure how well you are doing and make the best decisions to navigate the risks in front of you. It empowers your executive team and your managers by giving them budgets and objectives as well as the autonomy to execute.

In my opinion, it is the only way to take risks and drive a company forward. If you're used to business chaos—constantly putting out fire after fire—an annual plan isn't like a fire extinguisher. It's like a fire safety marshal who inspects a building to point out where problems *could* arise in the future. It gives you a chance to prepare and plan, so that the fires never break out in the first place.

A vNext Business can achieve business calm where so many others experience business chaos.

With your annual plan completed, we now turn to how to construct a go-to-market plan (GTM), which contains even more details and is the subject of our next chapter.

KEY POINTS FOR CREATING A VNEXT BUSINESS

1. Annual plans support your three-year strategic plan for the next twelve months.

2. Annual plans create a blueprint of sales, spend, and cash flow so you can navigate and adjust throughout the year.

3. They align everyone on OKRs to achieve the company's goals and strategic plans.

4. They give managers autonomy to execute with their spend and guidance on how to achieve goals and success.

5. Annual plans align departments and teams across the company to achieve a shared mission.

6. They allow you to invest over time to build new products, sales, and marketing capabilities over multiple years.

7. They permit you to take more calculated risks over the next few months and quarters.

8. Annual plans grant you the flexibility to make adjustments to OKRs, direction, and plans so you can pivot when you get new market information.

16

GO-TO-MARKET PLAN

In the previous two chapters, you read about the importance of strategic and annual plans. Now a final one—a go-to-market plan.

I think about these three plans in terms of a car.

- A strategic plan is like a car's frame, which gives the vehicle its shape. Its quality determines how fast the car can go, and its functionality tells us what kind of vehicle it will be—a pickup truck, a sports car, a minivan, or something else.

- An annual plan acts like a car's engine and onboard computer. It ensures all systems within the car's frame work efficiently together on a sustained basis.

- A go-to-market (GTM) plan is like a running manual for the independent systems within the car. Added into the framework, each system contributes to the vehicle's overall scale and scope.

The Infragistics go-to-market plan builds on our strategic and annual plans by detailing how we will achieve our yearly fiscal and sales objectives for each product or vertical market we serve.

So why might you want to employ go-to-market plans for your company?

If your business acts and works in a single country or you have a single product or service, your annual plan may contain sufficient information to preclude the need for a GTM plan. On the other hand, a GTM is vital if you have regional divisions in other countries or more than one product line. A GTM for each country helps account for the way different national identities and cultures may affect how customers buy, how they make decisions, and how you market to them.

Similarly, if you have more than one product (we have five) or are launching a new one, you *must* develop a GTM plan. It provides you with a way to predict and measure how your product will perform in the marketplace. The GTM plan also details what you need to learn to either maintain your product's success or pivot in a new direction.

Go-to-market plans wonderfully organize your sales team around a central strategy to achieve your targets. At Infragistics, before we started employing a GTM plan, our sales teams used a "kitchen sink" method. They tried approaches that could be achieved in the easiest way. Sometimes they quickly found something that worked. More often than not, they landed on something that didn't work or was unreproducible. Our GTM plan allows us to determine the most certain path to obtaining sales.

When we launched our collaboration platform, Slingshot, we relied heavily on a GTM plan. Without it, our sales team might have (understandably) focused their efforts on approaching existing clients or on acquiring license purchases from other software industry companies. But as I detail below, the research we put into Slingshot's GTM plan showed us a better way. We wound up targeting another market segment entirely.

A GTM plan also has another major benefit—it creates company alignment. When managers, employees, and new hires read, understand, and internalize the plan, they begin to see how our product or service interacts with our overall mission and goals. And that alignment makes it easier to transform individual employees into a team that is aimed at a specific goal.

So instead of discussing the theory of GTM plans, I thought it might be easier to understand them by taking a look at a real one. Here are some key elements of Slingshot's GTM plan.

SLINGSHOT'S GO-TO-MARKET PLAN

The Slingshot project took Infragistics away from our thirty-three-year comfort zone of successfully selling our core products. That journey into the unknown necessitated a document that would help us experiment, learn, adapt, align, and refocus again and again. This is the vNext scientific method in practice!

Ten of us, including myself, my direct reports, and several other department heads, crafted the GTM plan based on extensive research and collaboration. We answered questions such as:

- How difficult would it be for us to penetrate new markets with a new product?

- Who is our most likely purchasing audience?

- What are the decision levers of our most likely purchasing audience?

- Who are the established competitors in this space?

- What are the competition's advantages?

- What are the competition's product deficiencies that we can potentially answer?

- What is the white space within the market that we can fill?

As we arrived at answers, we formulated more questions to focus on how to most efficiently spend marketing resources to achieve sales:

- Who is the best point of contact within our target purchasing organizations?

- Is there a difference in the quality of the types of leads? In other words, which type of teams do we have the best chance of converting in a reasonable amount of time: financial teams, technology teams, or marketing teams?

Infragistics Vision/Purpose

Create simplicity, beauty, and happiness
in the world, one app at a time

Figure 16.1. Infragistics vision/purpose from the strategic plan

Armed with our research and strategic conclusions, we developed Slingshot's GTM plan.

In our annual plan and GTM plans, we always put in our vision/ purpose, key business goals/mission, and our core strategies from our strategic plan. This helps reinforce them as we use the plan to communicate our GTM for a product.

Vision Statement

Slingshot's GTM begins with the Infragistics vision: to create simplicity, beauty, and happiness in the world, one app at a time (see Figure 16.1). (I never miss an opportunity to repeat our vision to keep everyone rallied around this noble company goal. You should do the same for your company. Repeat, repeat, repeat.)

Mission/Business Goals

The GTM plan then discusses the *mission/business goals* for our main products and how any new offerings might fit within that mix (see Figure 16.2).

Two major goals for Infragistics over the next one to three years

Purpose: The most innovative digital experiences and the world's best developers and designers use Ignite UI and Indigo to build simple and beautiful apps.

Business goal: We will be #1 in the web UI framework market by the end of 2022.

Purpose: Slingshot unleashes the power of the team and drives extraordinary business growth for all who use it.

Business goal: We will have over 1M active users in Slingshot by the end of 2024.

Figure 16.2. Mission/objectives of Infragistics from the strategic plan

- Purpose: The most innovative digital experiences and the world's best developers and designers use Ignite UI, Indigo Design, and AppBuilder to build simple and beautiful applications.

- Business goal: Infragistics will be number one in the web UI framework market by the end of the calendar year.

- Purpose: Slingshot unleashes the power of the team and drives extraordinary business growth for all to use.

- Business goal: We will have one million active users in Slingshot within twenty-four months of shipping.

Core Strategies

We then move on to *core strategies*, among them a focus on beauty and simplicity, nurturing a learning organization, and our approach to sales. These core strategies are from our strategic plan (see Figure 16.3).

Executive Overview

Next, we use an executive overview.

An executive summary provides a brief overview of your GTM plan. In one or two pages at most, it describes the key results of your marketing,

Core Strategies

Deliver the **fastest grids and charts** on the web stack.

Deliver products from **design to code that integrate with popular tools** to produce incredible app experiences on modern UIs for web, cloud, and mobile.

In **one app**, though a digital workplace, connect everyone you work with to data analytics, projects, content, and chats to boost team and company results.

Focus on **beauty and simplicity** to help development teams embed dashboards and analytics to drive business insight on modern web and cloud technologies.

Nurture a **learning organization** to drive growth through growth hacking.

Execute a **three-prong approach to grow sales** via transactional engagements, opportunities in key accounts through ABM and ABS methodology, and a new Sales 2.0 structure to engage with Slingshot and Reveal market.

Figure 16.3. Infragistics key strategies from the strategic plan

sales, and product objectives. Its purpose is to outline the most important information for your short-term and long-term go-to-market plans.

Here's what we cover in our GTM plan executive overview:

- Anticipated sales revenue in the coming year

- Counts on current active users/customers

- Marketing channels used (digital marketing, social, events, PR, influencers, partners, product lead growth, etc.)

- Sales channels used (direct sales, partner channel, account-based marketing, land and expand, etc.)

- Anticipated return on investment (ROI) delivered via sales, marketing, and brand awareness

- Ideas for improving conversion rate and the customer experience through growth hacking (scientific method)

- How much we will increase brand awareness by the end of next year

- Product road map, which outlines what will be added to a product over the next twelve months

Transformation of Our Organization to Build a New Capability

The next section of Slingshot's GTM plan discusses how we will continue to transform Infragistics into a software-as-a-service (SaaS) company. This is an enterprise that hosts an application and makes it available remotely to customers over the internet. Up to now, we have been product driven. Becoming a SaaS company requires us to learn new skills and procedures to be successful.

This section is where you identify any transformational changes necessary to reshape your business to build the skills, processes, and people to implement your strategies. This can take more than a year, so these changes should also be in your strategic and annual plans, so you and your team are focusing on achieving these goals.

Marketplace Opportunities and Messaging

Any product is meant to solve a problem. Listing out the biggest problems that our product solves helps us align all the relevant strategies for that product.

For Slingshot, we identified four critical problems that our product solves for customers. Our conclusions are based on research we conducted with potential customers rather than speculation from product developers. Potential customers told us that our competitors' collaboration software was flawed because:

- *A lack of centralization* meant frequent app switching, which wasted user time and interrupted workflow.

- *A lack of access* to data limited team members' abilities to collaborate and solve problems through data.

- *A lack of the ability to create priorities* caused inefficient and burdensome workflow.

- *A lack of transparency* meant leaders didn't have visibility into their team members' progress, limiting opportunities for support.

By analyzing the problems that exist in the marketplace and studying what high-performing teams and companies do, we developed the following thesis:

High-performing teams and companies:

- Have a high degree of trust in the team

- Use data to make decisions

- Align on objectives, which they have the autonomy to execute

- Place accountability at the individual and team level

- Keep everyone in the know and display effective communications

Our thesis embraces the idea that Slingshot is not just a technology but a philosophy about what teams and leaders need to achieve great results together.

Thus, our potential problem-solution statement became: "Slingshot is a digital workplace that connects everyone you work with to everything they need—content, projects, analytics, chat—to boost team results."

It is amazing how many hours it took our team to boil down the true essence of our product into a few words, but our efforts were worthwhile because it clarifies what we are attempting to solve for our customers (see Figure 16.4).

Audience and Market Profiles

As we worked on the GTM plan and kept segmenting the potential market, our initial audience became clear: marketing teams. We allocated 80 percent of our sales efforts and financial resources to this target, with the rest focused on the general market for project management and business intelligence tools.

Marketing teams generally consist of:

Slingshot Go-to-Market Positioning

Keep everyone in the know

Save time finding information when everything is transparent and easily found. Make working across teams, departments, and external clients easy.

Use data insights to make better, faster decisions

Create a data-driven culture by making it easy for teams to turn data into actionable insights.

Strive to accomplish goals

Achieve greater success when everyone is aligned, focused, and engaged on the same objectives and strategies.

Increase performance with accountability

Give team members a greater sense of ownership of their responsibilities by providing complete visibility when tasks are assigned, prioritized, and completed.

Figure 16.4. Infragistics Slingshot product go-to-market positioning

- Chief marketing officer
- SEO specialist
- Creative director
- Content writer
- Marketing analysts and strategists

Different roles mean different priorities. As a learning organization, we continuously explore what features and functionality each role might need to solve problems (see Figure 16.5). In acquiring business, we must find our value-proposition sweet spot that speaks to our clients' objectives.

Market Opportunity

The next section of the GTM plan examines the market size and addressable market. Given the market size, we estimate how much of the market we are looking to win with our current resources and how competitive the market is (see Figure 16.6).

Marketing Team GTM

Personas enable marketing, sales development, and sales teams to communicate with buyers using their own language.

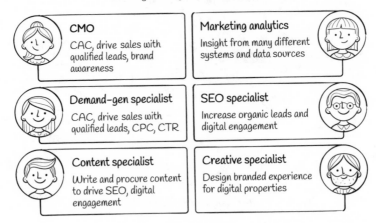

Figure 16.5. Infragistics Slingshot key personas

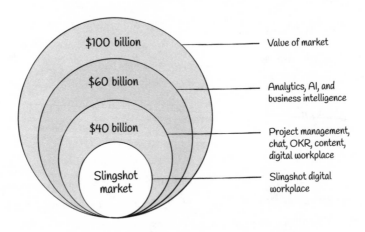

Figure 16.6. Infragistics Slingshot market opportunity

OKRs

When it comes to our GTM plan, we design OKRs (see Chapter 3 for a full explanation of OKRs) to keep our managers and employees focused on what is expected of them and to provide our organization opportunities to learn more about the market.

Figures 16.7–16.9 are some examples of the OKRs that we set up for Slingshot's GTM plan.

One of our objectives was to deliver X thousands in sales through digital sales, with the following key results:

- Deliver awareness and trials of product.

- Deliver X thousands through organic traffic.

- Deliver X thousands through paid efforts.

- Through the use of devices and channels, improve growth hacking and optimize our website.

- Use growth hacking to understand every point in the customer's journey so as to drive new seats and increase viral response.

- Deliver X thousand seats in 2022.

- Deliver X thousand leads per month.

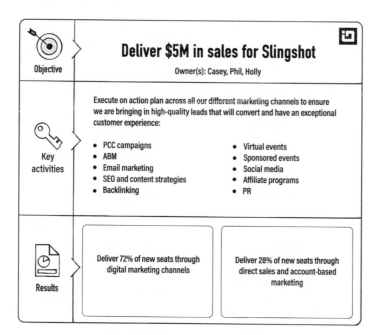

Figure 16.7. Infragistics Slingshot GTM OKR on sales

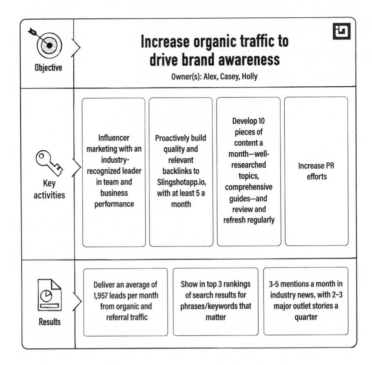

Figure 16.8. Infragistics Slingshot GTM OKR on brand awareness

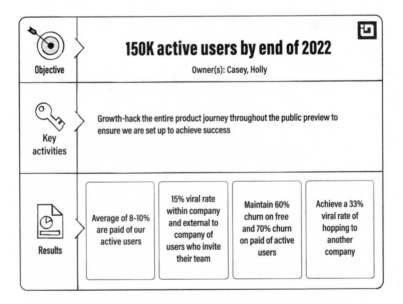

Figure 16.9. Infragistics Slingshot GTM OKR on users

- Convert page views to leads on average of X percent across all mediums.

- Convert X percent of leads to paid users.

These OKRs were based on the executive team's comprehensive research of other SaaS companies currently selling products to marketing teams.

While marketing teams are one of our key target markets, they're certainly not the *only* group we serve. Our GTM outlines other key demographic profiles such as accounting companies, public relations firms, marketing companies, digital businesses, and consultants (see Figure 16.10).

As a learning organization that makes data-driven decisions, we allocate money to understand other routes to market, to experiment, and to learn. For example, we tested going after the business intelligence market and the project management market along with the hybrid workplace. We continually reevaluate and test other routes to market to achieve our goals for Slingshot.

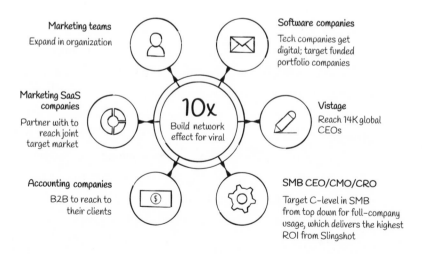

Figure 16.10. Infragistics Slingshot GTM example of segmentation of the plan

Appendix

Our GTM plan contains an appendix that includes a SWOT analysis, key competitors, and market analysis.

PUTTING THE GTM PLAN TO WORK

A vNext Business is agile. It's a learning organization. And with any plan—a strategic plan, an annual plan, or a GTM plan—there's always the potential pitfall of sitting on your heels after a plan is fully developed. The plan is the beginning, not the end.

As we finalize our GTM plan and receive feedback from the marketplace, we compare up-to-date results and revenue metrics to the assumptions we made in the OKRs. We look at our objectives and our results to see what is and is not working and then adjust the plan accordingly on an ongoing basis.

Throughout your implementation of the plan, you must constantly ask *why* questions to understand the buyer's journey, to find market fit, and to improve your ability to obtain market share.

As a vNext Business, you must be learning, updating, and pivoting. *Every. Single. Day.*

I know that sounds daunting. And in all honesty, it's not easy—at first. But as with any difficult task, it's simply a matter of starting. If your organization doesn't use GTM plans, try a simple one on for size. See if it doesn't create more alignment, more mobility, and more flexibility to achieve your organization's goals. I bet you'll like the results.

A good GTM plan is dynamic and always changing. We update ours throughout the year. As the campaign to sell Slingshot unfolded, we continuously examined whether we had correctly calibrated our mix of account-led growth and product-led growth.

Account-led growth involves different levels of your organization—account executives, inside sales team, sales consultants, and sales development representatives. On the other hand, product-led growth requires investing in your product and in its successful use by your customers. This effort assists the customer in learning and utilizing the product to maximize their own ROIs.

Both of these GTM strategies have the same objectives: to drive adoption of our product and service and to retain and expand our customer base.

But these two different approaches require different investments in people and work processes.

After examining all the data, we saw a pattern. Following a data-driven decision, we recalibrated Slingshot's GTM plan to put more emphasis on product-led growth. We hired additional data consultants. We agreed we needed to build software that would better help us ascertain a buyer's intent. We also hired customer-success professionals whose sole goal is to ensure our customers are getting the most possible value out of their experience with the product. Finally, we determined we had to provide more content, such as white papers, videos, and blogs focusing on best business practices to guide customers to be more successful with the product.

Remember, don't change too many things all at once. Change is necessary to achieve a different result, but if you change everything at once, you'll never identify the magic variable that yields the favorable outcome.

Even the best plans are only useful if those who are tasked with implementing them also *understand* them. That's why we review our GTM plan with everyone in our company after it is complete.

Implementing a GTM plan can have significant and measurable impacts on your business. Here's what they've done for my team:

- Increase chances of product/service success
- Support a sustainable rhythm of business
- Align everyone to the same value proposition and product messaging
- Outline where to focus our resources
- Identify our objectives and how they will be measured
- Increase accountability around key objectives

- Save a wealth of time by ensuring our team is moving in the same direction on a consistent basis

Most of all, like the strategic and annual plans, GTM plans provide business leaders with a strategy for adapting to a world that is constantly changing.

Despite the time they take to create, they are well worth the reward.

 ## KEY POINTS FOR CREATING A VNEXT BUSINESS

1. If you have a single product or service, your strategic plan and annual plan can be enough to align and execute your game plan, in which case you do not need a GTM plan.

2. GTM plans are more detailed than strategic plans and annual plans for a specific product or service execution.

3. Creating a GTM plan helps align and get intrinsic buy-in from key members of a team.

4. GTM plans help align and focus your sales, marketing, and product teams.

5. Include your vision, key objectives or mission, and core strategies in all your GTM plans.

6. GTM plans should cover sales targets, market size, key customer pain points you're addressing, how you are segmenting the market to focus resources, what marketing channels you will use, and detailed OKRs for sales, marketing, and product development.

7. Share your plan with all members of the GTM team.

8. The GTM plan serves as a guidepost for your monthly GTM rhythm-of-the-business meetings.

9. Focus on data to measure goal attainment and get insight into why things are happening.

10. Stay agile and be willing to change and update the plan as you learn and get market feedback on what is working and what is not working.

17

RECOVERY AND
SELF-CARE

The sudden, sharp pain in my left calf seemed to come out of the blue. Well, actually, out of the blue sky, since I'd been seated on a plane for about fifty hours that week. I'd been traveling almost nonstop for three months to Japan, India, Europe, and South America. Day and night, I'd been meeting with customers and employees, making presentations, solving problems, resolving conflicts. I was always "on," with scant time for any significant rest and relaxation; each night I'd collapse into a hotel bed and then get up and do it again.

I've been a workaholic my entire life. I grew up in an era when the mantra was "no pain, no gain." I felt I was invincible and the more hours I worked, the better my chances were of being successful.

This is *still* the prevailing business narrative in America.

There had been many other moments like this in the past when I was on the verge of mental and physical exhaustion, but I'd never paused to consider the impact this was having on my work, my life, and my relationships. I'd somehow recover and go right back to working nonstop. Like a lot of CEOs, I felt guilty if I was not constantly contributing to my company's success.

I thought I had a "charley horse," an old-school term for a sudden muscle cramp, the type that often occurs after some kind of physical exertion.

Usually, it disappears with rest and hydration. I tried to ignore my discomfort, but it persisted and grew worse by the time I returned home.

That night I woke up and could not breathe. My wife and I hurried to an emergency room, where I was diagnosed with a pulmonary embolism—a blood clot—that could escape to my lungs. I was hospitalized for four days and then placed on blood thinners for six months.

The blood clot taught me a valuable lesson. It prompted me to learn how to lead without literally killing myself. Over time, I learned I could be a *better* CEO, a better father, and a better husband if I took care of myself better. I realized that to take care of the people and things I really love, I first had to take care of myself.

After all—you can't fill another's cup with an empty pitcher.

This was a major shift in my professional perspective. But it's also one that has been occurring in sports and business in recent years. Elite athletes such as LeBron James are testaments to the effectiveness of new practices of self-care that are enabling them to perform at the highest levels into their late thirties and mid-forties—ages when most players have retired or suffered injuries or sharp declines in performance.[1]

Many leading businesses, such as Microsoft, Google, Apple, Procter and Gamble, McKinsey and Company, and Zappos have pioneered new approaches to health and wellness for their executives and employees. And instead of losing ground, their productivity and performance have increased.[2]

It makes sense. I get much more done when I am recharged and following self-care routines. Taking time for myself turns me into a more empathetic leader and better teammate. I look at problems and issues at Infragistics in fresh, new ways that lead me to resolve them more quickly and creatively.

I've found that the key ingredients of self-care are an understanding of (1) stress, (2) the importance of mindfulness and meditation, (3) the need for substantial rest, (4) exercise, and (5) maintaining relationships with loved ones.

Let's spend some time with each one.

STRESS

The chaos of business *is* stress. When I rode airplanes for fifty hours in a week and traveled to ten different countries in three months, I put incredible stress on my body.

Stress is to life what string tension is to a violin: too little and the music is flat and dull; too much and the string snaps. Stress can be the kiss of death or the spice of life. The issue, really, is how to manage it. Managed stress makes us productive and allows us to accomplish great things; mismanaged stress hurts our morale, leads to a lack of productivity, and can even kill.[3]

By allowing myself to endure such a grueling pace for so many months in a row, I tightened the strings way too hard. I was moving from what is known as acute stress to dangerous or chronic stress.

Acute stress comes from the demands and pressures of the recent past and anticipated demands and pressures of the near future.[4] Launching a new product with multiple interim deadlines over the course of a year generates this form of stress for myself and my teams. But this type of stress *can* be useful. It makes the journey exciting. It holds us to account. It keeps us on our toes and trying our best.

Acute stress is manageable. Self-care practices can mitigate the potential anger, irritability, anxiety, depression, tension headaches, back pain, and elevated blood pressure associated with this type of stress.[5]

Chronic stress, on the other hand, is the grinding, day-in-and-day-out stress that wears people out and destroys bodies and minds. This is the stress of unrelenting demands and pressure for an extended period of time, such as my business trip. It (or unmanaged acute stress) can lead to heart attacks, strokes, perhaps cancer, and, as in my case, life-threatening blood clots.[6]

Not only does stress have personal and health consequences, but it can also severely affect a business's bottom line.

New York Times business columnist David Gelles describes its impact in his book *Mindful Work*.[7] A study by insurance giant Aetna found a highly stressed employee costs the company an extra $2,000 per year in healthcare compared to their less-stressed peers. After instituting stress reduction practices, Aetna calculated productivity gains alone were about $3,000 per employee, equaling an eleven-to-one return on investment.[8]

If stress is so costly and dangerous, what do we do about it?

The work, the deadlines, the drive to succeed and win—they'll always be there. I've found one of the most powerful techniques for dealing with stress is the practice of mindfulness.

MINDFULNESS

Though it has its roots in Buddhist meditation, the secular practice of mindfulness entered mainstream American culture in the early and mid-1980s through the work of Harvard social psychologist Ellen J. Langer and Jon Kabat-Zinn's Mindfulness-Based Stress Reduction (MBSR) program at the University of Massachusetts Medical School.[9]

For these scholars and other researchers, mindfulness means maintaining a moment-by-moment awareness of our thoughts, feelings, bodily sensations, and surrounding environment. It's about living in the moment. And while you can acknowledge your past regrets and future concerns, it's about staying present in the present.

Mindfulness also involves acceptance, meaning we pay attention to our thoughts and feelings without *judging* them—without believing, for instance, that there's a "right" or "wrong" way to think or feel.

In my case, mindfulness helps me silence the self-doubt rolling around in my head, empowering me to be a more confident leader.

Since the mid-1980s, thousands of scientific studies have documented the physical and mental health benefits of mindfulness. In recent years, many business leaders have concluded mindfulness is a necessary twenty-first-century skill. As Yolanda Lau, cofounder and chief talent officer at FlexTeam, writing in *Forbes*, contends, "Businesses with mindful teams are better equipped to compete in today's ever-changing environment."[10]

She argues that mindfulness in the workplace can decrease stress levels while improving focus, thoughtfulness, decision-making abilities, and overall well-being. Mindfulness gives employees permission and space to think—to be present, which leads to mental agility, resilience, and self-awareness. In addition, mindfulness can decrease emotional exhaustion, increase openness to new ideas, and help develop compassion and empathy.[11]

Regular mindful meditation among project teams and departments also has long-lasting benefits, including building stronger bonds between employees, increasing productivity, and building up prosocial behavior such as honesty.[12]

In my business, success is contingent on staying calm and adapting quickly—with an open mind—to shifting market circumstances. Mindfulness provides that competitive advantage. Moreover, a mindful workplace is a powerful tool for recruiting the best and the brightest. It leads to high levels of commitment at work and reduces turnover.

How to Practice Mindfulness

Mindfulness should start in the morning. Do the following practices *before* checking your smartphone or email, or you may be flooded with intrusions that make it more difficult to achieve the calmness you seek.

Just like any other skill, learning these practices takes time. Don't judge yourself if you don't master them immediately. You will.

It is not about being right. It is about *being*.

1. *On waking, sit in your bed or a chair in a relaxed posture.* Close your eyes and connect with the sensations of your seated body. Make sure your spine is straight but not rigid.

2. *Take three long, deep, nourishing breaths.* Breathe in through your nose and out through your mouth. Let your breath settle into its own rhythm, as you follow it in and out, noticing the rise and fall of your chest and belly as you breathe. If your mind wanders, just bring it back by focusing on your breath. By the end of the practice, you should achieve a sense of calmness.

3. *Ask yourself: "What is my intention for today?"* For exam-
    ple, "Today, I will be kind to myself," or "I will be patient with
    others," or "I will stay grounded and persevere to finish my
    goal," or "I will listen carefully to the other members of my
    team," or anything else you feel is important. Your intention
    serves as a reminder that will help you to be your best self and
    perform well. Then, use these prompts as you think about the
    people and activities you will face:

    - How might I have the best impact?

    - What quality of mind do I want to strengthen and develop?

    - What do I need to do to take better care of myself?

    - During difficult moments, how might I be more compas-
      sionate to others and myself?

    - How could I feel more connected and fulfilled?

4. *Throughout the day, check in with yourself.* Pause, take a breath,
    and revisit your intention. Make it a habit—as you sit down
    to your desk, before lunch, or even on a trip to the bathroom.
    Notice, as you become more and more conscious of your inten-
    tions, how the quality of your communications, relationships,
    and mood will shift.

Given my blood clot experience, I use mindfulness to do a physical
check-in. I ask myself: How do I feel today? How is my head? How is my
heart? How are my lungs?

I'm an advocate for mindfulness when I talk with other CEOs. I
always get one or two skeptics who scoff and tell me that it can't possibly
be worth it—that it's just a bunch of New Age nonsense. But honestly,
I've never heard this complaint from anyone who made a concerted effort
to just try it.

Short Periods of Mindfulness

Mindfulness in even short bursts can have a significant effect. Wharton School of Business Professor Lindsey Cameron found even seven or eight minutes of mindfulness a day result in more productive, helpful, and pleasant employees. It also expanded their rational decision-making skills, improved their attention and focus, and increased "divergent thinking," which aids in the ability to generate new ideas.[13]

You can try the mini-mindfulness approach I sometimes take—breathe in on a count of four to seven, and then on a count of four to seven breathe out. See if it works for you.

MEDITATION

Mindfulness is part of a constellation of stress-reducing practices that include concentration on a word, movement-based meditation, cultivating positive emotions, and the spiritual practice of emptying.

These different practices of meditation can be learned through books, audio recordings, videos, online training, websites, smartphone apps, and by traditional in-person sessions. The past five years have seen an explosion of apps and programs for meditation and yoga such as Shine, Meditation Studio, Headspace, Yoga Ed, and Calm. I use Headspace and Calm for a twenty-minute meditation.

Try out different meditation practices until you find one that works best for you.

Many leaders are now incorporating a ninety-second meditation to begin or end a meeting, which can either set the tone for the discussion or help frame employee mindsets and manage stress levels.

Many major companies have fully embraced meditative practices; among them are Apple, Google, Nike, McKinsey and Company, and Procter and Gamble.

Apple

Steve Jobs promoted meditation at Apple. He took part in meditation retreats, was married in a Zen ceremony, and maintained lifelong friendships with many monks. He passed his love for meditation on to the workplace, allowing employees to take thirty minutes a day to meditate at work, providing classes on meditation and yoga, and creating meditation rooms.[14]

Google

In 2007, Google established the Search Inside Yourself program, which was designed to help employees breathe mindfully, listen better to their coworkers, and improve their emotional intelligence. The company also offers meditation spaces and meditation courses.[15]

Nike

The sneaker giant allows their employees access to "quiet" rooms where they can take a nap, pray, or meditate. They also can participate in meditation and yoga classes.[16]

McKinsey and Company

The famed management and consulting firm is deeply involved with meditation. As McKinsey partner and meditation booster Michael Rennie said, "What's good for the spirit is good for the bottom line." The company has developed meditation programs for its own employees and for a number of its corporate clients.[17]

Procter and Gamble

Former P&G CEO A. G. Lafley is dedicated to his own meditative practice and has said, "You cannot outwork a problem, you have to out meditation it."[18] P&G offers a wealth of health and fitness programs that include meditation classes and spaces.

THE IMPORTANCE OF REST

On my extended business trip, I got little rest. And even if I could have grabbed some, I wouldn't have taken the opportunity. Like most of us, I thought of rest as the absence of work—not something valuable that contributes to performance. Sometimes our hard-driving American culture even equates rest with laziness.

But nothing could be further from the truth.

I think my ability to be a good leader is like a battery. When I'm fully charged, I'm on point: good decisions, good interactions, good foresight, good empathy. When I'm drained, it's the exact opposite. And that's why taking time to recharge is critical for leaders.

As Silicon Valley–based consultant Alex Soojung-Kim Pang argues in *Rest: Why You Get More Done When You Work Less*, rest is an essential component of working well and working smart. In his book, he outlines research that shows how rest helps workers improve their thinking, become more innovative, and increase their productivity.[19]

How does rest do this? When we are not directly focused on a task, our mind is still active, plugging away at problems, examining possible answers, and searching for new information. By resting, we support our ability to solve problems in smart ways.

Sleeping

Sleeping is, of course, the ultimate form of rest. In *Macbeth*, Shakespeare wrote, "The innocent sleep, sleep that knits up the ravell'd sleeve of care, the death of each day's life, sore labor's bath, balm of hurt minds, great nature's second course, chief nourisher in life's feast."[20] Modern research bears out his wisdom by proving the mind and the body require regular sleep to repair the wear and tear of everyday life.

When you fall asleep, your body shifts into maintenance mode and devotes itself to storing energy and fixing or replacing damaged cells. At the same time, your brain cleans out toxins, reviews that day's experiences, and works on problems that have been occupying your waking mind.[21]

Sleep is particularly important for performance. Researchers who looked at anesthesiology interns found that after a couple of weeks of having night shifts or on-call duties, their work performance declined significantly.[22] And that is not a profession where you want significantly declined performance!

Regular sleep—between seven and eight hours a night—means going to bed and getting up at about the same time every day. You should avoid alcohol, nicotine, and caffeine, especially three hours before retiring.

Napping

Another major way to get enough rest is to take a nap at work. Napping increases alertness and decreases fatigue—if you do it correctly. A short nap of around twenty minutes boosts your ability to concentrate by giving your brain a chance to restore depleted energy. In one study, Sara Mednick, professor of cognitive science at the University of California, Irvine, and her colleagues tested participants on perception tasks and then divided them into three groups: one that didn't nap at all, and two that napped either for an hour or ninety minutes. Everyone was then retested in the evening. Those who hadn't napped performed worse in the evening, while those who'd napped performed either the same or dramatically better. Testing all of the groups the next day—after a night's sleep—again resulted in nappers performing better than non-nappers.[23]

You can even vary the timing of your nap, depending on your energy needs during the day.[24]

Stopping Work at the Right Time

Many of us may feel that pushing ourselves to work long, unbroken hours is the best way to be productive. I shared this belief for many years. But social science research suggests an effective form of deliberate rest is to stop working at just the right point—when you experience a dip of your circadian rhythm (the internal clock that regulates some of our biological processes, including wakefulness).[25]

Stopping when you have a little energy left makes it easier to get started the next day. It also prompts your subconscious mind to tackle work problems better. Leaving tasks undone causes your mind to continue without your conscious awareness. Such a strategy provides a boost to creativity and a buffer against stress.[26]

Vacations

Vacations are perhaps the best way to rest the body and the mind. And before I go any further—a vacation means *actually* shutting off. It's not a vacation if you're on your phone checking emails and micromanaging from afar.

I take a lot of them, up to eight weeks a year. I encourage my executive team and employees to also take vacations and other time off. They will return refreshed and eager to work, filled with ideas and energy.

I am not alone in my belief in the importance of vacations. According to a Glassdoor survey, vacations and paid time off are *more* important to employees than pay raises![27]

Employers reap several benefits when they provide generous paid time off. They see reduced levels of unscheduled absenteeism. Lost wages due to absenteeism cost employers $1,685 per employee per year, according to the Centers for Disease Control.[28] Employers can also expect employees to be more honest when allowed to take vacation and personal days. They tend not to lie about or hide their true reason for not coming in.

Unlimited Paid Time Off

In recent years, the idea of rest has expanded from paid vacations and some additional paid days off during the year to unlimited paid time off (PTO). In 2019, unlimited PTO ranked as the top emerging benefit according to MetLife's Employee Benefits Trends study. Researchers found that out of 2,600 employees surveyed, 72 percent wanted unlimited PTO. Workers desired this benefit above health and wellness plans and on-site benefits like medical clinics, gyms, and restaurants. The respondents placed a very high value on benefits that help create a better work-life balance.[29]

Many top companies such as HubSpot, Roku, Dropbox, General Electric, and Netflix have adopted unlimited PTO.[30] As UKG CEO Aron Ain stated, "We started this policy in January 2016, and in calendar 2016, we had the best year we ever had. Our engagement went to levels it had never reached before. Our voluntary turnover went to the lowest level it's ever been at."[31]

Under unlimited PTO, employees are not assigned a set number of paid days off at the start of the year. Instead, they take time off when needed, as long as it does not disrupt business. This includes vacation days, sick leave, personal leave, and sabbaticals.[32]

In a member's absence, their team must still function properly. A well-formed unlimited PTO policy should be mutually beneficial to both a business and its employees. As long as an employee's work meets their employer's expectations and they have coordinated their leave with other team members, they are free to take leave.[33]

The system does have the potential for abuse. Some employees may take excessive time off, which can lead to an increased workload for other team members as they cover their absent colleagues' work. Pay attention to employees who are abusing the system. Talk with them about their reasons for taking so much time off. Make it another learning opportunity. See if the absences involve issues that have not been discussed thoroughly by managers and employees. Then work to help the employees take advantage of unlimited PTO within the rules and responsibilities of the company.

At first, I was opposed to the idea of unlimited PTO. It was the old, hard-driving me failing to appreciate the evidence that so overwhelmingly pointed to its benefits. In the end, I realized unlimited PTO was consistent with all the other agility practices we have implemented at Infragistics to increase productivity and performance. Because we trust each other, I knew team members would always respond with the best interests of the team and the company in mind.

Our data shows that Infragistics employees on average take 21.5 days off per year. Before our new policy it was 20 days, with five-year employees getting 25 days off and employees with more than ten years at the company getting 30 days off.

We put in a few rules to make the policy effective:

- All paid time off is tracked.

- Employees must request paid time off, and their manager must approve it.

- There is a maximum of two consecutive weeks per request.

- Requests for two consecutive weeks in one three-month period need to be approved by a senior manager.

Unlimited PTO has worked out very well. In fact, after looking at the data, I had to encourage some team members to take off more time!

EXERCISE

We all know the importance of getting daily exercise. But the US Department of Health and Human Services reports that only one in three adults achieves the recommended amount of physical activity each week, and more than 80 percent of adults do not meet the guidelines for both aerobic and muscle-strengthening activities.[34]

I'll admit finding time to exercise can be difficult. Work, family, and social commitments make it hard to incorporate a regular workout routine.

But it has many benefits. Exercise reduces stress, helps keep the heart healthy, lowers blood pressure, prevents disease, and helps with weight loss.

From a business point of view, it helps boost productivity. Writing in the *Harvard Business Review*, Ron Friedman, a social psychologist and founder of ignite80, a consulting firm that helps companies build extraordinary workplaces, details multiple studies that confirm the positive impact exercise has on productivity by boosting mental abilities, enhancing creativity, improving learning, sharpening memory, and deepening concentration.[35]

Walking is my preferred form of exercise. I slap on my headset and listen to music or an audiobook while taking a refreshing walk.

Research has shown that walking facilitates creative thinking by helping our brains engage in a light kind of focus, which encourages the mind to wander and aids in creativity.[36]

Stanford University researchers conducted a series of experiments looking at the effects of walking on creativity as measured by a test of divergent thinking, which asks people to come up with novel ways of dealing with everyday problems.[37]

Their results showed that walking *and* being outside each led to better test performances. In one experiment, the researchers found the benefits of walking on creativity did not fade immediately but carried over into performance on future tests.[38]

Of course, walking is not for everyone. Find a type of exercise that works for you and your body—maybe swimming or yoga or whatever feels energizing rather than exhausting—and try to incorporate twenty to thirty minutes of it into your daily routine. You may be surprised by how much better you feel!

AN INVESTMENT IN SELF-CARE GOES A LONG WAY

Drawing on healing practices that are thousands of years old, heeding cutting-edge social science research that shows how to greatly increase productivity by simply taking a nap or a restful vacation, meditating, and getting some moderate exercise—these are all insights, along with others mentioned in this chapter, that I have drawn on in recent years. They have improved the health and performance of myself and everyone at Infragistics. They work. Try them. And as you do, you will discover how powerful they can be to change your life and the lives of those you care about at work.

 ## KEY POINTS FOR CREATING A VNEXT BUSINESS

1. Manage your stress, as it will make you more productive and allow you to accomplish great things. Mismanaged stress hurts morale, leads to a lack of productivity, and can even kill.

2. Performing at your highest level requires you to take care of your mind and body.

3. Mindfulness, sleep, time off, and exercise are four important elements of recovery and performing at your highest level.

4. Mindfulness means maintaining a moment-by-moment aware-ness of our thoughts, feelings, bodily sensations, and surrounding environment. It's about living in the moment.

5. There are many apps like Headspace and Calm that can help you meditate.

6. Meditating is not only for you but also for the people around you. You will be more calm, present, relaxed, and joyful to be around.

7. Sleep is one of the single biggest factors in boosting your mood and cognitive abilities. Getting seven to eight hours a day on

a consistent schedule will improve your health and business performance.

8. Taking naps will help your creativity. Twenty-minute naps are a magic number to get rest and wake up.

9. Taking vacations, disconnecting, and spending time in nature are important ways to recover and enhance work performance and reduce stress.

10. Any form of daily exercise will refresh your mind and body.

CONCLUSION

Imagine an organization that has been successful for more than forty years, constantly achieving excellence and profitability, consistently developing new products that delight and amaze its passionate customers, overcoming numerous obstacles—including the deaths of two of its most important founding members—yet still, somehow, exhibiting the highest levels of teamwork.

That's how I would describe my favorite band—AC/DC. They still rock, especially when cofounder and lead guitarist Angus Young—he of the schoolboy outfit—duck walks across the stage à la Chuck Berry, blazing out power chords in front of throngs of frenzied fans that pack stadiums around the world. Angus always brings it.

My favorite AC/DC song is "Thunderstruck." It never fails to energize me, and I often listen to it when I need to turn it up a notch before a big meeting or when I reach the last leg of an extended business trip. It gives me a jolt; it's as if the lightning bolt that separates the AC/DC logo jumps from my headphones into my head and heart.

Although the song's lyrics tell of a personal breakup and a wild ride through Texas to recover emotionally, "Thunderstruck" also expresses a sensibility that almost every entrepreneur feels multiple times in their life.

I was first thunderstruck when I was eight years old. I realized I could earn money to help my mother by assisting our condo's custodian and by selling eight-track mixtapes to my friends. This early success created a core of resilience and optimism that sustains me to this day.

I was thunderstruck again when I started Infragistics with a small amount of saved cash and an idea for an innovative product. Drawing on my relentless work ethic, I mastered the many different elements of growing and nurturing a small business and made Infragistics a success.

I later was thunderstruck again when we only had $618.00 in the bank and had to come up with more than $580,000 a month in expenses. Unless we moved beyond a one-man show, Infragistics would go under. During the next few years, I discovered how to build the cultural, organizational, and financial structures and processes that would enable us to become a learning organization. We became driven by data. Our teams worked effectively together. We all had fun designing products that delighted our customers. The insights I have gained on this journey formed the content of this book and constitute the core elements of a vNext Business.

I was thunderstruck a fourth time at the Center for Creative Leadership when I discovered there were parts of my personality and behavior that could endanger the culture of success I had built at Infragistics and even my own health. It led me to make many changes to my lifestyle. And I still keep working on improving myself.

Like all entrepreneurs, I find running Infragistics is an ongoing adventure. The world is constantly changing, and the pace of that change is accelerating faster and faster.

The digital revolution is well underway. Some companies are adept at creating the digital literacy their workforce needs to master to succeed in this new world. Many are less adept and face the threat of extinction. The need to become a vNext Business has never been more urgent.

A new kind of employee is emerging as well. Millennials and Gen Z are seeking a different kind of work environment. The necessity for shutdowns and work-from-home caused by COVID-19 in 2020 and 2021, accompanied by the loss of more than a million Americans, triggered what has been called the Great Resignation. Millions of young workers left their jobs and, in many cases, chose not to return, even when uncertain how they would survive financially. They just wanted out.[1]

To bring them back will require companies to be driven by a mission that gives these young people a sense of purpose and accomplishment. Businesses will have to utilize the skills that the Millennials and Gen Zs bring to the job—they are highly adept at asynchronous communication and generating an instant flow of information, and doing so in new and imaginative ways.[2]

AI and the rise of robots will revolutionize all our lives. Enterprises will need to respond by reconceptualizing the very nature of work.

Despite all of these challenges, on its best days, Infragistics is like a great band—a collective effort that creates something amazing, leaving me and my teams with feelings of joy and accomplishment. More than that, our approach is the source of our constantly victories in the marketplace.

It is possible to replicate our success.

You can be happy at work.

You can have an adaptable and profitable business.

You can build something that grows and evolves into something more than its individual parts.

You can plan for the future while achieving success in the present.

You can take an intentional and strategic approach to managing your teams.

You can create a culture in which your teams feel energized and motivated.

You can provide your customers and clients with simple and beautiful experiences.

And it all starts with the vNext approach.

It is my hope that by incorporating this book's lessons and implementing its prescriptions, you will be thunderstruck repeatedly. I can think of no better way to live a life or run a company.

Here's to doing the hard things that will lead you to success and happiness!

Appendix

THE INFRAGISTICS WAY

The Infragistics Way describes the practices that guide our actions and decisions. It's who we are, it's who we want to be, and it's essential to our success.

DO THE RIGHT THING, ALWAYS

Demonstrate an unwavering commitment to doing the right thing in every action you take and in every decision you make, especially when no one's looking. Always tell the truth, no matter the consequences. If you make a mistake, own up to it, apologize, and make it right.

DELIVER RESULTS

While we appreciate effort, we reward and celebrate results. Follow up on everything and take responsibility to ensure that tasks get completed. Set high goals, use measurements to track your progress, and hold yourself accountable for achieving those results.

DELIGHT THE CUSTOMER

It's all about the experience. In every interaction, do the little things, as well as the big things, that delight people. Exceed expectations and deliver the "wow" factor every chance you get. We're here to make our customers' jobs easier, and we do that by remaining focused on beauty and simplicity in all that we produce.

BE FANATICAL ABOUT RESPONSE TIME

Respond to questions and concerns quickly, whether it's in person, on the phone, or by email. This includes simply acknowledging that we got the question and we're "on it," as well as keeping those involved continuously updated on the status of outstanding issues.

BE CURIOUS AND INNOVATE

In the search for the best solutions, be curious. Ask thoughtful questions and listen intently to the answers. Dig deeper to go beyond the expected. Take intelligent risks. Innovation, improvement, and success come from a thoughtful and intentional willingness to try the unconventional and to ask, "What if?" Don't be afraid to make mistakes. Use sound judgment and validate your ideas with stakeholders whenever possible.

CHECK YOUR EGO AT THE DOOR

It's not about you. Don't let your ego get in the way of doing what's best for the team. Worrying about who gets credit or taking things personally is counterproductive. Make sure every decision is based solely on advancing team goals and doing what's best for the customer.

BE DATA DRIVEN

Analyze situations and use available data with a relentless focus on improvement. Learn the facts before jumping to conclusions. Collect input from all relevant sources and avoid data bias. Without a data-driven culture, we're running blind.

SHOW GRIT AND "BRING IT" EVERY DAY

Persevere and be passionate about the long-term goal! Don't be afraid to make mistakes. Make the most of each day by approaching every task with energy, focus, purpose, and enthusiasm. Be courageous—act despite the risk of failure, be conscientious in your work, be tenacious in the face of challenges, and go for excellence over perfection! Learn from the successes or setbacks that result.

DELIVER AN EFFORTLESS EXPERIENCE

Find ways to make working with others easier. Provide simple and complete instructions. Focus on a seamless, friction-free user experience for internal and external customers. When in doubt, do more rather than pushing the work back. Streamline your processes. Simplify everything. Be ridiculously helpful.

MAKE CRAFTSMANSHIP PERSONAL

Demonstrate a passion for excellence and take pride in the quality of everything you touch and everything you do. The goal is to get things right, not simply to get them done. Have a healthy disdain for mediocrity. While we always want to work with a sense of urgency, sometimes we need to slow down to speed up. Allow time for the creative juices to flow and to think of all the options. Always ask yourself, "Is this my best work?"

PRACTICE HUMAN-CENTERED DESIGN

Develop solutions for your customers that are rooted in a deep and thorough understanding of their needs, situations, and known and unknown challenges. Immerse yourself in your customers' world to deliver the best possible experience and/or solution.

PRACTICE BLAMELESS PROBLEM-SOLVING

Demonstrate a relentless solution focus, rather than pointing fingers or dwelling on problems. Identify lessons learned, socialize them, and use those lessons to improve your processes and outcomes so you don't make the same mistake twice. Get smarter with every mistake. Learn from every experience.

HONOR COMMITMENTS

Do what you say you're going to do, when you say you're going to do it. This includes being on time for all phone calls, appointments, meetings, and promises. If a commitment can't be fulfilled, notify others early and agree on a new deliverable to be honored.

LOOK FROM THE OUTSIDE IN

Understand your customers' world. Know their challenges and frustrations. See the world from their perspective. The better you understand them, the more effectively you can anticipate and meet their needs. Engage with customers and keep their perspectives top of mind.

FIND A WAY

Adopt an ownership mentality. Take personal responsibility for making things happen. Respond to every situation by looking for how you can do it, rather than explaining why it can't be done. Be resourceful and show initiative. Don't make excuses or wait for others to solve the problem. See issues through to their completion.

BE RELENTLESS ABOUT IMPROVEMENT

What got us here won't get us to the next level. Regularly reevaluate every aspect of your job to find ways to improve. Don't be satisfied with the status quo. "Because we've always done it that way" is not a reason. Be excited by the possibilities that change brings and find ways to get things done better, faster, and more efficiently. Become a lifelong learner. Learn faster than the other folks.

LISTEN GENEROUSLY

Listening is more than simply "not speaking." Give others your undivided attention. Be present and engaged. Minimize the distractions and let go of the need to agree or disagree. Suspend your judgment and be curious to know more, rather than jump to conclusions. Above all, listen to understand.

SPEAK STRAIGHT

Speak honestly and simply in a way that helps to make progress. Say what you mean, and be willing to ask questions, share ideas, or raise issues that may cause conflict when it's necessary for team success. Be courageous enough to say what needs to be said. Address issues directly with those who are involved or affected.

SHOW MEANINGFUL APPRECIATION

Recognizing people doing things right is more effective than pointing out when they do things wrong. Regularly extend meaningful acknowledgment and appreciation—in all directions throughout your organization.

ASSUME POSITIVE INTENT

Work from the assumption that people are good, fair, honest, and that the intent behind their actions is positive. Set aside your own judgments and preconceived notions. Give people the benefit of the doubt.

COLLABORATE

Be inclusive. Share information and work together. Learn to ask yourself, "Who else needs to know this?" Be available for your teammates. Take responsibility, both formally and informally, to coach, guide, teach, and mentor others. Collaborate internally and with your customers and partners to find better solutions. Collaboration generates better ideas than working alone.

LIVE HEALTHY AND KEEP THINGS FUN

Take care of yourself at home and at the office. Exercise, get adequate sleep, and focus on a healthy diet. Support each other in making healthy choices. Keep perspective. Don't take things personally or take yourself too seriously. While our passion for excellence is real, remember that the world has bigger problems than the daily challenges that make up our work. Stuff happens. Laugh every day.

—

To learn more about the book and about Slingshot, scan the following codes:

deanguida.com   slingshotapp.io

NOTES

CHAPTER 1

1. Carolyn Dewar and Reed Doucette, "Culture: 4 Keys to Why It Matters," McKinsey and Company, March 27, 2018, https://www.mckinsey .com/capabilities/people-and-organizational-performance/our-insights/ the-organization-blog/culture-4-keys-to-why-it-matters.

2. Dewar and Doucette, "Culture."

3. Dewar and Doucette, "Culture."

4. Gallup, "State of the Global Workplace: 2022 Report," 2022, https://www.gallup .com/workplace/349484/state-of-the-global-workplace.aspx.

5. Marie-Claire Ross, "5 Reasons Why Mission-Driven Leaders Are the Most Successful," LinkedIn, December 14, 2015, https://www.linkedin.com/ pulse/5-reasons-why-mission-driven-leaders-most-successful-ross-gaicd/.

CHAPTER 2

1. Dale Carnegie, *How to Win Friends and Influence People* (New York: Gallery Books, 2022).

2. Carnegie, *How to Win Friends*.

3. Carnegie, *How to Win* Friends.

4. Carnegie, *How to Win Friends*, 85.

5. Carnegie, *How to Win Friends*.

6. Frances Bridges, "10 Ways to Make People Like You, from 'How to Win Friends and Influence People,'" *Forbes*, February 7, 2018, https://www.forbes.com/sites/ francesbridges/2018/02/07/10-ways-to-make-people-like-you-from-how-to -make-friends-and-influence-people/?sh=7f189a124bb4.

7. Napoleon Hill, *Think and Grow Rich* (Shippensburg, PA: Sound Wisdom, 2016).

8. Joseph Adebisi, "The 13 Essential Principles of *Think and Grow Rich*," *Shortform*, July 21, 2021, https://www.shortform.com/blog/principles-of-think-and-grow-rich/.

9. Jocko Willink and Leif Babin, *Extreme Ownership: How U.S. Navy SEALs Lead and Win* (New York: St. Martin's Press, 2017).

10. Willink and Babin, *Extreme Ownership*.

11. Tushar Vakil, "What Makes Teams Successful—Google's Project Aristotle Came Up with These 5 Factors That Matter," New Age Leadership, accessed December 22, 2022, https://newageleadership.com/what-makes-teams-successful-googles-project-aristotle-came-up-with-these-five-factors-that-matter/.

12. Vakil, "What Makes Teams Successful."

13. Vakil, "What Makes Teams Successful."

14. Vakil, "What Makes Teams Successful."

15. Vakil, "What Makes Teams Successful."

CHAPTER 3

1. London Business School, "Why Senior Managers Can't Name Their Firm's Top Priorities," December 7, 2015, https://www.london.edu/news/two-thirds-of-senior-managers-cant-name-their-firms-top-priorities.

2. Deloitte, "Becoming Irresistible: A New Model for Employee Engagement," *Deloitte Review*, no. 16 (January 27, 2015), https://www2.deloitte.com/us/en/insights/deloitte-review/issue-16/employee-engagement-strategies.html.

3. PerformYard, "What Are Cascading Goals and How to Use Them in 2023," accessed June 3, 2023, https://www.performyard.com/articles/what-are-cascading-goals-and-how-to-use-them#.

4. PerformYard, "What Are Cascading Goals."

5. PerformYard, "What Are Cascading Goals."

6. William Harke, "What Companies Use OKRs?" Weekdone, accessed June 3, 2023, https://blog.weekdone.com/what-companies-use-okrs/.

7. Andrew Constable, "Early-Stage Companies, Stop Chasing the Next Shiny Object: Use OKRs to Focus," *Forbes*, July 2, 2021, https://www.forbes.com/sites/forbescoachescouncil/2021/07/02/early-stage-companies-stop-chasing-the-next-shiny-object-use-okrs-to-focus/?sh=2b97ac414890.

8. John Doerr, *Measure What Matters: How Google, Bono and the Gates Foundation Rock the World with OKRs* (New York: Portfolio, 2018).

9. Doerr, *Measure What Matters*.

10. Doerr, *Measure What Matters*.

11. Doerr, *Measure What Matters*.

12. Doerr, *Measure What Matters*.

13. Doerr, *Measure What Matters*.

14. Doerr, *Measure What Matters*.

15. Doerr, *Measure What Matters*.

16. Doerr, *Measure What Matters*.

17. Doerr, *Measure What Matters*.

18. Patrick Lencioni, *Silos, Politics, and Turf Wars* (San Francisco: Josey-Bass, 2006), 2.

19. Brent Gleeson, "The Silo Mentality: How to Break Down the Barriers," *Forbes*, October 2, 2013, https://www.forbes.com/sites/brentgleeson/2013/10/02/the-silo-mentality-how-to-break-down-the-barriers/?sh=7cb56148c7e9.

20. Scott D. Anthony and Mark Johnson, "What a Good Moonshot Is Really For," *Harvard Business Review*, May 14, 2013, https://hbr.org/2013/05/what-a-good-moonshot-is-really-2.

21. Anthony and Johnson, "Moonshot."

22. Anthony and Johnson, "Moonshot."

23. Anthony and Johnson, "Moonshot."

24. Christopher McFadden, "From DVDs to Streaming, Here's the Incredible History of Netflix," *Interesting Engineering*, July 4, 2020, https://interestingengineering.com/culture/the-fascinating-history-of-netflix.

25. Doerr, *Measure What Matters*.

26. Jim Collins and Jerry Porras, *Built to Last: Successful Habits of Visionary Companies* (New York: HarperBusiness, 2004).

27. Will Kenton, "What Is a Big Hairy Audacious Goal (BHAG)? Categories and Examples," *Investopedia*, November 26, 2022, https://www.investopedia.com/terms/b/big-hairy-audacious-goal-bhag.asp.

28. Jim Collins, "The Story of Starbucks' Journey to Find Its BHAG," accessed June 3, 2023, https://www.jimcollins.com/media_topics/TheStoryOfStarbucks.html; Gennaro Cuofano, "What Is a Big Hairy Audacious Goal (BHAG)? The Big Hairy Audacious Goal in a Nutshell," FourWeekMBA, January 25, 2023, https://fourweekmba.com/big-hairy-audacious-goal-bhag/#; Brad Giles, "Meta BHAG, the Trust Problem, the Greatest Trade of All Time, Mailchimp and the Dangerous Thing about Focusing on Your Competition," *Evolution Partners Newsletter*, October 31, 2021, https://evolutionpartners.com.au/meta-bhag-the-trust-problem-the-greatest-trade-of-all-time-mailchimp-the-dangerous-thing-about-focusing-on-your-competition.html.

29. Lisa Shufro, "Committed vs. Aspirational OKRs: What Is the Difference?" *What Matters*, accessed June 3, 2023, https://www.whatmatters.com/faqs/committed-aspirational-okrs-examples-difference#.

30. Shufro, "Committed vs. Aspirational OKRs."

31. David Curry, "Microsoft Teams Revenue and Usage Statistics (2022)," *Business of Apps*, September 6, 2022, https://www.businessofapps.com/data/microsoft-teams-statistics/; Patrick Watson, "Has Microsoft Teams Growth Reached Its Peak?" Cavell Group, July 28, 2021, https://cavellgroup.com/microsoft-teams-growth/#.

32. Betterworks, "How to Create OKRs for Personal Development,"October 6, 2021, https://www.betterworks.com/magazine/how-to-create-okrs-for-personal-development/.

33. Betterworks, "How to Create OKRs."

CHAPTER 4

1. Sean Ellis and Morgan Brown, *Hacking Growth: How Today's Fastest-Growing Companies Drive Breakout Success* (New York: Crown, 2017).

2. Ellis and Brown, *Hacking Growth.*

3. Adam Heitzman, "6 Growth Hacking Successes That Catapulted Business Success," *Inc.*, June 1, 2018, https://www.inc.com/adam-heitzman/6-growth-hacking-successes-that-catapulted-business-success.html. For a detailed discussion of growth hacking, see Infragistics, "Growth Hacking: Why You Need It and How to Do It," Slingshot, February 25, 2022, https://www.slingshotapp.io/whitepapers/growth-hacking.

4. Fortune Business Insights, "With 13.2% CAGR, Team Collaboration Software Market Size to Reach USD 40.79 Billion [2022–2028]," November 22, 2022, https://www.globenewswire.com/news-release/2022/11/22/2560560/0/en/With-13-2-CAGR-Team-Collaboration-Software-Market-Size-to-Reach-USD-40-79-Billion-2022-2028.html; Moshe Beauford, "The State of Team Collaboration in 2022," GetVoIP, January 25, 2022, https://getvoip.com/blog/2021/03/26/team-messaging-stats/.

5. Rocketspace, "How 3 Startups Achieved Product-Market Fit," September 18, 2018, https://www.rocketspace.com/tech-startups/how-3-startups-achieved-product-market-fit.

CHAPTER 5

1. Joe Smith, "How the Lightening's Michael Peterson Became an NHL Analysis Pioneer," *The Athletic*, November 24, 2020, https://theathletic.com/2213294/2020/11/24/tampa-bay-lightning-nhl-analytics-michael-peterson-stanley-cup/.

2. Arik Parnass, "Analytics, Not Statistics, Driving NHL Evolution," *NHL*, February 22, 2015, https://www.nhl.com/news/analytics-not-statistics-driving-nhl-evolution/c-754099.

3. William Craig, "The History of the Internet in a Nutshell," WebFX, August 12, 2022, https://www.webfx.com/blog/web-design/the-history-of-the-internet-in-a-nutshell/.

4. Keith D. Foote, "A Brief History of Big Data," Dataversity, December 14, 2017, https://www.dataversity.net/brief-history-big-data/.

5. Hugo Delgado, "Web 2.0 History, Evolution and Characteristics," Akus.net, August 22, 2022, https://disenowebakus.net/en/web-2.

6. Rebecca Murtagh, "Mobile Now Exceeds PC: The Biggest Shift since the Internet Began," *Search Engine Watch*, July 8, 2014, https://www.searchenginewatch.com/2014/07/08/mobile-now-exceeds-pc-the-biggest-shift-since-the-internet-began/.

7. M. G. Siegler, "Eric Schmidt: Every Two Days We Create as Much Information as We Did Up to 2003," *TechCrunch*, August 4, 2010, https://techcrunch.com/2010/08/04/schmidt-data/.

8. Jason Wise, "How Much Data Is Generated Every Day in 2023?" *Earthweb*, April 7, 2023, https://earthweb.com/how-much-data-is-created-every-day/.

9. Wise, "How Much Data."

10. Emanuel Younanzadeh, "Are You Really a Data-Driven Organization?" *Forbes*, December 29, 2021, https://www.forbes.com/sites/forbescommunicationscouncil/2021/12/29/are-you-really-a-data-driven-organization/?sh=7060e65f3906.

11. Randy Bean, "NewVantage Partners Releases 2021 Big Data and AI Executive Survey," *Business Wire*, January 4, 2021, https://www.businesswire.com/news/home/20210104005022/en/NewVantage-Partners-Releases-2021-Big-Data-and-AI-Executive-Survey.

12. Lyndsee Manna, "The Changing Value of Data and the Need for Data Literacy," *TDWI Upside*, February 4, 2022, https://tdwi.org/articles/2022/02/04/bi-all-changing-value-of-data-and-need-for-data-literacy.aspx.

13. Lars Fiedler, Till Großmaß, Marcus Roth, and Ole Jørgen Vetvik, "Why Customer Analytics Matter," McKinsey and Company, May 26, 2016, https://www.mckinsey.com/capabilities/growth-marketing-and-sales/our-insights/why-customer-analytics-matter.

14. Harsha, "Who Is More Intelligent: Sherlock Holmes or Mycroft Holmes?" *News Fetcher*, August 13, 2021, https://www.thenewsfetcher.com/who-is-more-intelligent-sherlock-or-mycroft-holmes/.

15. Arthur Conan Doyle, "The Adventure of the Bruce-Partington Plans," *Strand Magazine*, December 1908.

16. Randy Bean, "Why Becoming a Data-Driven Organization Is So Hard," *Harvard Business Review*, February 24, 2022, https://hbr.org/2022/02/why-becoming-a-data-driven-organization-is-so-hard.

17. Kasey Panetta, "A Data and Analytics Leader's Guide to Data Literacy," Gartner, August 26, 2021, https://www.gartner.com/smarterwithgartner/a-data-and-analytics-leaders-guide-to-data-literacy.

18. Panetta, "A Data and Analytics Leader's Guide."

19. Parnass, "Analytics, Not Statistics."

20. Nicole Janssen, "The Data Science Talent Gap: Why It Exists and What Business Can Do about It," *Forbes*, October 11, 2022, https://www.forbes.com/sites/forbestechcouncil/2022/10/11/the-data-science-talent-gap-why-it-exists-and-what-businesses-can-do-about-it/?sh=12b819b62398.

21. Othmane Lamrani, "The Emergence of Citizen Data Scientist: The Democratization of Analytics," RestApp, April 12, 2022, https://restapp.io/blog/citizen-data-scientist/.

22. Lamrani, "The Emergence."

CHAPTER 6

1. David A. Garvin, "Building a Learning Organization," *Harvard Business Review* 71, no. 4 (July–August 1993), https://hbr.org/1993/07/building-a-learning-organization.

2. Peter Senge, *The Fifth Discipline: The Art and Practice of the Learning Organization* (New York: Currency, 2006), 3.

3. "Building a Learning Organization," *Atlas of Public Management*, October 19, 2017, https://www.atlas101.ca/pm/concepts/building-a-learning-organization/.

4. Andrew Chen, *The Cold Start Problem: How to Start and Scale Network Effects* (New York: Harper Business, 2021).

5. Sidharta Chatterjee, "Constraints in Organizational Learning, Cognitive Load and Its Effect on Employee Behavior," MPRA Paper no. 47707, January 11, 2013, https://mpra.ub.uni-muenchen.de/47707/8/MPRA_paper_47707.pdf.

CHAPTER 7

1. Jonathan Trevor and Barry Varcoe, "How Aligned Is Your Organization?" *Harvard Business Review*, February 7, 2017, https://hbr.org/2017/02/how-aligned-is-your-organization.

2. Trevor and Varcoe, "How Aligned Is Your Organization?"

3. Brent Gleeson, "6 Steps for Ensuring Leadership Alignment: Alignment within Any Leadership Team in Any Environment Is Critical to Mission Success," *Inc.*, August 29, 2016, https://www.inc.com/brent-gleeson/6-steps-for-ensuring-leadership-alignment.html.

4. Lili Duan, Emily Sheeren, and Leigh M. Weiss, "Tapping the Power of Hidden Influencers," *McKinsey Quarterly*, March 1, 2014, https://www.mckinsey.com/capabilities/people-and-organizational-performance/our-insights/tapping-the-power-of-hidden-influencers.

5. Duan, Sheeren, and Weiss, "Tapping the Power of Hidden Influencers."

CHAPTER 8

1. Stefan Ellerbeck, "The Great Resignation Is Not Over! A Fifth of Workers Plan to Quit in 2022," World Economic Forum, June 24, 2022, https://www.weforum.org/agenda/2022/06/the-great-resignation-is-not-over/.

2. Jamie Johnson, "9 Reasons Your Best Employees Are Quitting," U.S. Chamber of Commerce, October 5, 2022, https://www.uschamber.com/co/run/human-resources/top-reasons-why-employees-quit.

3. Aaron De Smet, Bonnie Dowling, Marina Mugayar-Baldocchi, and Bill Schaninger, "Great Attrition or Great Attraction? The Choice Is Yours," *McKinsey Quarterly*, September 8, 2021, https://www.mckinsey.com/capabilities/people-and-organizational-performance/our-insights/great-attrition-or-great-attraction-the-choice-is-yours.

CHAPTER 9

1. Lexi Croswell, "How Open and Honest Communication Impact Employee Engagement," Culture Amp, accessed June 5, 2023, https://www.cultureamp.com/blog/open-and-honest-communication.

2. Jim Harter, "Employee Engagement on the Rise in the U.S.," Gallup, August 26, 2018, https://news.gallup.com/poll/241649/employee-engagement-rise.aspx.

3. Susan Scott, *Fierce Conversations: Achieving Success at Work and in Life One Conversation at a Time* (New York: Berkley, 2004).

4. Michael Beer, *Fit to Compete: Why Honest Conversation about Your Company's Capabilities Are the Key to a Winning Strategy* (Cambridge, MA: Harvard Business Press, 2020).

5. Kim Scott, *Radical Candor: Be a Kick-Ass Boss without Losing Your Humanity* (New York: St. Martin's Press, 2019).

6. Ray Dalio, "Work Principle 1: Trust in Radical Truth and Radical Transparency," LinkedIn, November 26, 2018, https://www.linkedin.com/pulse/ work-principle-1-trust-radical-truth-transparency-ray-dalio/.

7. Julie Musilek, "Courageous Conversations at Work: A Guide to the Discussion You Are Scared Of," Great Place to Work, February 12, 2021, https://www .greatplacetowork.com/resources/blog/a-guide-to-the-discussion-you-are-scared -to-have-right-now.

CHAPTER 10

1. Warren G. Bennis and Patricia Ward Biederman, *Organizing Genius: The Secrets of Creative Collaboration* (New York: Basic Books, 1997), 210.

2. John Beeson, "Deconstructing Executive Presence," *Harvard Business Review*, August 22, 2012, https://hbr.org/2012/08/de-constructing-executive-pres.

3. Mike Myatt, "Leadership and Presence," N2Growth, accessed June 5, 2023, https://www.n2growth.com/never-let-them-see-you-sweat/.

4. Lisa Rosh and Lynn Offerman, "Be Yourself, but Carefully," *Harvard Business Review*, October 7, 2013, https://hbr.org/2013/10/be-yourself-but-carefully.

5. Rosh and Offerman, "Be Yourself, but Carefully."

6. Amy Cuddy, "Your Body Language May Shape Who You Are," TEDGlobal, 2012, https://www.ted.com/talks/amy_cuddy_your_body_language_may_shape _who_you_are?language=en.

7. Cuddy, "Your Body Language."

8. Kim Elsesser, "Power Posing Is Back: Amy Cuddy Successfully Refutes Criticism," *Forbes*, April 3, 2018, https://www.forbes.com/sites/kimelsesser/2018/04/03/ power-posing-is-back-amy-cuddy-successfully-refutes-criticism/?sh=231e03843b8e.

9. Nicky Champ, "Why Amy Cuddy's TED Talk Has Been Viewed More than 41 Million Times," Business Chicks, accessed June 5, 2023, https://businesschicks .com/why-amy-cuddys-tedtalk-has-been-viewed-more-than-41-million-times/.

CHAPTER 11

1. Gallup, "What Is Employee Engagement and How Do You Improve It?" accessed June 5, 2023, https://www.gallup.com/workplace/285674/improve-employee -engagement-workplace.aspx.

2. Saberr, "Coaching vs Managing Employees: Differences and Examples of Both," March 8, 2022, https://blog.saberr.com/coaching-vs-managing.

CHAPTER 12

1. Peter R. Scholtes, Brian L. Joiner, and Barbara J. Streibel, *The Team Handbook* (Madison, WI: Oriel, 2003).

2. Jack Covert and Todd Sattersten, *The Hundred Best Business Books of All Time: What They Say, Why It Matters and How They Can Help You* (New York: Portfolio, 2009).

3. W. Edward Deming, *Quality Productivity and Competitive Position* (Cambridge: Massachusetts Institute of Technology, 1982).

4. Scholtes, Joiner, and Streibel, *The Team Handbook*, 3–8.

5. Scholtes, Joiner, and Streibel, *The Team Handbook*, 3–5.

CHAPTER 13

1. World Rugby, "Beginner's Guide to Rugby," accessed June 5, 2023, https://www .world.rugby/the-game/beginners-guide/safety.

2. Hirotaka Takeuchi and Ikujiro Nonaka, "The New New Product Development Game," *Harvard Business Review*, January 1986, https://hbr.org/1986/01/ the-new-new-product-development-game.

3. Jeff Sutherland, *The Art of Doing Twice the Work in Half the Time* (New York: Crown, 2014), 3–25.

4. SolidSolutions, "Traditional vs Modern Approaches to Product Development," accessed July 23, 2023, https://www.arenasolutions.com/white-papers/ new-era-of-product-development/traditional-vs-modern-approach-to-npd/.

5. Visual Paradigm, "How Scrum Team Works? A Brief Guide," accessed June 5, 2023, https://www.visual-paradigm.com/scrum/how-scrum-team-works/.

6. Visual Paradigm, "How Scrum Team Works?"

7. Visual Paradigm, "How Scrum Team Works?"

8. Professional Development, "Who Uses Scrum?" accessed June 5, 2023, https:// www.professionaldevelopment.ie/who-uses-scrum.

9. "Key Takeaways from the Gallup State of the American Workplace Study," *Lighthouse Blog*, accessed June 5, 2023, https://getlighthouse.com/blog/gallup-state-of-the-american-workplace-study/.

CHAPTER 14

1. Catherine Cote, "Why Is Strategic Planning Important?" Harvard Business School Online, October 6, 2020, https://online.hbs.edu/blog/post/why-is-strategic-planning-important#.

2. Tracy Maylett, "Why a Successful Business Strategy Depends on Listening to Your Employees," *Forbes*, September 8, 2021, https://www.forbes.com/sites/forbeshumanresourcescouncil/2021/09/08/why-a-successful-business-strategy-depends-on-listening-to-your-employees/?sh=6e8646116bcc.

3. Gary Gagliardi, "Peter Drucker on Strategic Planning," Science of Strategy Institute, accessed June 6, 2023, http://scienceofstrategy.org/main/content/peter-drucker-strategic-planning; Lucidchart, "How to Define Strategy Using Porter's Five Forces," accessed June 6, 2023, https://www.lucidchart.com/blog/what-is-strategy.

4. Robert S. Kaplan and David P. Norton, *The Balanced Scorecard: Translating Strategy into Action* (Cambridge, MA: Harvard Business Review Press, 1996); Robert S. Kaplan and David P. Norton, *The Strategy-Focused Organization: How Balanced Scorecard Companies Thrive in the New Business Environment* (Cambridge, MA: Harvard Business Review Press, 2000).

5. Robert S. Kaplan and David P. Norton, "Mastering the Management System," *Harvard Business Review,* January 2008, https://hbr.org/2008/01/mastering-the-management-system. See also Cote, "Why Is Strategic Planning Important?"

6. Cote, "Why Is Strategic Planning Important?"

7. Quoted in Cote, "Why Is Strategic Planning Important?"

8. Bernard Marr, "Why Every Company Needs a Plan-on-a-Page," Bernard Marr and Co., accessed June 6, 2023, https://bernardmarr.com/why-every-company-needs-a-plan-on-a-page/#.

9. Bruno Dubuc, "Short-Term Memory: Up to 7 Items, but Highly Volatile," *The Brain from Top to Bottom*, accessed June 6, 2023, https://thebrain.mcgill.ca/flash/capsules/experience_jaune03.html#.

10. Clara Moskowitz, "Mind's Limit Found: 4 Things at Once," *Live Science*, April 27, 2008, https://www.livescience.com/2493-mind-limit-4.html.

11. Bernard Marr, "How Many Strategic Goals Should a Company Have?" Bernard Marr and Co., accessed June 6, 2023, https://bernardmarr.com/how-many-strategic-goals-should-a-company-have.

12. Robin Mejia, "Red Team, Blue Team: How to Run an Effective Simulation," *Network World*, April 27, 2008, https://www.networkworld.com/article/2278686/red-team--blue-team--how-to-run-an-effective-simulation.html.

13. David Norton, "Why Strategies Fail? Devising a Strategy Execution System for Certain Success," Business Results Group, August 22, 2014, https://www.brg.co.za/strategy-fails/.

CHAPTER 17

1. Andrew Heffernan and Michael Easter, "How Tom Brady, LeBron James, and Other GOAT Athletes Stay in Game Shape," *Men's Health*, April 26, 2021, https://www.menshealth.com/fitness/a36256825/tom-brady-lebron-fitness/.

2. Michele McDaniel, "Employee Wellbeing: The New Bellwether of Corporate Success?" *Microsoft XC Research Blog*, July 20, 2021, https://www.microsoft.com/en-us/research/group/customer-insights-research/articles/employee-wellbeing-the-new-bellwether-of-corporate-success/; Lily Martis, "7 Companies with Epic Wellness Programs," Monster, accessed June 6, 2023, https://www.monster.com/career-advice/article/companies-good-wellness-programs.

3. Lyle H. Miller, Alma Dell Smith, and Larry Rothstein, *The Stress Solution: An Action Plan to Manage the Stress in Your Life* (New York: Pocket Books, 1993), 14–16.

4. Miller, Smith, and Rothstein, *The Stress Solution*, 17.

5. Miller, Smith, and Rothstein, *The Stress Solution*, 18.

6. Miller, Smith, and Rothstein, *The Stress Solution*, 20–21.

7. David Gelles, "How to Be More Mindful at Work," *New York Times*, accessed June 6, 2023, https://www.nytimes.com/guides/well/be-more-mindful-at-work.

8. Alicia Caramenico, "Aetna Building a Case for a 'Mind-Body' Approach to Stress Management," *Fierce Healthcare*, February 22, 2011, https://www.fiercehealthcare.com/healthcare/aetna-building-a-case-for-a-mind-body-approach-to-stress-management.

9. Ellen J. Langer, *Mindfulness*, 25th Anniversary Ed. (Boston: Da Capo, 2014); Jon Kabat-Zinn, *Full Catastrophe Living: Using the Wisdom of Your Body and Mind to Face Stress, Pain, and Illness* (New York: Bantam, 2013).

10. Yolanda Lau, "Increasing Mindfulness in the Workplace," *Forbes*, October 5, 2020, https://www.forbes.com/sites/forbeshumanresourcescouncil/2020/10/05/increasing-mindfulness-in-the-workplace/?sh=5b218c016956.

11. Lau, "Increasing Mindfulness in the Workplace."

12. Lau, "Increasing Mindfulness in the Workplace."

13. "Mindfulness at Work: A Little Bit Goes a Long Way," *Knowledge at Wharton*, September 30, 2019, https://knowledge.wharton.upenn.edu/article/mindfulness-at-work/.

14. James Duffy, "10 Big Companies That Promote Employee Meditation," More than Accountants, January 2, 2020, https://www.morethanaccountants.co.uk/10-big-companies-promote-employee-meditation/.

15. Duffy, "10 Big Companies."

16. Duffy, "10 Big Companies."

17. Duffy, "10 Big Companies."

18. Duffy, "10 Big Companies."

19. Alex Soojung-Kim Pang, *Rest: Why You Get More Done When You Work Less* (New York: Basic Books, 2018).

20. William Shakespeare, *The Complete Works of William Shakespeare*, vol. 2, *Macbeth*, ed. W. G. Clark and W. Aldis Wright (Garden City, NY: Nelson Doubleday, 1950), 799.

21. Eric Suni, "What Happens When You Sleep?" Sleep Foundation, August 29, 2022, https://www.sleepfoundation.org/how-sleep-works/what-happens-when-you-sleep.

22. Miller, Smith, and Rothstein, *The Stress Solution*, 53–54.

23. Josh Jones, "How to Take the Perfect Nap, According to Cognitive Scientist Sara Mednick," Open Culture, May 18, 2021, https://www.openculture.com/2021/05/how-to-take-the-perfect-nap-according-to-cognitive-scientist-sara-mednick.html.

24. Jeff Kahn, "A Sleep Doctor's Guide to the Best Nap Length for You," Rise, May 16, 2023, https://www.risescience.com/blog/best-nap-length.

25. Kahn, "A Sleep Doctor's Guide."

26. Pang, *Rest*.

27. Glassdoor, "A Guide for Not Limiting Yourself with Unlimited PTO," July 25, 2022, https://www.glassdoor.com/blog/dont-limit-yourself-with-unlimited-pto/.

28. CDC Foundation, "Worker Illness and Injury Costs U.S. Employers $225.8 Billion Annually," January 28, 2015, https://www.cdcfoundation.org/pr/2015/worker-illness-and-injury-costs-us-employers-225-billion-annually.

29. MetLife, "Thriving in the New Work-Life World," 2019, https://www.metlife
.com/content/dam/metlifecom/us/ebts/pdf/MetLife-Employee-Benefit-Trends
-Study-2019.pdf.

30. K. Jared Wright, "Need a Vacation? These 8 Companies Offer Unlimited
PTO," *Employee Benefit News*, July 7, 2021, https://www.benefitnews.com/
list/8-companies-that-offer-unlimited-paid-time-off.

31. Scott Mautz, "This CEO Launched an Unlimited Vacation Policy: Here's How
It Worked Out," *Inc.*, November 14, 2017, https://www.inc.com/scott-mautz/this
-ceo-launched-an-unlimited-vacation-policy-heres-how-it-worked-out.html.

32. Jamie Birt, "What Is Unlimited Paid Time Off (PTO)? (With Pros and
Cons)," Indeed, May 26, 2022, https://www.indeed.com/career-advice/
career-development/unlimited-pto.

33. Birt, "What Is Unlimited Paid Time Off?"

34. Anthony Dominic, "Only 23 Percent of Americans Meet National Exercise
Guidelines," *Club Industry*, July 5, 2018, https://www.clubindustry.com/
fitness-studies/only-23-percent-americans-meet-national-exercise-guidelines.

35. Ron Friedman, "Regular Exercise Is Part of Your Job," *Harvard Business Review*,
October 3, 2014, https://hbr.org/2014/10/regular-exercise-is-part-of-your-job.

36. Mayo Clinic Staff, "Walking: Trim Your Waistline, Improve Your Health," Mayo
Clinic, May 19, 2021, https://www.mayoclinic.org/healthy-lifestyle/fitness/
in-depth/walking/art-20046261.

37. May Wong, "Stanford Study Finds Walking Improves Creativity,"
Stanford News, April 24, 2014, https://news.stanford.edu/2014/04/24/
walking-vs-sitting-042414/.

38. Wong, "Stanford Study."

CONCLUSION

1. Emily Rose McRae and Peter Aykens, "9 Future of Work Trends for 2023,"
Gartner, December 22, 2022, https://www.gartner.com/en/articles/9-future
-of-work-trends-for-2023; Amy Fontinelle, "What Is the Great Resignation?
Causes, Statistics and Trends," *Investopedia*, November 30, 2022, https://www
.investopedia.com/the-great-resignation-5199074.

2. Ed O'Boyle, "4 Things Gen Z and Millennials Expect from Their Workplace,"
Gallup, March 30, 2021, https://www.gallup.com/workplace/336275/things-gen
-millennials-expect-workplace.aspx.

INDEX

Italic page numbers indicate material in figures or tables.

ABOUT THE AUTHOR

**T**ech entrepreneur and CEO Dean Guida knows there's a limit to what you can build with grit alone.

At sixteen, Dean bought the first IBM PC and fell in love with writing software. He went on to receive a bachelor of science degree in operation research from the University of Miami. After graduating, he was a freelance developer and wrote many systems for IBM and on Wall Street. At twenty-three, he started Infragistics to build UX/UI tools for professional software developers.

Seemingly overnight, Dean had to go from early internet coder to business operator—a feat that forced him to learn some of business's biggest lessons on the job. He immediately began navigating the nuances of scaling a company, hiring and growing teams, and becoming a leader, a manager, and a mentor.

Fast-forward thirty-five years, and Dean's tech company now has operations in six countries. More than two million developers use Infragistics software, and its client roster boasts 100 percent of the S&P 500, including Fidelity, Morgan Stanley, Exxon, Intuit, and Bank of America.